Fodor's InFocus

CHARLESTON

1st Edition

Where to Stay and Eat
for All Budgets

Must-See Sights
and Local Secrets

Ratings You Can Trust

Fodor's Travel Publications   New York, Toronto, London, Sydney, Auckland
www.fodors.com

FODOR'S IN FOCUS CHARLESTON

Editor: Douglas Stallings

Writer: Eileen Robinson Smith

Editorial Production: Evangelos Vasilakis, Astrid deRidder

Maps & Illustrations: Ed Jacobus, David Lindroth and Mark Stroud; *cartographers*; Bob Blake and Rebecca Baer, *map editors*

Design: Fabrizio La Rocca, *creative director*; Guido Caroti, *art director*; Ann McBride, *designer*; Melanie Marin, *senior picture editor*

Cover Photo: Bob Krist/eStock Photo

Production/Manufacturing: Amanda Bullock

SPECIAL SALES

This book is available for special discounts for bulk purchases for sales promotions or premiums. Special editions, including personalized covers, excerpts of existing books, and corporate imprints, can be created in large quantities for special needs. For more information, write to Special Markets/Premium Sales, 1745 Broadway, MD 6-2, New York, New York, NY 10019, or e-mail specialmarkets@randomhouse.com.

AN IMPORTANT TIP & AN INVITATION

Although all prices, opening times, and other details in this book are based on information supplied to us at press time, changes occur all the time in the travel world, and Fodor's cannot accept responsibility for facts that become outdated or for inadvertent errors or omissions. **So always confirm information when it matters,** especially if you're making a detour to visit a specific place. Your experiences—positive and negative—matter to us. If we have missed or misstated something, **please write to us.** We follow up on all suggestions. Contact the Charleston editor at editors@fodors.com or c/o Fodor's at 1745 Broadway, New York, NY 10019.

Be a Fodor's Correspondent

Your opinion matters. It matters to us. It matters to your fellow Fodor's travelers, too. And we'd like to hear it. In fact, we *need* to hear it. When you share your experiences and opinions, you become an active member of the Fodor's community. Here's how you can help improve Fodor's for all of us.

Tell us when we're right. We rely on local writers to give you an insider's perspective. But our writers and staff editors also depend on you. Your positive feedback is a vote to renew our recommendations for the next edition.

Tell us when we're wrong. We update most of our guides every year. But things change. If any of our descriptions are inaccurate or inadequate, we'll incorporate your changes in the next edition and will correct factual errors at fodors.com *immediately*.

Tell us what to include. You probably have had fantastic travel experiences that aren't yet in Fodor's. Why not share them with a community of like-minded travelers? Share your discoveries and experiences with everyone directly at fodors. com. Your input may lead us to add a new listing or a higher recommendation.

Give us your opinion instantly at our feedback center at www. fodors.com/feedback. You may also e-mail editors@fodors.com with the subject line "Charleston Editor." Or send your nominations, comments, and complaints by mail to Charleston Editor, Fodor's, 1745 Broadway, New York, NY 10019.

Happy Traveling!

Tim Jarrell, Publisher

CONTENTS

MAPS

ABOUT THIS BOOK

Our Ratings

We wouldn't recommend a place that wasn't worth your time, but sometimes a place is so experiential that superlatives don't do it justice: you just have to be there to know. These sights, properties, and experiences get our highest rating, **Fodor's Choice,** indicated by orange stars throughout this book. Black stars highlight sights and properties we deem **Highly Recommended** places that our writers, editors, and readers praise again and again for consistency and excellence.

Credit Cards

AE, D, DC, MC, V following restaurant and hotel listings indicate whether American Express, Discover, Diners Club, MasterCard, and Visa are accepted.

Restaurants

Unless we state otherwise, restaurants are open for lunch and dinner daily. We mention dress only when there's a specific requirement and reservations only when they're essential or not accepted.

Hotels

Unless we tell you otherwise, you can assume that the hotels have private bath, phone, TV, and air-conditioning. We always list facilities but not whether you'll be charged an extra fee to use them, so when pricing accommodations, find out what's included.

Many Listings

⋆	Fodor's Choice
★	Highly recommended
✉	Physical address
↔	Directions
✆	Mailing address
☎	Telephone
🖷	Fax
⊕	On the Web
✉	E-mail
🎟	Admission fee
✆	Open/closed times
Ⓜ	Metro stations
🖃	Credit cards

Hotels & Restaurants

🏨	Hotel
⌂	Number of rooms
⅋	Facilities
❍	Meal plans
✕	Restaurant
⌂	Reservations
↘	Smoking
⅋	BYOB
✕🖾	Hotel with restaurant that warrants a visit

Outdoors

⚐	Golf
⛺	Camping

Other

☺	Family-friendly
⇒	See also
✉	Branch address
☞	Take note

WHEN TO GO

There really is no bad time to visit Charleston. Spring and fall are high season, when the temperatures are best and hotel rates and occupancy are at their highest. But there are a myriad of reasons why these seasons are most attractive. The blooming of cherry blossoms is followed by a profusion of azaleas, dogwoods, and camellias in April and apple blossoms in May. Spring and fall temperatures are delightful during the day, and mild at night. Art shows, craft fairs, and music festivals (including the famous Spoleto USA festival) take place in summer. During the fall, golfers are out in full force, and though it may be too cool to swim, beachcombing is a popular activity out on the sea islands. During the high season it's important to make your reservations as far in advance as possible for both hotels and restaurants.

Climate

Spring and fall temperatures are delightful during the day, and mild at night. Summer can be hot and humid, though temperatures are a bit more temperate on the coastal islands. Mild winter weather can be punctuated by brief bouts of frigid conditions. Thunderstorms are common in the spring and summer. Hurricane season stretches from May through November, and storms occasionally strike the area.

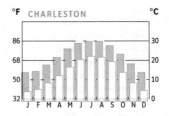

°F CHARLESTON °C

Welcome to Charleston

WORD OF MOUTH

"I hope you plan to stay in the historic district. A walking map is all you need. Go to the [Old City Market] for fun flea market shopping. Slip into an old church for a rest. Be cheesy . . . take a carriage ride. Eat shrimp and grits. Read some Pat Conroy before you go."

—twigsbuddy

By Eileen
Robinson
Smith

WELCOME TO CHARLESTON. You will hear that phrase over and again during the course of your stay here, where people are genuinely happy to share their city with you. And even though the city is driven by forward-thinking policies and recent achievements, residents have not forgotten their manners. Indeed, Charleston was lauded as the most mannerly city in the United States by the late queen of etiquette, Marabelle Young Stewart, for 11 consecutive years.

Charleston is one of those places where people say, "What's not to like?" She is beguiling. An incredible mix of architectural styles dating as far back as the 1600s includes pastel row houses; white-pillared antebellum mansions; and stylish, brick-and-glass waterfront condominiums. Purple wisteria wraps around the black iron grillwork of garden gates that lead to hidden courtyards. Photographers love the city, for its hundreds of church spires and its palm-fringed coastline. A city with more than a little culture, it is internationally known for its annual Spoleto USA performing arts festival, which makes late May and early June one of the best times to visit.

One of the South's most iconic cities, Charleston now has top-flight hotel accommodations and is becoming a popular go-to spot for celebrities, former presidents, and the well-heeled. Even these sophisticated world travelers are impressed by the range of shopping possibilities, from edgy boutiques to classy antique shops to upscale stores specializing in home decor. And the restaurants offer a wealth and variety of choices uncommon in a midsize city; look for dining spots that serve classic Lowcountry dishes, contemporary fusion cuisine, and even ethnic bistros.

Budget-conscious travelers don't have to be left out of the picture. There are many well-priced lodging options both within the city and in the outlying areas, and some of the atmospheric bed-and-breakfasts are relatively inexpensive. Family restaurants and seafood shacks will provide you a good southern time along with your fried shrimp and hush puppies.

It is the simple pleasures of biking the historic streets and islands and swimming at gorgeous beaches—just kicking back—that keep travelers returning and sometimes turning into long-term residents.

CHARLESTON TOP 5

Beaches: The Lowcountry has been blessed with a coastline of exceptional long stretches of taupe beaches just outside of the city of Charleston and on its renowned barrier islands, like Kiawah. Nearby Hilton Head is South Carolina's largest barrier island, with amazing beaches that go for miles, many of which are largely undeveloped.

Great Lodging: Charleston has a mélange of exceptional accommodations, including historic B&Bs and inns, boutique hotels, and full-service hotels. Nearby Beaufort also has a handful of atmospheric B&Bs and inns. And Hilton Head is known for its resort complexes, condos, and villas.

Lowcountry Cuisine: Charleston began its food revolution in the 1980s, and as the pool of talented chefs evolved, contemporary adaptations of regional Lowcountry specialties gained national media coverage. You'll also eat well in both Beaufort and Hilton Head.

Outdoor Activities: More than a day at the beach, outdoor activities in the Charleston area include golf, biking, tennis, all manner of boating and fishing, water sports, and horseback riding. Major family fun is found at resorts offering children's programs and at the region's city and state parks.

Nightlife: Charleston locals love to have a good time, and the city's social calendar is filled with several great annual festivals, during which the streets are filled with piano bars, lounges with live jazz, rooftop bars, and restaurants with live music.

HISTORY OF CHARLESTON

The Carolina colony was the southernmost of the original English colonies of the 1600s. By 1680, the settlement that is now Charleston had grown, but with assaults from Spanish and French rivals, Indian raids, and, later, pirate attacks, life there was not easy. The original settlers of Charles Town, named for King Charles I, were Anglicans, but the Scottish and Irish came, too, and the city was also a refuge for Catholics, French Huguenots, and German Protestants. By 1800, Sephardic Jews of Spanish and Portuguese ancestry had also immigrated here, becoming an important part of the city's merchant class and establishing what would soon become one of the largest Jewish communities in North America.

By the mid-18th century, Charleston was the largest and wealthiest city in the South and a port with an enviable shipping industry. As the local Carolinians thrived, their relationship with England deteriorated. Anger that they were being taxed too heavily played an important roll in getting the Carolina colony to join the revolutionary cause. Mel Gibson's movie *The Patriot,* which was filmed in and around Charleston, colorfully portrays Charleston's history in the Revolutionary War.

In 1860, the same vehemence and pride that Charlestonians displayed in the Revolutionary War led them into another fight. They were adamant about two issues: states' rights and the right to hold slaves. Slaves were the primary labor force in the city and were essential to running South Carolina's plantations, where cotton, rice, and indigo were cash crops. The plantation economy had made the Lowcountry wealthy, and South Carolina was the first Southern state to secede from the Union. The following year, violent opposition to Abraham Lincoln's antislavery views instigated the start of the Civil War, and the first shots of the war were fired from Charleston's Fort Johnson onto the Union-occupied Fort Sumter.

By 1865, after the South was defeated and antebellum society ruined, it widely was thought that the South would never rise again. That changed with the discovery of vast phosphate deposits (used to make fertilizer) in the local riverbanks. By 1867, Charleston had become the world's major phosphate exporter. Many of the former plantation families became movers and shakers in the phosphate trade, allowing them to restore their family manses and revitalize the community.

Alas, the tides of fortune went against this resilient city once again, and due to high taxation (this time by the state) and competition, the industry dried up. But by the late-19th century, Charleston's reputation as a cultural oasis helped tourism to boom. And to replace the phosphate industry in the city's economy, the Charleston Naval Shipyard was created in 1901 and became the city's major employer for decades, thriving particularly during the two world wars, until its demise in the 1990s. By then, Charleston had grown from a regional to a national tourist destination. Today, the city thrives, growing annually as transplants and retirees move here, seeking a less stressful urban lifestyle, a warm, coastal haven, and genteel ways.

Here Comes the Bride

With all the charms of a Southern belle, Charleston is guaranteed to capture the hearts of the betrothed. With its hundreds of historic churches, picturesque plantations, historic homes, and myriad other reception sites, Charleston has become known as a wedding destination. The endless Lowcountry beaches, notably on Hilton Head, are ideal for a sunset wedding ceremony. Symphony musicians can fill the air with their classical refrains, or a Gullah chorus can sing *Hallelujah!*

Both Charleston and Hilton Head are fully equipped for this market. Many of the hotels and resorts have wedding coordinators and offer special packages. A host of professional florists, photographers, musicians, caterers, and wedding professionals can provide the flawless planning that every bride requires. They combine tradition, elegance, and Southern hospitality to make a wedding one enchanting evening. For an auspicious beginning, the Lowcountry with its moss-laden, ancient oaks and marsh-hugging rivers provides one of the most picturesque backdrops in the country.

A PROGRESSIVE CITY ROOTED IN HISTORY

Charleston is the kind of place where you may dream about living after spending your first 24 hours. Indeed, many visitors have made the decision to stay permanently and then never look back. Mayor Joseph Riley, Jr., who has retained his office for more than 25 years, is recognized as a visionary who has transformed Charleston from a provincial, dated, and insular town to a progressive, forward-thinking city that is a model community for the entire country. It was he who convinced composer Gian Carlo Menotti to bring the Spoleto festival to Charleston in 1977. Riley also inaugurated such tourism attractions as downtown's Waterfront Park, the South Carolina Aquarium, and, most recently, the Old Slave Mart Museum. He also replaced two well-worn bridges to the upscale suburb of Mount Pleasant with the stunning Arthur Ravenel Jr. Bridge, one of the largest single-span bridges in North America. Tourism is an important part of the city's economy. The most interesting part of Charleston is the Historic District, where fortunate residents have renovated their homes to look as good as the most beautiful house museums.

But the Charleston story is not all tourism-related. The city's economic development plan has attracted such manufacturers as BMW and the software company Blackbaud on Daniel Island, which built a state-of-the-art soccer stadium for the region. Hospitals in and around the city, notably the Medical University of South Carolina (MUSC), give Charleston high ratings nationally for quality of care, a major draw for retirees. Known for its medical research, MUSC has attracted thousands of doctors, nurses, and research scientists. Its medical school has an internationally diverse student body, including a laudably large percentage of women.

A "young" town, thanks to the centuries-old College of Charleston (1770) which has seen amazing growth in recent decades, the city sees many grads stay on after their education is complete. As it has expanded, the "C of C," as it is known locally, has done the city justice by revitalizing the Calhoun Street corridor. Downtown neighborhoods that were once marginal now boast contemporary architecture, including the college's new brick-and-glass library on Calhoun Street. Decaying, wood-frame homes have been renovated into administrative offices and fraternity houses. Anyone can stroll through the college's grassy Cistern area, with its majestic, mossy oaks and the beautiful, white-pillared Randolph Hall (c. 1828). Another local institution of higher learning is the famous Citadel, the Military College of South Carolina.

IF YOU LIKE . . .

HISTORY YOU CAN SEE AND DO

Charleston has a wealth of historic homes and churches where you can see just how well the prosperous Charlestonians lived and worshipped. The former plantations, open to the public, are another slice of yesteryear and the so-called plantocracy. Nearby Beaufort is also filled with history. These buildings tell the story of wars, wealth, and collapse, but also of rebirth.

The drive along the half-mile Avenue of Oaks at Boone Hall Plantation & Gardens is itself an attraction, but this working plantation is the oldest of its kind in the Charleston area. The **Coastal Discovery Museum in** Hilton Head is a great way to learn about the Lowcountry, this museum is even better because admission is free. **Middleton Place** is one of the

1

grandest of the antebellum estates, Middleton's gardens are a delight, and though the main house was burned during the Civil War, the "gentlemen's wing" has been restored to its former glory. **The Nathaniel Russell House,** built in 1808, is one of the nation's finest surviving examples of Adamstyle architecture. **The Old Sheldon Church Ruins,** northwest of Beaufort, are worth a stopover if you are driving from Charleston or Beaufort to Edisto Island. The namesake of famous Church Street, the graceful late-Georgian **St. Philip's Episcopal Church** dates from 1838.

ENJOYING THE GREAT OUTDOORS

The Atlantic Ocean is the Lowcountry's backyard, but the area is crisscrossed with rivers like the Ashley and the Cooper that flow into the ocean, as well as a myriad of creeks and estuaries. Water plays a major part in the recreation possibilities here, especially fishing, dolphin-watching trips, and kayaking. On land, tennis and golf are the top tickets, especially on Kiawah and Hilton Head islands. But the region has dozens of good golf courses and hundreds of tennis courts.

One of the greatest pleasures of being in the coastal waters is the opportunity to do some fishing in the Gulf Stream. These charters aren't cheap, but the fishing is excellent. Paddling on your own or on a guided tour of the marshes, the Ashley River, Beaufort's Ace Basin, or even around Hilton Head's coastal waters is a great way to appreciate the area's natural environment. The Lowcountry and its waterscapes are simply gorgeous.

AFRICAN-AMERICAN & GULLAH HISTORY

"Gullah" is the name given to the descendants of slaves in the Lowcountry. It can refer to the people themselves, to their language, or to their culture. African slaves were a part of the religious community here, and the Emanuel A.M.E. Church grew from those early roots. The black community has a number of churches downtown and welcomes visitors to their lively services. Foot-stompin' gospel performances can be heard at several churches during the Piccolo Spoleto Festival. Within the main Spoleto USA Festival, a number of events with African-American performers, notably jazz musicians, are very popular.

Gullah Tours, which take place in Charleston, Beaufort, and Hilton Head, give you a glimpse into the authentic history of the Gullah and their culture. The Moja Arts Festival, which takes place during the last week of September and first week of October, celebrates African heritage and Caribbean influences on African-American culture. The history of slavery in Charleston is recounted in what may be the only remaining slave auction house still standing, the Old Slave Mart Museum. **Avery Research for Afro-American History & Culture** is part museum and part archive, and was once a school for freed slaves; today, it's a learning center where you can see artifacts and documentation of the slave era and hear the riveting story in a short film. **The Penn Center,** which is on St. Helena Island near Beaufort, is the unofficial Gullah headquarters, preserving the culture and developing opportunities for Gullahs.

SHOPPING

Charleston has metamorphosed into a shopper's haven, having gone full circle from a district with tourist shops with tired, dated offerings to a city full of unique, individually-owned boutiques with trendy—even edgy—fashions, interspersed between quality chain stores and restaurants where ladies do lunch. Most of the shopping action happens on King Street, and Upper King has added its Design District, with a new wave of antique, furniture, and home fashion stores. Add to this more than 25 art galleries predominately in the French Quarter. On Hilton Head, you can find great shopping, too.

One of many laudable galleries in Charleston, Beaufort, and Hilton Head, the Martin Gallery displays and sells the works of both international and local artists. It's easily the city's most impressive gallery. **King Street,** Charleston's major shopping street, has a little bit of everything, from the haute designer shops and the quality chains of Middle King, to the antique shops of Lower King and the young, edgy shops in and around Calhoun Street. The **Old City Market has** a great concentration of shops at both the high- and low-ends, with a little bit for everyone. The sweetgrass baskets weaved and sold here are of high quality, but beware of the prices. The major shopping center on Hilton Head, the Sea Pines Center is memorable not only for its shops but also for its park benches, landscaping, and outdoor alligator sculpture.

Exploring
Charleston

WORD OF MOUTH

"There are so many things to do in the area—walking tours, visiting historic homes/buildings, seeing the Hunley, Ft. Sumter, outlying plantations, the aquarium, dining, carraige tours, shopping, the ocean, nature excursions, etc., that having a basic want-to-do-list is probably the place to start."

—dsgmi

By Eileen
Robinson
Smith

WANDERING THROUGH THE CITY'S HISTORIC DISTRICT, you would swear it was a movie set. The spires and steeples of more than 180 churches punctuate the low skyline, and the horse-drawn carriages pass centuries-old mansions and carefully tended gardens overflowing with heirloom plants. It's known for its quiet charm, and has been called the most mannerly city in the country.

Immigrants began settling in large numbers in 1670. They flocked to Charleston initially for religious freedom and later for prosperity (compliments of the rice, indigo, and cotton plantations). Preserved through the poverty that followed the Civil War, and natural disasters like fires, earthquakes, and hurricanes, many of Charleston's earliest public and private buildings still stand. And thanks to a rigorous preservation movement and strict Board of Architectural Review, the city's new structures blend with the old. In many cases, recycling is the name of the game— antique handmade bricks literally lay the foundation for new homes. But although locals do live—on some literal levels—in the past, the city is very much a town of today.

Take the internationally heralded Spoleto Festival, for instance. For two weeks every summer, arts patrons from around the world come to enjoy local and international concerts, dance performances, operas, improv shows, and plays at venues citywide. Day in and out, diners can feast at upscale Southern restaurants, shoppers can look for museum-quality paintings and antiques, and outdoor adventurers can explore all of Charleston's outlying beaches, parks, and marshes. But as cosmopolitan as the city has become, it's still the South, and just outside the city limits are farm stands cooking up boiled peanuts, recently named the state's official snack.

ORIENTATION & PLANNING

GETTING ORIENTED

The heart of the city is on a peninsula, sometimes just called "downtown" by the nearly 60,000 residents who populate the area.

North of Broad. The main part of the Historic District, where you'll find the lion's share of the Historic District's homes, B&Bs, and restaurants is the most densely packed area of the city and will be of the greatest interest to tourists. King Street, Charleston's main shopping street, is here as well.

The Battery & South of Broad. The southern part of the Historic District is heavily residential, but it still has a few important sights and even some B&Bs, though many fewer restaurants and shops.

Mount Pleasant & Vicinity. East of Charleston, across the Arthur Ravenel Jr. Bridge, Mount Pleasant, an affluent suburb just across the river from Charleston, will be of some interest to tourists. Farther afield, the outlying islands have the region's best beaches and resorts. There are a few good places to stay in Mount Pleasant itself.

West of the Ashley River. Beyond downtown, the area of Charleston west of the Ashley River will be of some interest to tourists, though the sights here are spread out over a much greater area than in the historic downtown.

PLANNING YOUR TIME

The best way to get acquainted with Charleston is to take a carriage ride, especially one that takes you through the South of Broad neighborhood. After the ride, carriage companies drop you off near the Old City Market in the North of Broad neighborhood, where you can wander looking for souvenirs. You can get acquainted with Charleston's Historic District at your leisure, especially if you can devote at least three days to the city. You'll have time to explore some of the plantations west of the Ashley River. With another day, you can explore Mount Pleasant, and if you have more time, head out to the coastal islands, where trips to the golf course or the beach are the order of the day; for a longer say, you can even rent condo or villa on one of the coastal island to enjoy the fresh sea breezes.

EXPLORING CHARLESTON

The main downtown Historic District is roughly bounded by Lockwood Boulevard on the Ashley River to the west, Calhoun Street to the north, East Bay Street on the Cooper River to the east, and the Battery to the south. Nearly 2,000 historic homes and buildings occupy this fairly compact area of 800 acres. The peninsula is divided up into several neighborhoods, starting from the south and moving north, including The Battery, South of Broad, Lower King Street, and Upper King Street ending near the "Crosstown," where

CHARLESTON TOP 5

Dining Out: Charleston has become a culinary destination, with talented chefs who offer innovative twists on the city's traditional cuisine. Bob Waggoner at the Charleston Grill is one outstanding example.

Seeing Art: The city is home to more than 100 galleries, so you'll never run out of places to see world-class art. The Charleston Museum and dozens of others add to the mix.

Spoleto Festival USA: If you're lucky enough to visit in late May and early June, you'll find a city under siege: Spoleto's flood of indoor and outdoor performances (opera, music, dance, and theater) is impossible to miss and almost as difficult not to enjoy.

The Battery: The views from the point—both natural and man-made—are the loveliest in the city. Look west to see the harbor; to the east you'll find elegant Charleston mansions.

Historic Homes: Charleston's preserved 19th-century houses, including the Nathaniel Russell House, are highlights; outside the city, plantations like Boone Hall, with its extensive garden and grounds, make for scenic excursions.

U.S. 17 connects downtown to Mount Pleasant and West Ashley. You won't need a car in Charleston since almost everything is within walking distance; for those who prefer not to walk, there are bikes, pedicabs, tour buses, water taxis, and the Carta trolley buses. Street parking is irksome, as meter readers are among the city's most efficient public servants. Parking garages, both privately and publicly owned, charge around $1.50 an hour, and most of the hotels charge a fee to park your car.

You'll see no skyscrapers in the downtown area because building heights are strictly limited to maintain the city's historic setting. In the 1970s, most department stores decamped for suburban malls, turning King Street into rows of (very architecturally significant but) empty building shells. Soon, preservation-conscious groups began to save these Art Deco beauties, and by the mid-1980s the shopping district was revived with the addition of the Omni Hotel (now Charleston Place). Big-name retailers quickly saw the opportunity in this attractive city and settled in as well. Although Lower King thrives, Upper King is still in the process of revitalization.

Beyond downtown, the Ashley River hugs the west side of the peninsula, and the region on the far shore is called West Ashley. The Cooper River runs along the east side of the peninsula, with Mount Pleasant on the opposite side and the Charleston Harbor in between. Lastly, there are outlying sea islands with many beaches to choose from—James Island with its Folly Beach, John's Island, Kiawah and Seabrook Islands, Isle of Palms, and Sullivan's Island—with their own appealing attractions. Everything that entails crossing the bridges is best explored by car or bus.

NORTH OF BROAD

Large tracts of available land made the area North of Broad ideal for suburban plantations during the early 1800s. A century later the peninsula had been built out, and today the area is a vibrant mix of residential neighborhoods and commercial clusters, with verdant parks scattered throughout. This area is comprised of three primary neighborhoods: Upper King, the Market area, and the College of Charleston. Though there are a number of majestic homes and pre-revolutionary buildings in this area (including the oldest public building in the city, the Old Powder Magazine), the main draw is the area's collection of stores, museums, restaurants, and historic churches.

As you explore, note that the farther north you travel (up King Street in particular), the newer and more commercial development becomes. Although pretty much anywhere on the peninsula is considered prime real estate these days, the farther south you go, the more expensive the homes become. In times past, Broad Street was considered the cutoff point for the most coveted addresses. Those living in the area Slightly North of Broad were called mere "SNOBs," and their neighbors South of Broad were nicknamed "SOBs."

Numbers in the margins correspond to numbers on the Downtown Charleston map.

MAIN ATTRACTIONS

❷ Charleston Museum. Founded in 1773, the country's oldest museum is housed in a contemporary complex. (The original Greek Revival pillars are all that remain standing at the museum's former home on Rutledge Avenue.) The museum's decorative-arts holdings and its permanent Civil War exhibit are extraordinary. There are more than 500,000 items in the collection, including silver, toys, snuffboxes,

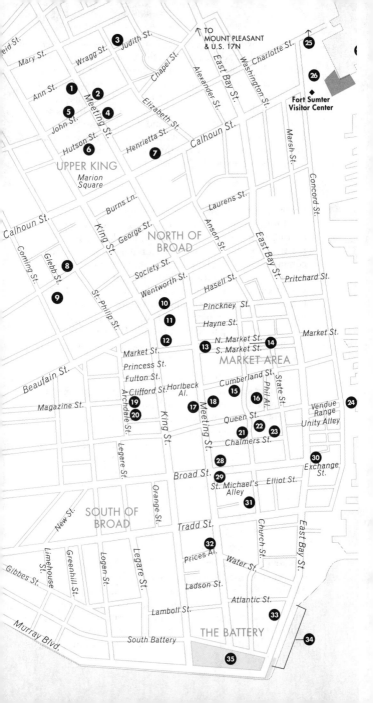

27

TO FORT SUMTER

Charleston
Maritime Center

Downtown Charleston

Cooper River

Aiken-Rhett House, **3**	The Hunley, **25**
Avery Research Center, **9**	Joseph Manigault House, **4**
The Battery, **34**	Kahal Kadosh Beth Elohim Reform Temple, **10**
Charleston Museum, **2**	Market Hall, **13**
Charleston Place, **12**	Nathaniel Russell House, **32**
Charleston Visitor Center, **1**	Old Citadel, **6**
Children's Museum of the Lowcountry, **5**	Old City Market, **14**
Circular Congregational Church, **18**	Old Exchange Building /Provost Dungeon, **30**
City Hall, **28**	Old Powder Magazine, **15**
College of Charleston, **8**	Old Slave Mart Museum, **23**
Dock Street Theatre, **21**	St. John's, **19**
Edmondston-Alston House, **33**	St. Mary's, **11**
Emanuel African Methodist Episcopal Church, **7**	St. Michael's, **29**
	St. Philip's, **16**
Fort Sumter, **27**	South Carolina Aquarium, **26**
French Protestant (Huguenot) Church, **22**	Unitarian Church, **20**
Gibbes Museum of Art, **17**	Waterfront Park, **24**
Heyward-Washington House, **31**	White Point Gardens, **35**

0 ——— 1/4 mi
0 ——— 400 meters

and Indian artifacts. There are also fascinating exhibits on natural history, archaeology, and ornithology. The suspended whale skeleton (the museum's mascot to many locals) is a must-see. ■TIP→**Combination tickets that give you admission to the Joseph Manigault House and the Heyward-Washington House are a bargain at $22.** ⊠*360 Meeting St., Upper King* ☎*843/722–2996* ⊕*www.charlestonmuseum. org* ☎*$10* ⊘*Mon.–Sat. 9–5, Sun. 1–5.*

⓬ **Charleston Place.** The city's most renowned hotel is flanked
★ by upscale boutiques and specialty shops. Stop by for afternoon tea at the classy Thoroughbred Club. The city's finest public restrooms are downstairs by the station. Entrances for the garage and reception area are on Hasell Street between Meeting and King streets. ⊠*130 Market St., Market area* ☎*843/722–4900.*

❶ **Charleston Visitors Center.** The center's 20-minute film *Forever Charleston* is a fine introduction to the city. ■TIP→**The first 30 minutes are free at the parking lot, making it a real bargain.** ⊠*375 Meeting St., Upper King* ☎*843/853–8000 or 800/868–8118* ⊕*www.charlestoncvb.com* ☎*Free* ⊘*Apr.– Oct., daily 8:30–5:30; Nov.–Mar. 31, daily 8:30–5.*

❺ **Children's Museum of the Lowcountry.** Hands-on exhibits at
☾ this top-notch museum keep kids up to age 12 occupied
★ for hours. They can climb on a replica of a local shrimp boat, play in exhibits that show how water evaporates, and wander the inner workings of a medieval castle. ⊠*25 Ann St., Upper King* ☎*843/853–8962* ⊕*www.explorecml.org* ☎*$7* ⊘*Tues.–Sat. 10–5, Sun. 1–5.*

NEED A BREAK? When you get overheated, stop for an icy treat at Paolo's Gelato Italiano (⊠*41 John St., Upper King* ☎*843/577–0099*). Flavors include various fruits and florals, as well as traditional flavors like pistachio. It also serves crepes covered with delicious sauces.

⓲ **Circular Congregational Church.** The first church building erected on this site in the 1680s gave bustling Meeting Street its name. The present-day Romanesque structure, dating from 1890, is configured on a Greek-cross plan and has a breathtaking vaulted ceiling. Explore the graveyard, the oldest in the city, with records dating back to 1696. ⊠*150 Meeting St., Market area* ☎*843/577–6400* ⊕*www. circularchurch.org.*

8 College of Charleston. Randolph Hall—an 1828 building with a majestic Greek-revival portico designed by Philadelphia architect William Strickland—anchors the central Cistern area of the college. Draping oaks envelop the Cistern's lush green quad, where graduation ceremonies and concerts take place. The college was founded in 1770. Scenes from *Cold Mountain* were filmed here. ⌧*St. Philip and George Sts., College of Charleston Campus* ⊕*www.cofc.edu.*

21 Dock Street Theatre. Incorporating the remains of the Old Planter's Hotel (circa 1809) and with a New Orleans French Quarter feel, this theater is draped in red-velvet curtains and has wonderful woodwork. At this writing, it is closed for a much-needed renovation and not expected to reopen until mid-2010. Call to check opening date. ⌧*135 Church St., Market area* ☎*843/720–3968* ⊕*www. charlestonstage.com.*

27 Fort Sumter National Monument. The first shot of the Civil War was fired at Fort Sumter on April 12, 1861. After a 34-hour battle, Union forces surrendered the fort, which became a symbol of Southern resistance. The Confederacy continued to hold it, despite almost continual bombardment, from August 1863 to February of 1865. When it was finally evacuated, the fort was a heap of rubble. Today, the National Park Service oversees it, and rangers conduct guided tours. To reach the fort, you have to take a ferry; boats depart from Liberty Square Visitor Center and from Patriot's Point in Mount Pleasant. There are six crossings daily between mid-March and mid-August. The schedule is abbreviated the rest of the year, so call ahead for details. ⌧*Charleston Harbor* ☎*843/577–0242* ⊕*www.nps.gov/ fosu* ⌑*Fort free; ferry $15, kids 9 and under $5.* ⊙*mid-Mar.–early Sept., daily 10–5:30; early Sept.–Mar., daily 10–4 (11:30–4 Jan.–Feb.).*

The **Fort Sumter Liberty Square Visitor Center,** next to the South Carolina Aquarium, contains exhibits on the Civil War. This is a departure point for ferries headed to the island where you can find Fort Sumter itself. ⌧*340 Concord St., Upper King* ☎*843/577–0242* ⌑*Free* ⊙*Daily 8:30–5.*

HISTORY LESSON. A ferry ride to Fort Sumter is a great way to sneak in a history lesson for the kids. For about the same price as a standard harbor cruise you get a narrated journey that points out the historic sites and explains how the Civil War began.

㉒ French Protestant (Huguenot) Church. The tiny Gothic-style church is the only one in the country still using the original Huguenot liturgy. English-language services are held Sunday at 10:30. ⊠*136 Church St., Market area* ☎*843/722–4385* ⊕*www.frenchhuguenotchurch.org* ⊙*Mid-Mar.–mid-June and mid-Sept.–mid-Nov., Mon.–Thurs. 10–4, Fri. 10–1.*

⑰ Gibbes Museum of Art. Housed in a beautiful Beaux-Arts building, this museum boasts a collection of 10,000 works, principally American with a local connection. Each year there are a dozen special exhibitions, often of contemporary art. The museum shop is exceptional, with artsy, Charlestonian gifts. ⊠*135 Meeting St., Market area* ☎*843/722–2706* ⊕*www.gibbesmuseum.org* ⊡*$9* ⊙*Tues.–Sat. 10–5, Sun. 1–5.*

❹ Joseph Manigault House. An outstanding example of Federal architecture, this home was designed by Charleston architect Gabriel Manigault for his brother in 1803. It's noted for its carved-wood mantels, grand staircase, elaborate plasterwork, and garden "folly." The pieces of rare tricolor Wedgwood are noteworthy. ⊠*350 Meeting St., Upper King* ☎*843/722–2996* ⊕*www.charlestonmuseum.org* ⊡*$10* ⊙*Mon.–Sat. 10–5, Sun. 1–5.*

❻ Old Citadel Building. A fortresslike building on Marion Square was the first home of the Carolina Military College and once housed troops and arms. It is now part of an Embassy Suites hotel. The present-day Citadel is in Hampton Park on the Ashley River. ⊠*341 Meeting St., Upper King* ☎*843/723–6900.*

⑭ Old City Market. This area is often called the Slave Market ⊙ because it's where house slaves once shopped for produce and fish. Today, stalls are lined with restaurants and shops selling children's toys, leather goods, and regional souvenirs. Local "basket ladies" weave and sell sweetgrass, pine-straw, and palmetto-leaf baskets—a craft passed down through generations from their West African ancestors. ⊠*N. and S. Market Sts., between Meeting and E. Bay Sts., Market area* ☎*No phone* ⊙*Daily 9–dusk.*

★ **Fodor's**Choice **Old Slave Mart Museum.** This is likely the only ㉓ building still in existence that was used for slave auctioning, which ended in 1863. It is part of a complex called Ryan's Mart, which contains the slave jail, the kitchen, and the morgue. The history of Charleston's role in the slave trade is recounted here. ⊠*6 Chalmers St., Market*

JOHN JAKES'S BEST BETS

Fort Sumter. A boat ride to the famous Civil War fort is an attraction that shouldn't be missed by any visitor who appreciates history. Close your eyes just a bit and you can imagine Sumter's cannon blasting from the ramparts—maybe even spot a sleek, gray blockade-runner from Liverpool sneaking into the harbor at dusk.

Carriage Rides. We lived in the Lowcountry for years before I took one of the carriage rides that originate next to the outdoor market. I had a misguided scorn for such tours until I jumped impulsively into a vacant carriage one day. I found the young guide enormously informative, and learned a lot, even some years after writing *The North and South Trilogy*. Caution: Carriage routes are determined by where they start from; try to avoid those that take you away from the real jewel featured in the others—the Historic District.

Boone Hall Plantation. This finely preserved property just a few miles north of the city stood in for Mont Royal, Patrick Swayze's home in the David L. Wolper miniseries *The North and South*. The avenue of live oaks leading to the house is well worth the visit. Alas, Patrick doesn't live here any more. —John Jakes

area ☎843/958–6467 ⊕*www.charlestoncity.info* 🖃*$7* ⊗*Mon.–Sat. 9–5.*

★ **Fodor'sChoice St. Philip's (Episcopal) Church.** The namesake of ⓰ Church Street, this graceful late-Georgian building is the second on its site: the congregation's first building burned down in 1835 and was rebuilt in 1838. During the Civil War, the steeple was a target for shelling; one Sunday a shell exploded in the churchyard. The minister bravely continued his sermon. Afterward, the congregation gathered elsewhere for the duration of the war. Notable Charlestonians like John C. Calhoun are buried in the graveyard. ⊠*146 Church St., Market area* ☎843/722–7734 ⊕*www. stphilipschurchsc.org* ⊗*Church weekdays 9–11 and 1–4; cemetery daily 9–4.*

㉖ **South Carolina Aquarium.** The 380,000-gallon Great Ocean ☾ Tank has the tallest aquarium window in North America. ★ Exhibits display more than 10,000 creatures, representing more than 500 species. You travel through the five major regions of the Southeast Appalachian Watershed: the Blue Ridge Mountains, the Piedmont, the coastal plain, the coast, and the ocean. Little ones can pet stingrays at one touch tank and horseshoe crabs and conchs at another. ✉*100 Aquarium Wharf, Upper King* ☎*843/720–1990 or 800/722–6455* ⊕*www.scaquarium.org* ⚄*$16* ⊙*Mid-Apr.–mid-Aug., Mon.–Sat. 9–5, Sun. noon–5; mid-Aug.–mid-Apr., Mon.–Sat. 9–4, Sun. noon–4.*

⑳ Unitarian Church. Completed in 1787, this church was remodeled in the mid–19th century using plans inspired by the Chapel of Henry VII in Westminster Abbey. The Gothic fan-tracery ceiling was added during that renovation. An entrance to the church grounds is at 161½–163 King Street and leads to a secluded, overgrown Victorian-style graveyard that invites contemplation. Sunday service is at 11 AM. ✉*8 Archdale St., Market area* ☎*843/723–4617* ⚄*Free* ⊙*Church Fri. and Sat. 10–1, graveyard daily 9–5.*

㉔ Waterfront Park. Enjoy the fishing pier's porch-style swings,
★ stroll along the waterside path, or relax in the gardens overlooking Charleston Harbor. Two fountains can be found here: one, the adulated "Pineapple Fountain"; the other, a walk-in (or jump-in) fountain that is refreshing on hot summer days. The park is at the foot of Vendue Range, along the east side of Charleston Harbor and Cooper River. ✉*Prioleau St., Market area* ☎*843/724–7321* ⚄*Free* ⊙*Daily 6 AM–midnight.*

ON THE CHEAP. **A $44.95 Charleston Heritage Passport, sold at the Charleston Visitors Center, gets you into the Charleston Museum, Gibbes Museum of Art, the Nathaniel Russell House, the Edmondston-Alston House, the Aiken-Rhett House, Drayton Hall, and Middleton Place. It's good for two days. It can now be bought online, too, at** ⊕*www.travelocity.com.*

ALSO WORTH SEEING
❸ Aiken-Rhett House. This stately 1818 mansion still has its original wallpaper, paint schemes, and even some of its furnishings. The kitchen, slave quarters, and work yard are much as they were when the original occupants lived here, making this one of the most complete examples of urban slave life. Confederate general P. G. T. Beauregard made his headquarters here in 1864. ✉*48 Elizabeth St., Upper King* ☎*843/723–1159* ⊕*www.historiccharleston. org* ⚄*$10; $16 with admission to Nathaniel Russell House* ⊙*Mon.–Sat. 10–5, Sun. 2–5.*

⑨ Avery Research Center for African-American History and Culture.
This center, part museum and part archive, was once a school for freed slaves. Collections include slavery artifacts like badges, manacles, and bills of sale. A riveting mural chronicles the Middle Passage—the journey slaves made from Africa to Charleston's shores. The free tours include a brief film. ⊠*125 Bull St., College of Charleston Campus* ☎*843/953–7609* ⊕*www.cofc.edu* ☎*Free* ☉*Weekdays noon–5, mornings by appointment.*

⑦ Emanuel African Methodist Episcopal Church. Home of the South's oldest African Methodist Episcopal congregation, the church had its beginnings in 1818. Authorities closed it in 1822 when they suspected freedman Denmark Vesey was using the sanctuary to plan a massive slave uprising. The church reopened on the present site after the Civil War ended. ⊠*110 Calhoun St., Upper King* ☎*843/722–2561* ☎*Donations accepted* ☉*Daily 9–4.*

㉕ The Hunley. The *Hunley* became the world's first successful submarine when it was built for the Confederacy in 1864, and then suddenly disappeared into the depths of the sea. Lost for over a century, it was found in 1995 off the coast of Sullivan's Island and raised in 2000. It is being preserved and excavated in a 90,000-gallon tank. A full military funeral with honors was given in 2000 for those men who perished aboard. Tour tickets can be ordered in advance online or over the phone, but you have to pay a service charge. ⊠*1250 Supply St., Old Charleston Naval Base* ☎*843/743–4865 Ext. 10, 877/448–6539 for tour reservations* ⊕*www.hunley.org, www.etix.com (for tour reservations only)* ☎*$12* ☉*Sat. 10–5, Sun. noon–5.*

⑩ Kahal Kadosh Beth Elohim Reform Temple. Considered one of the nation's finest examples of Greek-revival architecture, this temple was built in 1840 to replace an earlier one. The original was the birthplace of American Reform Judaism in 1824. Tours are conducted Sunday to Friday. ⊠*90 Hasell St., Market area* ☎*843/723–1090* ⊕*www.kkbe.org* ☎*Free* ☉*Weekdays 10–noon, Sun. 12:30–3:45.*

⑬ Market Hall. Built in 1841, this imposing restored landmark was modeled after the Temple of Nike in Athens. The hall contains the **Confederate Museum,** in which the United Daughters of the Confederacy displays flags, uniforms, swords, and other Civil War memorabilia. ⊠*188 Meeting St., Market area* ☎*843/723–1541* ☎*$5* ☉*Tues.–Sat. 11–3:30.*

15 **Old Powder Magazine.** Built in 1713, the oldest public building in South Carolina is the only one that remains from the time of the Lords Proprietors. The city's volatile—and precious—gunpowder was kept here during the Revolutionary War. The building's thick walls were designed to implode (rather than explode) if its stores were detonated, thus saving Charleston from the destructive capability of its large gunpowder reserve. ✉*79 Cumberland St., Market area* ☎*843/722–9350* 🎫*$2* 🕐*Tues.–Sat. 11–3:30.*

BUILDING BOOM. Charleston boomed with the plantation economy in the years before the Civil War. South Carolina's rice, indigo, and cotton crops produced an extraordinary concentration of wealth. Seeking a social and cultural lifestyle to match its financial success, the plantocracy entertained itself in style. The city was also renowned for its talented goldsmiths, silversmiths, gunsmiths, tobacconists, brewers, and cabinetmakers. More than 200 private residences were built during this period, and the city was one of the top shopping places in North America.

19 **St. John's Lutheran Church.** This Greek-revival church with delicate wrought-iron gates was completed in 1817 for a congregation that was established in 1742. Its most noteworthy leader, Dr. John Bachman, served as preacher 1815–74 and was known for ministering to local African-Americans and for collaborating on two books with his friend, naturalist John James Audubon. ✉*5 Clifford St., Market area* ☎*843/723–2426* ⊕*www.stjohnscharleston.org.*

11 **St. Mary's Catholic Church.** Beautiful stained glass, wall paintings, and an interesting cemetery tucked between stone walls are highlights of the earliest Roman Catholic church in the Carolinas and Georgia. The white-pillar structure was constructed in 1839. ✉*95 Hasell St., Market area* ☎*843/722–7696* 🕐*By appointment.*

SOUTH OF BROAD

Locals have long joked that just off the Battery (at Battery Street and Murray Boulevard), the Ashley and Cooper rivers join to form the Atlantic Ocean. Such a lofty proclamation speaks volumes about the area's rakish flair. To observe their pride and joy, head to the point of the downtown peninsula. Here, handsome mansions surrounded by elaborate gardens greet incoming boats and passersby. The look is reminiscent of the West Indies with good reason:

before coming to the Carolinas in the late–17th century, many early British colonists had first settled on Barbados and other Caribbean isles where homes with high ceilings and broad porches caught the sea breezes.

OLD-FASHIONED WALK. In spring and summer, Charleston's gardens are in full glory. In fall and winter the homes are dressed in their holiday finest. Twilight strolls are a Dickensian experience, with homes lit from within showing off one cozy scene after another.

The heavily residential area south of Broad Street and west of the Battery brims with beautiful private homes, most of which bear plaques with a short written description of the property's history. Mind your manners, but feel free to peek through iron gates and fences at the verdant displays in elaborate gardens. Although an open gate once signified that guests were welcome to venture inside, that time has mostly passed—residents tell stories of how they came home to find tourists sitting in their front porch rockers. But you never know when an invitation to look around from a friendly owner-gardener might come your way. Several of the city's lavish house museums call this famously affluent neighborhood home.

Numbers in the margins correspond to numbers on the Downtown Charleston map.

MAIN ATTRACTIONS

★ Fodor'sChoice **Battery.** From the intersection of Water Street and East Battery you can look east toward the city's most photographed mansions; look west for views of Charleston Harbor and Fort Sumter. Walk south along East Battery to White Point Gardens, where the street curves and becomes Murray Boulevard. ✉*East Bay St. and Murray Blvd., South of Broad.*

Heyward-Washington House. The area where rice planter Daniel Heyward built his home in 1772 is believed to have been the inspiration for the folk opera *Porgy and Bess*. President George Washington stayed in the house during his 1791 visit. The period furnishings include the Holmes Bookcase, one of the finest remaining American furniture pieces of the late–18th century. Pay attention to the restored kitchen, the only one like it in Charleston open to the public. ✉*87 Church St., South of Broad* ☎*843/722–2996* ⊕*www.charlestonmuseum. org* ✐*$8* ☉*Mon.–Sat. 10–5, Sun. 1–5.*

IF THE SHOE FITS. Wear good walking shoes, because the sidewalks, brick streets, and even Battery Promenade are very uneven. Take a bottle of water, or take a break to sip from the fountains in White Point Gardens, as there are practically no shops south of Broad Street.

★ Fodor's Choice **Nathaniel Russell House.** One of the nation's finest
③② examples of Adam-style architecture, the Nathaniel Russell House was built in 1808. The interior is distinguished by its ornate detailing, its lavish period furnishings, and the "free flying" staircase that spirals three stories with no visible support. The garden is well worth a stroll. ⌂ *51 Meeting St., South of Broad* ☎*843/724–8481* ⊕*www.historiccharleston.org* ☞*$10; $16 with admission to Aiken-Rhett House* ☉*Mon.–Sat. 10–5, Sun. 2–5.*

㉙ **St. Michael's Episcopal Church.** The first cornerstone of St. Michael's was set in place in 1752, making it Charleston's oldest surviving church. Through the years other elements were added: the steeple clock and bells (1764); the organ (1768); the font (1771); and the altar (1892). The pulpit—original to the church—was designed to maximize natural acoustics. ⌂ *14 St. Michael's Alley, South of Broad* ☎*843/723–0603* ⊕*www.stmichaelschurch.net* ☉*Weekdays 9–4:30, Sat. 9–noon.*

㉟ **White Point Gardens.** Pirates once hung from gallows here;
☉ now it's a serene park with Charleston benches—small
★ wood-slat benches with cast-iron sides—and views of the harbor and Fort Sumter. Children love to climb on the replica cannon and pile of cannonballs. ⌂ *Murray Blvd. and E. Battery, South of Broad* ☎*843/724–7327* ☉*Weekdays 9–5, Sat. 9–noon.*

OLD-FASHIONED WALK. In spring and summer, Charleston's gardens are in full glory. In fall and winter the homes are dressed in their holiday finest. Twilight strolls are a Dickensian experience, with homes lit from within showing off one cozy scene after another.

ALSO WORTH SEEING

㉘ **City Hall.** The intersection of Meeting and Broad streets is known as the Four Corners of Law, representing the laws of nation, state, city, and church. On the northeast corner is the graceful, pale pink City Hall, dating from 1801. The second-floor council chambers double as a museum where you can find John Trumbull's 1791 satirical portrait of George

Washington and Samuel F.B. Morse's likeness of James Monroe. ✉ *80 Broad St., North of Broad* ☎ *843/577–6970 or 843/724–3799* ✍ *Free* ⊙ *Weekdays 8:30–5.*

㉝ **Edmondston-Alston House.** First built in 1825 in late-Federal style, the Edmondston-Alston House was transformed into the imposing Greek-revival structure you see today during the 1840s. Tours of the home—furnished with antiques, portraits, silver, and fine china—are informative. ✉ *21 E. Battery, South of Broad* ☎ *843/722–7171* ⊕ *www.middleton place.org* ✍ *$10; $41 with combination ticket for Middleton Place* ⊙ *Tues.–Sat. 10–4:30, Sun. and Mon. 1:30–4:30.*

㉚ **Old Exchange Building & Provost Dungeon.** Originally a customs ☾ house with a waterside entrance, this building was used by the British to house prisoners during the Revolutionary War. Today, costumed guides bring the revolutionary era to life. ✉ *122 E. Bay St., South of Broad* ☎ *843/727–2165* ⊕ *www.oldexchange.com* ✍ *$7* ⊙ *Daily 9–5.*

MOUNT PLEASANT & VICINITY

East of Charleston, across the Arthur Ravenel Jr. Bridge, the largest single-span bridge in North America, is the town of Mount Pleasant, named not for a mountain or a hill but for a plantation in England from which some of the area's settlers hailed. In its Old Village neighborhood are antebellum homes and a sleepy, old-time town center with a drugstore where patrons sidle up to the soda fountain and lunch counter for egg-salad sandwiches and floats. Along Shem Creek, where the local fishing fleet brings in the daily catch, several seafood restaurants serve the area's freshest (and most deftly fried) seafood. Other attractions in the area include military and maritime museums, plantations, and, farther north, the Cape Romain National Wildlife Refuge.

MAIN ATTRACTIONS

★ **Boone Hall Plantation & Gardens.** A ½-mi drive through a live-oak alley draped in Spanish moss introduces you to the still-operating plantation, the oldest of its kind. Tours take you through the 1935 mansion, the butterfly pavilion, the heirloom rose garden, and nine antebellum-era brick slave cabins. Seasonal Gullah culture performances in the theater are laudable. Stroll along the winding river, or tackle the fields to pick your own strawberries, pumpkins, or tomatoes. Across the highway are a farmers' market and gift shop. *North and South, Queen,* and Nicholas Sparks's *The Notebook* were filmed here. ▪TIP→ **Plan your**

FODOR'S FIRST PERSON:

PAT CONROY, WRITER

"I know of no more magical place in America than Charleston's South of Broad. I remember seeing this area near the Battery when I was a kid and I was stunned as to how beautiful it was. In meeting with my Doubleday publisher about writing this latest book, now entitled *South of Broad,* which is set there, she wanted to understand the big draw of this neighborhood. I said, "It is the most beautiful area of this gorgeous city. It is what the Upper East Side is to Manhattan, what Pacific Heights is to San Francisco, or what Beverly Hills is to Los Angeles. SOB is mysterious. It keeps drawing you back like a magnetic force. I am fortunate that my writer friend Ann Rivers Simms lets me stay in her carriage house there when I come to town. As a cadet at The Citadel, I would walk along the Battery and watch the ships come in and out of port. They looked so close you thought you could touch them."

Conroy talks of other Charleston favorites: "When my children come to town I go to the aquarium with my grandchildren. It is small enough to take in. Aquariums always make me believe in God. Why? You see the incredible shapes of things and the myriad capacity for different forms of animals. And there is that wonderful outdoor area where you can look at the fish tanks and then look out to the river and see porpoises playing."

"Thanks to Mayor Riley (the city's mayor for more than 30 years), who has been like Pericles for Charleston, there are so many parks and open spaces. Waterfront Park is a great example."

"And one of the true joys of Charleston in these last decades is its restaurant renaissance."

visit to coincide with annual events like June's Blue Grass Festival and January's Oyster Festival. ⊠*1235 Long Point Rd., off U.S. 17 N, Mount Pleasant* ☎*843/884–4371* ⊕*www.boonehallplantation.com* ⊠*$17.50* ☉*Apr.–early Sept., Mon.–Sat. 8:30–6:30, Sun. 1–5; early Sept.–Mar., Mon.–Sat. 9–5, Sun. 1–4.*

☾ **Fort Moultrie National Monument.** Here Colonel William Moultrie's South Carolinians repelled a British assault in one of the first Patriot victories of the Revolutionary War. Completed in 1809, this is the third fort on this site at **Sullivan's Island,** reached on Route 703 off U.S. 17 N (10 mi southeast of Charleston). A 20-minute film tells the history of the fort.

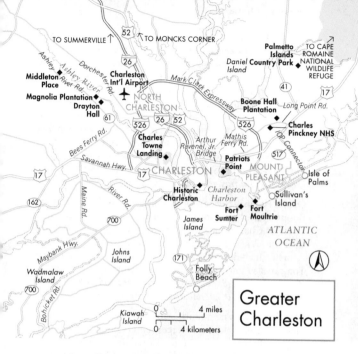

Greater Charleston

■TIP→Plan to spend the day bicycling through Sullivan's Island, which is characterized by its cluster of early-20th-century beach houses. ⌖*1214 Middle St., Sullivan's Island* ☎*843/883-3123* ⊕*www.nps.gov* ⌖*$3* ☉*Daily 9–5.*

☪ **Patriots Point Naval & Maritime Museum.** Ships berthed here
★ include the aircraft carrier USS *Yorktown,* the World War II submarine USS *Clamagore,* the destroyer USS *Laffey,* and the Coast Guard cutter *Ingham,* responsible for sinking a U-boat during World War II. A Vietnam exhibit showcases naval air and watercraft used in the military action. ⌖*Foot of Ravenel Bridge, Mount Pleasant* ☎*843/884-2727* ⊕*www.patriotspoint.org* ⌖*$15* ☉*Daily 9–6:30.*

BASKET LADIES. Drive along U.S. 17 N, through and beyond Mount Pleasant, to find the basket ladies set up at rickety roadside stands, weaving sweetgrass, pine-straw, and palmetto-leaf baskets. Baskets typically cost less on this stretch than in downtown Charleston. Each purchase supports the artisans, who are becoming fewer and fewer each year. Nevertheless, be braced for high prices.

ALSO WORTH SEEING

Cape Romain National Wildlife Refuge. A grouping of barrier islands and salt marshes, this 60,000-acre refuge is one of the most outstanding in the country. The **Sewee Visitor & Environmental Education Center** has information and exhibits on the refuge, trails, and rescued or breeding live birds of prey and red wolves. ■TIP→ **From Cape Romain National Wildlife Refuge you can take a $30 ferry ride to Bull Island. The island is a nearly untouched wilderness; the beach here, strewn with bleached driftwood, is nicknamed Boneyard Beach.** ✉*5821 U.S. 17 N, Awendaw* ☎*843/928–3368* ⊕*caperomain.fws.gov* ⌚*Free* ⊙*Tues.–Sun. 9–5.*

Charles Pinckney National Historic Site. Across the street from Boone Hall Plantation, this is a remnant of the country estate of Charles Pinckney, drafter and signer of the Constitution. A self-guided tour focuses on African-American farm life, including the plantation owner–slave relationship. You can also tour an 1820s tidewater cottage. ✉*1254 Long Point Rd., off U.S. 17N, Mount Pleasant* ☎*843/881–5516* 🖷*843/881–7070* ⊕*www.nps.gov* ⌚*Free* ⊙*Daily 9–5.*

Old Village. This neighborhood is distinguished by white-picket-fenced colonial cottages, antebellum manses, tiny neighborhood churches, and restored (or new) waterfront homes with price tags in the millions. It's a lovely area to stroll or bike. The Blessing of the Fleet seafood festival takes place each April. ✉*South of Alhambra Park, Mount Pleasant.*

⟳ **Palmetto Islands County Park.** This 943-acre park has a playground, paved trails, an observation tower, and boardwalks extending over the marshes. You can rent bicycles and paddleboats, or pay an extra fee for entrance to a small water park. ✉*Long Point Rd., ½ mi past Boone Hall Plantation, Mount Pleasant* ☎*843/884–0832* ⊕*www.ccprc.com* ⌚*$2* ⊙*Apr., Sept., and Oct., daily 9–6; May–Aug., daily 9–7; Nov.–Feb., daily 10–5; Mar., daily 10–6.*

WEST OF THE ASHLEY RIVER

Ashley River Road, Route 61, begins a few miles northwest of downtown Charleston, over the Ashley River Bridge. Sights are spread out along the way and those who love history, old homes, and gardens may need several days to explore places like Drayton Hall, Middleton Place, and Magnolia Plantation and Gardens. Spring is a peak time

Cruising from Charleston

For almost 300 years Charleston, the queen of port cities, has been known for its active commercial port, but it has been less than five years since it became a port of embarkation for Caribbean cruises. It started with just two cruise lines and two ports of call. On the arrival calendar you will now see such names as Cunard, Royal Caribbean, Holland America, Princess, and Carnival. The *Norwegian Majesty,* which accounted for a large number of Charleston cruise calls, was sold to Louis Cruise Lines and will have no future here after May 2009. Charleston is actively seeking a replacement to preserve their premier destination for cruising embarkations and is negotiating with Norwegian Cruise Line for a replacement ship. Beginning in 2009, the *Celebrity Mercury* will call here four times between November 2009 and February 2010 on its nine-night itineraries from Baltimore; two other cruises will originate in Charleston in February and April 2010.

City officials have gone to great lengths to accommodate the needs of cruise-ship passengers. For example, the parking and shuttle to Union Pier is now down to a science. Passengers can often opt to stay at an outlying property and leave their car there without charge for the duration of the cruise. Several hotels, both in the city and in Mount Pleasant, work with the various cruise lines to offer passengers special discounted packages. Most cruise passengers do extend their stay or arrive a couple of days early. Charleston has been cited with several remarkable awards by cruisers, who have named the city one of the most romantic in the U.S.

For the latest cruise news, schedules, and for package information, visit the Web site for the port of Charleston: ⊕ *www.scspa.com.*

for the flowers, although the gardens are in bloom throughout the year.

MAIN ATTRACTIONS

🌣 **Magnolia Plantation & Gardens.** The extensive informal garden, begun in 1685, has evolved into an overflowing collection of plants that bloom year-round, including a vast array of azaleas and camellias. You can take a tram or boat to tour the grounds, travel through the 125-acre Waterfowl Refuge, or explore the 30-acre Audubon Swamp Garden by foot using its new network of boardwalks and bridges. You can traverse the more than 500 acres of trails. (Regrettably, you can no longer rent a canoe or a bike, though you can bring them into the grounds.) There are also a petting zoo, a miniature-horse ranch, and an antebellum cabin (a guide gives a talk about slavery.) You can tour the 19th-century plantation house, which originally stood in Summerville (the original burned.) The home was taken apart, floated down the Ashley River, and reassembled here. The Audubon Swamp Garden is the only individual attraction that can be visited without first paying the $15 admission fee for the grounds. ⊠*3550 Ashley River Rd., West Ashley* ☎*843/571–1266 or 800/367–3517* ⊕*www.magnolia plantation.com* ⊠*Grounds $15; tram $7; boat $7; house tour $7; Audubon Swamp Garden $7* ☉*Daily 8–5:30.*

★ Fodor'sChoice **Middleton Place.** Blooms of all seasons form floral
☘ *allées* (alleys) along terraced lawns and around ornamental lakes shaped like butterfly wings. Much of the year, the landscaped gardens, begun in 1741, are ablaze with camellia, magnolia, azalea, and rose blossoms. A large part of the mansion was destroyed during the Civil War, but the gentlemen's wing has been rebuilt and now displays the house's impressive collections of silver, furniture, paintings, and historic documents. In the stable yard, craftspeople use authentic tools to demonstrate spinning, weaving, and other skills from the plantation era. Farm animals, peacocks, and other creatures roam freely. The Middleton Place Restaurant serves Lowcountry specialties for lunch and dinner. It has a cozy character, a real sense of history, and is a charming, tranquil spot. (You do not have to pay admission to have dinner, and dinner guests can walk the grounds from 5 until dusk.) There is also a delightful museum gift shop that carries local arts, crafts, and souvenirs; a garden shop sells rare seedlings. You can sign up for kayak, bike, wagon, or carriage rides. Finally, you can stay overnight at the contemporary Middleton Inn, where floor-to-ceiling windows splendidly frame the Ashley River. ⊠*4300 Ashley River Rd., West Ashley* ☎*843/556–6020 or 800/782–3608* ⊕*www.middleton place.org* ⊠*Grounds $25, house tour $10, carriage tours $15; all-inclusive day-pass $45* ☉*Grounds daily 9–5; house tours Tues.–Sun. 10–4:30, Mon. noon–4:30.*

ALSO WORTH SEEING

☘ **Charles Towne Landing State Historic Site.** Commemorating the
★ site of the original 1670 Charleston settlement, this park has a reconstructed village and fortifications, a new museum, which allows you to relive the first colonists' experiences up to modern-day life, and English park gardens with

2

bicycle trails and walkways. A new replica of the colonists' 17th-century sailing vessel is being constructed, and at this writing was moored in the tidal creek in late 2008. In the animal park (Charleston's only zoo), more than 20 native (American) species roam freely—among them alligators, bison, pumas, bears, and wolves. Bicycle rentals are available. The site has a new and inviting entrance which winds through a preserved wooded area. The paths will take you to the marshes, creek, and animal park. ✉ *1500 Old Towne Rd., Rte. 171, West Ashley* ☎ *843/852–4200* ⊕ *www.south carolinaparks.com* ✍ *$5* ⊙ *Daily 8:30–5.*

Drayton Hall. Considered the nation's finest example of unspoiled Georgian–Palladian architecture, this mansion is the only plantation house on the Ashley River to have survived the Civil War. A National Trust historic site, built between 1738 and 1742, it's an invaluable lesson in history as well as in architecture. Drayton Hall has been left unfurnished to highlight the original plaster moldings, opulent hand-carved woodwork, and other ornamental details. Watch *Connections,* which details the conditions under which slaves were brought from Africa. You can also see copies of documents that recorded the buying and selling of local slaves. Tours depart on the hour; guides are known for their in-depth knowledge of the era. ✉ *3380 Ashley River Rd., West Ashley* ☎ *843/769–2600* ⊕ *www. draytonhall.org* ✍ *$14* ⊙ *Mar.–Oct., daily 9:30–4; Nov.– Feb., daily 9:30–3.*

SIDE TRIPS FROM CHARLESTON

Gardens, parks, and the charming town of Summerville are good reasons to travel a bit farther afield for day trips. As Charleston and the surrounding suburbs—particularly Mount Pleasant—grow up, it is good to know that Southern country towns still exist close to Charleston. Sit out on a screen porch after some Southern home cooking, paddle around a haunting cypress swamp, and tell preternatural stories, the kind that Southern children are raised on. If the closest you have ever been to an abbey is watching *The Sound of Music,* you can visit Mepkin Abbey and see the purity of the simple religious life. If an overnight at the stellar Woodlands is out of your budget range, go for a memorable fine-dining experience; Sunday Brunch there is both celebratory and more affordable. Drive the tars and gravel and let the towering pines shade you. Turn off the

Charleston Preserved

It's easy to think Charleston is a neverland, sweetly arrested in pastel perfection. But look at Civil War–era images of the Battery mansions on East Bay Street, one of the most photographed areas in town today, and you see the surrounding homes disfigured with crippling battle scars. Because of the poverty that followed the Civil War, on the whole locals simply couldn't afford to build anew from the late 1860s through the early part of the 20th century, so they put the homes they had back together.

In the 1920s it was community activism that rescued the old homes from being destroyed. According to Jonathan Poston, author of *Buildings of Charleston*, the preservation movement began when an Esso gas station was slated to take the place of the Joseph Manigault House. Citizens formed the Society for the Preservation of Old Dwellings (the first such group in the nation) and saved what's now a popular house museum. By 1931, Charleston's City Council had created the Board of Architectural Review (BAR), and designated the Historic District protected from unrestrained development—two more national firsts. The Historic Charleston Foundation was established in 1947, and preservation is now second nature (by law).

As you explore, look for Charleston single houses: just one room wide, they were built with the narrow end street-side and multistory south or southwestern porches (often called piazzas) to catch prevailing breezes. Cool air drifts across these shaded porches, entering the homes through open windows.

You'll see numerous architectural vestiges along Charleston's preserved streets. Many houses have plaques detailing their history, and others have Carolopolis Awards given for fine restoration work. Old fire insurance plaques are more rare; they denote the company that insured the home and that would extinguish the flames if a fire broke out. Notice the bolt heads and washers that dot house facades along the Battery; some are in the shape of circles or stars, and others are capped with lion heads. These could straighten sagging houses when tightened via a crank under the floorboards.

Note the iron spikes that line the tops of some residential gates, doors, walls, and windows. Serving the same purpose as razor wire atop prison fences, most of these *cheveux de frise* (French for "frizzy hair") were added after a thwarted 1822 slave rebellion to deter break-in—or escape.

a/c and breath in the fresh air. This is a less touristed part of South Carolina.

MONCKS CORNER

30 mi northwest of Charleston on U.S. 52.

This town is a gateway to a number of attractions in Santee Cooper Country. Named for the two rivers that form a 171,000-acre basin, the area brims with outdoor pleasures centered on the basin and nearby Lakes Marion and Moultrie.

Explore the inky swamp waters of **Cypress Gardens** in a flat-bottom boat; walk along paths lined with moss-draped cypress trees, azaleas, camellias, daffodils, wisteria, and dogwood; and marvel at the clouds of butterflies in the butterfly house. The swamp garden was created from what was once the freshwater reserve of the vast Dean Hall rice plantation. It's about 24 mi north of Charleston via U.S. 52, between Goose Creek and Moncks Corner. ⊠ *3030 Cypress Gardens Rd., 29461* ☎ *843/553–0515* ☜ *$10* ☉ *Daily 9–5; last admission at 4.*

Francis Marion National Forest consists of 250,000 acres of swamps, vast oaks and pines, and little lakes thought to have been formed by falling meteors. It's a good place for picnicking, hiking, camping, horseback riding, boating, and swimming. ⊠ *U.S. 52* ☎ *843/336–3248* ☜ *Free* ☉ *Daily 9–4:30.*

Mepkin Abbey is an active Trappist monastery overlooking the Cooper River. The site was the former plantation home of Henry Laurens and, later, of publisher Henry Luce and wife Clare Boothe Luce. You can tour the gardens and abbey or even stay here for a spiritual retreat—one- to six-night stays are open to anyone, including married couples, willing to observe the rules of the abbey (like breakfast at dawn) and who don't mind spartan accommodations. To hear the monks sing and to attend the annual Spoleto event here is a peaceful and spiritual experience. The simplicity of the abbey is very grounding. (Reservations are required, and donations are greatly appreciated.) The gift shop carries items the monks have produced—soaps, honey, and sweets—derived from ingredients farmed on the premises. Tours depart at 11:30 and 3. ⊠ *1098 Mepkin Abbey Rd., off Dr. Evans Rd.* ☎ *843/761–8509* ⊕ *www.mepkinabbey.org* ☜ *Grounds free; tours $5* ☉ *Tues.–Fri. and Sun. 9–4:30, Sat. 9–4.*

♥ On the banks of the Old Santee Canal is the **Old Santee Canal Park,** which you can explore on foot or by canoe. The park includes a 19th-century plantation house. The on-site Berkeley Museum focuses on cultural and natural history, and the history of Berkeley County. The Interpretive Center goes into the history of the canal. ✉*900 Stony Landing Rd., off Rembert C. Dennis Blvd.* ☎*843/899–5200* ⊕*www.oldsanteecanalpark.org* ☞*$3* ⊘*Daily 9–5.*

For more information about area lakes and facilities, contact **Santee Cooper Counties Promotion Commission & Visitors Center** ✉*9302 Old Hwy. 6, Drawer 40, Santee* ☎*803/854–2131* ⊕*www.santeecoopercountry.org.*

WHERE TO STAY

$–$$ 🏠**Rice Hope Plantation.** On a former rice plantation outside of Moncks Corner, 45 minutes west of Charleston, this inn overlooks the Cooper River. The grounds, studded with live oaks, were designed by landscape architect Loutrell Briggs. Antiques and reproductions fill the big, sprawling house with five working fireplaces. Guest rooms have wood floors and four-poster beds. This is not a white-pillared mansion, though; it's a more modest farmhouse. You have use of the kitchen and you will get a full Lowcountry breakfast. **Pros:** very country in style, and the family and staff exude Southern hospitality; a true getaway from all that is overly sophisticated and stressful. **Cons:** you will not find any trendy restaurants or nightspots out here; don't expect luxury at the old homestead. ✉*206 Rice Hope Dr., Moncks Corner* ☎*843/849–9000 or 800/569–4038* ⊕*www.ricehope.com* ☞*4 rooms, 1 suite* ♿*In-room: Wi-Fi. In-hotel: tennis court, water sports, Wi-Fi, parking (free), no-smoking rooms* ▤*AE, MC, V* ⦿*BP.*

SUMMERVILLE

25 mi northwest of Charleston via I–26 and Rte. 165.

Victorian homes, many of which are listed on the National Register of Historic Places, line the public park. Colorful gardens brimming with camellias, azaleas, and wisteria abound. Downtown and residential streets curve around tall pines, as a local ordinance prohibits cutting them down. Visit for a stroll in the park, or to go antiquing on the downtown shopping square. Summerville was built by wealthy planters. It has become a town that is being populated with young, professional families and well-to-do retirees transplanted from the cold climes. It has an artsy bent to it and some trendy eateries have opened. The presence of the revered resort The Woodlands adds a lot to the genteel, aristocratic ambience.

For more information about Summerville, stop by the **Greater Summerville/Dorchester County Chamber of Commerce and Visitor Center** (⊠*402 N. Main St.* ☎*843/873–2931* ⊕*www.summervilletourism.com*).

WHERE TO STAY & EAT

★ Fodor'sChoice 🔝 **Woodlands Resort & Inn.** With the distinct feel
$$$$** of an English country estate, this Relais & Châteaux property has individually decorated rooms with nice touches like Frette linens. This 1906 Revival-style inn completed a much-needed, major refurbishment of its interior and all of its guest rooms in 2008. A new casual dining option was created, too. The service and quality of the accommodations are exceptional, and the restaurant ($$$$) is one of the finest in this part of the country. Talented young chef Tarver King continues to prove himself with every challenging, multicourse tasting menu. Diners can also choose from the à la carte menu. Sunday brunch is locally popular, too, but there is no Sunday dinner. The wine events, cooking demonstrations, and tastings are well worth doing. Wine pairings by long-standing sommelier Stéphane Peltier are perfection. **Pros: a country retreat excellent for de-stressing; well-geared for weddings and honeymoons; luxurious bedding and electronic blinds (with drapes) make it ideal for sleeping. **Cons:** far (45 minutes) from downtown Charleston, so not a good base for exploring the city; not near any beaches; very traditional style might feel stuffy to some. ⊠*125 Parsons Rd.29483* ☎*843/875–2600 or 800/774–9999* ⊕*www. woodlandsinn.com* ↪*10 rooms, 9 suites* ⬡*In-room: safe, DVD, Wi-Fi. In-hotel: restaurant, tennis courts, pool, spa, bicycles, parking (free), some pets allowed, no-smoking rooms* ▤*AE, D, DC, MC, V* ⦿*EP.*

Where to Eat in Charleston

WORD OF MOUTH

"Do you by any chance enjoy lamb? If so dine at Slightly North of Broad in Charleston and order their rack of lamb with the Cabernet sauce. I can still remember that dish and wish I could have it ever time I think of it."

—LoveItaly

"Jestine's Kitchen is a great place for lunch with down-to-earth, authentic Lowcountry cooking."

—LawrenceJ

By Eileen
Robinson
Smith

EATING IS A SERIOUS PASTIME IN CHARLESTON. You can dine at nationally renowned restaurants serving the best modern Southern creations or, if you prefer, a waterfront shack with some of the best fried seafood south of the Mason-Dixon line. Big-name chefs, including Bob Waggoner of the Charleston Grill, Robert Carter of the Peninsula Grill, Ken Vedrinkski of Sienna, Frank Lee of Slightly North of Broad, Mike Lata of FIG, and Craig Deihl of Cypress, have earned reputations for preparing Lowcountry cuisine with a contemporary flair. Incredible young talents include Tarver King of the Woodlands, Aaron Deal of Tristan, FISH's Nico Romo, and Sean Brock of McCrady's.

The local food revolution began in the early 1980s, with the reintroduction of original Lowcountry cuisine onto restaurant menus. As Lowcountry cuisine evolved and contemporary adaptations became commonplace, the city's remarkable pool of talented chefs grew, and Charleston began to be thought of as a destination for foodies. Here, dinner conversation, even around the kitchen table, often centers around the latest restaurant news, whether the name of the major chef who just left for Chicago, the opening or the closing of this or that restaurant, or what landmark received a negative review in Thursday's *Post and Courier.* Enjoy the marvelous restaurants here, and don't even say the "D" (diet) word.

Reservations are a good idea for dinner year-round, especially on weekends, as there is almost no off-season for tourism. Tables are especially hard to come by during the Southeastern Wildlife Expo (President's Day weekend in February) and the Spoleto Festival (late May to mid-June). The overall dress code is fairly relaxed: casual khakis and an oxford or polo shirt for men, casual slacks (or a skirt), top, and sandals for women work in most places just fine, but in the fine-dining restaurants, particularly on the weekends, people tend to dress up.

PRICES

Fine dining in Charleston can be expensive. One option to keep costs down might be to try several of the small plates that many establishments offer. To save money, drive over the bridges or go to the islands, including James and John's islands.

WHAT IT COSTS				
¢	$	$$	$$$	$$$$
RESTAURANTS				
under $10	$10–$14	$15–$19	$20–$24	over $24

Restaurant prices are for a main course at dinner, not including
taxes (7.5% on food, 8.5% tax on liquor).

NORTH OF BROAD

$ ✕ **Andolini's Pizza.** *Pizza.* A cheap-date spot, Andolini's caters
to college students who hide out in the tall booths or on the
rear patio. The dough and sauce are made daily, and the
cheese is freshly grated. Toppings include the expected, as
well as banana peppers, feta, jalapeños, and extra-tasty Italian sausage. Call in advance for takeout. ✉*82 Wentworth
St., Lower King* ☎*843/722–7437* ☰*AE, D, MC, V.*

$$$– ✕ **Anson.** *Lowcountry.* Nearly a dozen windows afford views
$$$$ of the passing horse-drawn carriages. The softly lighted,
gilt-trimmed dining room is romantic, though some locals
prefer the more casual scene downstairs. The cuisine is
traditional Lowcountry, including shrimp with grits, and
oysters fried in cornmeal (both served as appetizers). The
she-crab soup is one of the best around. The chef takes
liberties with some classics, including the crispy flounder
in apricot sauce and the roasted red snapper with succo-
tash and shrimp, giving them a more contemporary spin.
Gooey, molten chocolate cake with house-made peanut
butter ice cream is a favorite. ✉*12 Anson St., Market area*
☎*843/577–0551* ☰*AE, D, DC, MC, V* ⊘*No lunch.*

$$ ✕ **A.W. Shuck's Seafood Restaurant & Oyster Bar.** *Seafood.*
Well-known for bacon-wrapped stuffed shrimp, seafood
jambalaya, and oysters on the half shell, the restaurant
has recently renovated its patio that overlooks Market
Street, making it an ideal spot for people watching. The
oyster bar is a great place to drop by for a refuel the way
locals do—with beer and a half-dozen oysters. The main
dining room is very family friendly, even a little hectic, but
the young servers care and are friendly in that distinctly
Southern way. ✉*35 S. Market St., Market area* ☎*843/
723–1151* ☰*AE, D, MC, V.*

$$ ✕ **Blossom.** *Southern.* Exposed white rafters and linenless
tables make this place casual and yet upscale. The terrace

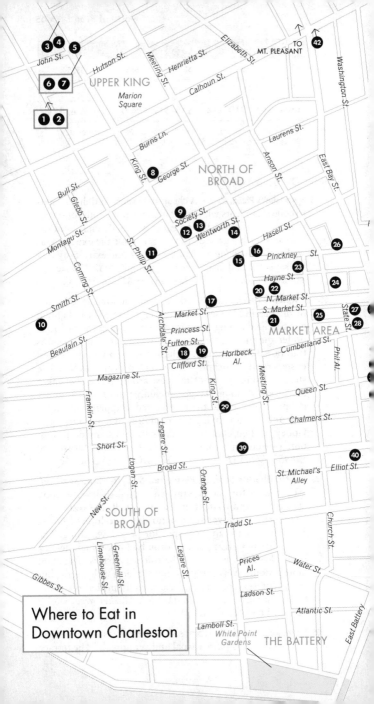

Where to Eat in Downtown Charleston

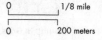

Andolini's Pizza, **11**

Anson, **24**

A.W. Shuck's, **27**

Blossom, **36**

Boathouse
Restaurant, **42**

Bubba Gump, **21**

Carolina's, **41**

Charleston Crab House, **28**

Charleston Grill, **17**

Circa 1886, **10**

Coast bar & Grill, **7**

Cru Café, **26**

Cypress Lowcountry Grille, **37**

82 Queen, **29**

FIG, **16**

Fish, **3**

Five Loaves Cafe, **1**

Fleet Landing, **31**

Fulton Five, **18**

Gaulart & Maliclet Café, **39**

Grill 225, **30**

Hank's Seafood, **23**

High Cotton, **32**

Hominy Grill, **2**

Il Cortile del Re, **19**

Jestine's Kitchen, **14**

La Fourchette, **5**

Magnolias, **34**

McCrady's, **38**

Mercato, **22**

Modica, **8**

Muse, **9**

Oak Steakhouse, **40**

Peninsula Grill, **20**

Pita King, **4**

Robert's of Charleston, **35**

Sermet's Corner, **12**

Slightly North of Broad, **33**

Sticky Fingers, **15**

39 Rue de Jean, **6**

Tristan, **25**

Wentworth Grill, **13**

BEST LOCAL SPECIALTIES

Shrimp 'n Grits. This is the quintessential Charleston specialty that you will hear about as soon as you hit the bricks. To be truly decadent, you need to finish this starch off with heavy cream and a slab of butter. Each chef has his or her own guarded recipe, but traditionally, local, wild shrimp is sautéed with onions, garlic, and fresh tomatoes. Contemporary takes on it can be truly innovative.

Oysters. This homely bivalve lives in the banks of the tidal creeks and has been a main source of protein in the Lowcountry since the early Colonial days. Steamed oysters—rather than raw, on the half-shell—are a local tradition, especially when they are cooked over an outdoor fire. Oysters may be lightly battered and fried, often made into an oyster po'boy.

Blue Crabs. Charlestonians love their crustaceans, and although these blue-backed, clawed creatures are expensive, this does not stop them from ordering cream-based she-crab soup, a Charleston specialty, which is served with a splash of dry sherry.

Crab cakes are perennial favorites on local menus, and of course, come spring, during the molting season, plump, soft-shell crabs are deftly fried.

Charleston Bouillabaisse. Just like the specialty of Marseilles, this rich seafood stew is made from a variety of fish and shellfish, which might include local wild shrimp, sea scallops, grouper, flounder, oysters, crabmeat, mussels, and if you are lucky, a little lobster. It's served steaming hot in an oversized soup bowl and includes the classic French fish broth and saffron threads.

Pecans. These popular nuts have grown in Southern backyards in the Lowcountry for generations. Pecan pies continue to be a common entry on local dessert menus. You may also see a pecan praline parfait, or you can just pick up some pralines, which are made with fresh pecans and a molten brown sugar mix; they are sold at candy emporiums in the Old City Market. You might also see pecan-crusted grouper.

with a view of St. Philip's majestic spire, the dining room, and the bar are heavily populated with young professionals. The open, exhibition kitchen adds to the high-energy atmosphere. Lowcountry seafood is a specialty, and the pastas are made on the premises. Special seasonal menus can be expected and the new bar menu is available as late as 1 AM on Friday and Saturday nights. ⊠*171 E. Bay St., Market area* ☎*843/722–9200* ⊟*AE, DC, MC, V.*

$$-$$$$ ✕ **Boathouse Restaurant.** *Seafood.* Large portions of fresh seafood at reasonable prices make both Charleston-area branches of this restaurant wildly popular. The shrimp hush puppies with spicy mayonnaise and lightly battered fried shrimp and oysters are irresistible. Entrées come with mashed potatoes, grits, collard greens, or blue-cheese coleslaw. The original Isle of Palms location is right on the water, so tables are hard to come by. At the Upper King branch, which is in a more central location, the architecture is strikingly contemporary, with a fisherman's boat hoisted at the bar. Brunch is popular on Sunday. ⊠*549 E. Bay St., Upper King* ☎*843/577–7171* ⊠*101 Palm Blvd., Isle of Palms* ☎*843/886–8000* ⌂*Reservations essential* ⊟*AE, DC, MC, V* ⊗*No lunch Mon.–Sat.*

$$ ✕ **Bubba Gump.** *Seafood.* If you loved Forrest, Jenny, Lieutenant Dan, and the others from the movie *Forrest Gump,* then head to this chain eatery. The food, particularly the shrimp with mango-pineapple salsa, can be surprisingly good. You won't be able to resist the chocolate-chip-cookie sundae. Children who weren't even born when the movie came out in 1994 adore the "Gumpisms" scrawled on the walls of the indoor dining room, and that if you flip the license plate on the table, the server will come back. Young kids love to race the rubber duckies in the mock creek and to get a slushy drink in a glowing plastic cup that is available in the cutesy gift shop. ⊠*96 S. Market St., Market area* ☎*843/723–5665* ⊟*AE, DC, MC, V.*

★ Fodor'sChoice ✕ **Charleston Grill.** *Southern.* Bob Waggoner's
$$$$ groundbreaking New South cuisine is now served in a dining room highlighted by pale wood floors, flowing drapes, and elegant Queen Anne chairs. A jazz ensemble adds a hip, yet unobtrusive, element. As it was hoped, the Grill, which has been reborn in a more relaxed form, now attracts a younger and more vibrant clientele than its original incarnation. The affable and highly talented chef raised the culinary bar in this town and continues to provide what many think of as its highest gastronomic experience. He utilizes only the best produce, such as the organic vegetables used in the golden beet salad. The menu is now in four quadrants: simple, lush (foie gras and other delicacies), cosmopolitan, and Southern. A nightly tasting menu offers a way to sample it all. The pastry chef sends out divine

creations like chocolate caramel ganache. Sommelier Rick Rubel has 1,300 wines in his cellar, with many served by the glass. ⊠*Charleston Place Hotel, 224 King St., Market area* ☎*843/577–4522* ⌂*Reservations essential* ⊟*AE, D, DC, MC, V* ⊘*No lunch.*

$$$$ ✕**Circa 1886.** *Southern.* If you're celebrating, come to this
★ dining room in a carriage house behind the Wentworth Mansion, where the sound level is low enough that you needn't strain to hear your companions. There's a formality here, and the wait staff has both skill and decorum. Chef Marc Collins has created dishes that are real originals; don't resist the Vidalia onion cream soup or the foie gras with crushed almonds. Crab is the central ingredient in his signature soufflé. The coffee-rubbed strip loin with corn pudding, asparagus, and truffles is remarkable. After all that beef, you may experience a chemical need for dessert—try the chocolate tasting with wonders like chocolate-chunk-brownie gelato. ⊠*149 Wentworth St., Lower King* ☎*843/853–7828* ⌂*Reservations essential* ⊟*AE, D, DC, MC, V* ⊘*Closed Sun. No lunch.*

$$–$$$ ✕**Coast Bar & Grill.** *Seafood.* Tucked off a little alley in a restored warehouse, Coast has pared-down trappings like exposed brick-and-wood floors, but the recent renovation has it looking spiffy indeed. Fried fare and heavy sauces are staples, but lighter dishes such as the fish tacos and ceviche make it a standout. The best dishes include oak-grilled fish and lobster served with pineapple-chili salsa, white-wine-and-lemon sauce, or rémoulade. The room can be noisy, but it's always fun, especially if you like a festive atmosphere. You can watch the cooks in the heat of the open-kitchen in the front room or go in the back dining room where it is cooler. The bar menu served from 5 to 7 has some great small plates like tuna carpaccio. There's usually live music on Sunday evening, sometimes a delightful "gypsy" guitarist. ⊠*39D John St., Upper King* ☎*843/722–8838* ⊟*AE, D, DC, MC, V* ⊘*No lunch.*

$$–$$$ ✕**Cru Café.** *Southern.* One reason people come to this 18th-century house is to have lunch on the sunny wraparound porch, but it's the inventive menu that keeps them coming back. Fried chicken breasts are topped with poblano peppers and mozzarella, and the duck confit is served with caramelized pecans and goat cheese, topped with fried shoestring onions, and dressed with port-wine vinaigrette. Chef John Zucker likes to go heavy on the starches, and his flavorful whipped potatoes are made with heavy cream. The four-cheese mac' is a favorite. Meat dishes come with sauces made with green peppercorns, port wine, pear sherry, chipotle peppers, and horseradish cream. ⊠*18 Pinckney St., Market area* ☎*843/534–2434* ▭*AE, DC, MC, V* ⊙*Closed Sun. and Mon.*

$$$–
$$$$
★
×**Cypress Lowcountry Grille.** *Eclectic.* From the owners of Magnolias and Blossom comes a renovated 1834 brick-wall building with an urbane contemporary decor. Rust-color leather booths, a ceiling with light sculptures that change color, and a "wine wall" of 5,000 bottles keeps things interesting. The cuisine is high-end Southern-American, with fresh local ingredients accented with exotic flavors, notably from the Pacific Rim. Try fabulous salads, like the hearts of palm and baby greens with local goat cheese topped with a walnut vinaigrette. The duck is a good entrée choice, as is the filet cooked over hickory wood and topped with a Madeira wine sauce. Executive chef Craig Deihl consistently creates simple yet elegant fare, and you can do the same with his cookbook called, of course, *Cypress*. ⊠*167 E. Bay St., Market area* ☎*843/727–0111* ⚑*Reservations essential* ▭*AE, DC, MC, V* ⊙*No lunch.*

$$$ ×**82 Queen.** *Southern.* In a city with a vibrant but ever-evolving restaurant scene, this is one of the landmarks. Wildly popular as a social meeting ground in the 1980s, it has settled down into its primary role as an atmospheric, fine-dining establishment. Multiple dining areas in both indoor and garden settings make this a great place to linger, perhaps under a gazebo or in an elegant, art-rich (and air-conditioned) room inside the historic residence. Also notable is the genuinely caring service and extensive wine list featuring new varietal blends (no house wine here) which have earned it high and consistent praise. As always, its food has strong southern leanings, with seafood highlights including Charleston bouillabaisse; don't miss the creamy grits (perfection) or authentic fried green tomatoes. ⊠*82 Queen St., Lower King* ☎*843/723–7591* ⚑*Reservations essential* ▭*AE, MC, V.*

$$$ ×**FIG.** *Eclectic.* Acronyms are popular here; this name, for instance, stands for Food Is Good. Chef Michael Lata's mantra is KIS, a reminder for him to keep it simple. Spend an evening here for fresh-off-the-farm ingredients cooked with unfussy, flavorful finesse. The menu changes frequently, but the family-style vegetables might be as simple

as young beets in sherry vinegar placed in a plain white bowl. His dishes do get more complex: there's the pureed cauliflower soup with pancetta, incredible veal sweetbreads with smoked bacon and escarole, and grouper with a perfect golden crust accompanied by braised artichokes. Serene, abstract oceanscape art was added to the stark decor and has really warmed up the dining room. The bar scene is lively, especially on Tuesday, when there's smokin' live jazz. ⊠*232 Meeting St., Market area* ☎*843/805–5900* ▤*AE, D, DC, MC, V* ⊗*No lunch.*

$$$ ✕**Fish.** *Eclectic.* Since its European chef, Nico Romo, raised
★ it to a high culinary level, settling into the niche of French/ Asian cuisine with the freshest seafood, the popularity of Fish has soared. The fact that it is in the newly-revitalized Upper King neighborhood has made it an "in" place for the young sophisticates who gather at the purple heart-wood bar. Savvy foodies have also adopted it. The dim sum appetizer is more beautiful than a flower arrangement. The sweet-chili calamari and other petite plates give the menu a new kick. The bouillabaisse with coconut-lemongrass broth and ginger croutons is one-of-a-kind. Increasing business has triggered a major redo of the spaces, which blend antiqued mirrors and stainless steel, and a new dining room has gone into the adjacent building. The original bar has tripled in size. Some "jazzy" contemporary musicians play on "Wine Wednesdays," when bottles of wine are half-price from 6 to 8. ⊠*440–442 King St., Upper King* ☎*843/722–3474* ⚑*Reservations essential* ▤*AE, MC, V* ⊗*Closed Sun. No lunch Sat.*

$–$$ ✕**Five Loaves Cafe.** *Eclectic.* This good-for-you, healthy café sadly had to vacate its original King Street location when the building sold, so you will have to either visit the new downtown location on Cannon Street or go over the bridge to Mt. Pleasant. Each day there are five new soups—if you're lucky, one of them will be pureed eggplant. A favorite is the spinach salad with grilled polenta croutons, fresh mozzarella, and toasted almonds. The mix-and-match lunch options are ideal, particularly for small appetites. You can choose a cup of soup or a small salad and half a sandwich. And happily, the café is now open for dinner. On Tuesday and Friday, a bottle of wine is half-price. Everything is super healthful (if you can resist the sinful desserts). ⊠*43 Cannon St., Upper King* ☎*843/937–4303* ⊠*1065 Johnnie Dowd Blvd., Mount Pleasant* ☎*843/937–1043* ▤*AE, DC, MC, V* ⊗*Closed Sun.*

$$$ ✕ **Fleet Landing.** *Seafood.* A great place to meet for drinks or dinner, this restaurant overlooking the harbor is right at the cruise-ship terminal. The structure is a renovated 1940s navy debarkation building smack-dab on the water offering views from every table. Sit out on the deck and watch the harbor action while you tempt the seagulls. Your best choices are among the many seafood entrees (many fried) and oysters (either raw or steamed, in season). Shrimp and grits with Tasso ham and fried leeks is a best seller, as is local grouper with a choice of eight sauces that include charred tomato vinaigrette. A popular lunch choice is the mahimahi marinated in coconut and snuggled in an onion *ciabatta* roll brushed with coconut aioli. A brunch and lunch menu is offered on weekends. ✉ *186 Concord St., Market area* ☎ *843/722–8100* ▭ *AE, D, MC, V.*

$$$$ ✕ **Fulton Five.** *Italian.* In the antiques district, this romantic restaurant has chartreuse walls and brass accents. In warm weather you can opt for a seat on the second-floor terrace. Wherever you sit, the northern Italian specialties are worth savoring. Mushroom risotto with sweet corn accompanies the beef with porcini mushrooms. There's pappardelle with rabbit, and crabmeat and tarragon-laced butter flavor the spinach gnocchi. ✉ *5 Fulton St., Lower King* ☎ *843/853–5555* ▱ *Reservations essential* ▭ *AE, DC, MC, V* ☾ *Closed Sun. and late Aug.–early Sept. No lunch.*

★ Fodor'sChoice ✕ **Grill 225.** *Steak.* This atmospheric establishment has been stockpiling accolades over the years and has never been better. Its popularity and status as a special occasion restaurant makes it popular year-round as a superior dining experience with a staggering array of excellent wines and professional, caring service. Dress up and add to the elegance created by wood floors, white linens, and red-velvet upholstery. It makes sense to opt for the prime USDA handpicked steaks; the filet with foie gras with a fig demi-glace (hold the béarnaise) may be the best you will ever have anywhere. You will need to share a side or two, such as the mashed sweet potatoes with Boursin cheese. Presentation is at its best with appetizers like the tuna tower tartare. Expect hefty portions, but save room for the pastry chef's shining creations, which include a contemporized version of baked Alaska with a nutty crust, flambéed tableside. ✉ *Market Pavilion Hotel, 225 E. Bay St., Market area* ☎ *843/266–4222* ▭ *AE, D, DC, MC, V.*

$$$– $$$$ ✕**Hank's Seafood.** *Seafood.* A lively spot with a popular bar and a community table flanked by paper-topped private tables, Hank's is an upscale fish house with such Southern adaptations as Lowcountry bouillabaisse. Seafood platters come with sweet-potato fries and cole slaw. It has a true bistro atmosphere, with waiters in long white aprons buzzing about. It's super popular with the thirtysomething crowd and those who live inland and want the freshest seafood. With a location just off the Old Market, the sister restaurant to the fancy-pants Peninsula Grill is a noteworthy landmark on Charleston's dining scene. ✉*Church and Hayne Sts., Market area* ☎843/723–3474 ▭*AE, D, DC, MC, V* ◷*No lunch.*

$$$– $$$$ ★ ✕**High Cotton.** *Southern.* Chef Anthony Gray, who has been with the restaurant since 1991, has taken over as chef, and so far the transition has gone smoothly. Lazily spinning paddle fans, palm trees, and brick walls still create a plantation ambience. As for the food, Gray combines wonderful flavors and flawless presentation for memorable meals. His Southern and Italian background translates to such specialties as homemade sausages and excellent sauces and marinades for meat. You can feast on bourbon-glazed pork and white-cheddar grits. The chocolate soufflé with blackberry sauce and the praline soufflé are both remarkable. Sunday brunch is accompanied by musicians who sweeten the scene. At night the bar is enlivened with jazz. ✉*199 E. Bay St., Market area* ☎843/724–3815 ◿*Reservations essential* ▭*AE, D, DC, MC, V* ◷*No lunch weekdays.*

$–$$ ✕**Hominy Grill.** *Southern.* The wooden barber poles from the last century still frame the door of this small, homespun café. Chalkboard specials are often the way to go here, whether you are visiting for breakfast, lunch, or dinner. Chef Robert Stehling is a Carolina boy who lived in New York; that dichotomy shows in his "uptown" comfort food. Here, you can have the perfect soft-shell crab sandwich with homemade fries, but leave room for the tangy buttermilk pie or the chocolate peanut butter pie. The bottom line: whatever Robert cooks tastes good. There is usually a line for Sunday brunch, and the young servers are sometimes frantic. The outdoor patio seating is more relaxing. ✉*207 Rutledge Ave., Canonboro* ☎843/937–0930 ▭*AE, MC, V* ◷*No dinner Sun.*

$$–$$$ ✕**Il Cortile del Re.** *Italian.* The translation is "House of the King" in Italian, and when walking to the antique district

CLOSE UP

Lowcountry Cuisine

Colonial settlers to Charles Towne found maritime forests, winding rivers, and vast marshes along a flat coastal plain, which came to be called the Lowcountry. This expansive backyard provided a cornucopia of sustenance—seafood, game, and produce—and the recipes French and English settlers brought from their homeland were altered to match the ingredients found here. After slaves were brought in from the West Indies and West Africa to work the rice fields, the Gullah language—a rollicking Creole dialect that uses both English with African words and accents—and culture developed. Because blacks and whites were in such close proximity (slaves outnumbered whites for generations), languages, accents, and cuisines melded. The mix of Continental recipes and African flavors, made by using the harvest of the region, became known as Lowcountry cooking.

Rice, rice, and more rice is ever-present in Lowcountry dishes, including *pilau*, also spelled *purlieu* (both pronounced pur-*low*), which is a pilaf—rice cooked in meat or vegetable broth. Salty-sweet shrimp and grits are on menus of every price category in Charleston. You can buy creamy she-crab soup in restaurants and stores. Other essential dishes are Hoppin' John (rice and beans), and Frogmore Stew (with shrimp, sausage, and corn). Okra, eggplant, *hominy* (cooked grits), tomatoes, butter beans, benne seeds, ham, shrimp, fish, and game are all part of the regional cuisine. Southern favorites like fried green tomatoes, fried fish and oysters, baconwrapped shad roe, and stuffed quail are popular here, too. But Charleston cuisine is not all about things past; true to the spirit of Lowcountry cooking, "city" chefs continue to innovate and create using the local harvest of farm-fresh heirloom vegetables and seafood caught daily just offshore.

3

of Lower King Street, you will know you have arrived when you see the Italian flag waving outside. Hearty soups and pastas, fresh cheeses and breads, and great wines make this a slice of Tuscany. This trattoria has an Italian-born chef whose dishes couldn't be more authentic: braised lamb shank, porcini-mushroom ravioli, baby arugula salad. The charming, centuries-old building has as much character as the staff. The animated bar is popular with locals, though some patrons prefer the quieter garden seating out back.

✉*193A King St., Lower King* ☎*843/853–1888* ▭*MC, V* ☉*Open Sun. No lunch Sun.–Wed.*

$ ✕ **Jestine's Kitchen.** *Southern.* Enjoy dishes made from family recipes that have been passed down through the generations—like sweet chicken with lima beans—at the last of the true down-home, blue-plate Southern restaurants in the historic district. This casual eatery is known for its fried everything: chicken, okra, shrimp, pork chops, and green tomatoes. The cola cake and coconut-cream pie are divine. Tourists apparently have heard about this bit of old Charleston; lines form outside nearly every day. ✉*251 Meeting St., Lower King* ☎*843/722–7224* ▭*MC, V* ☉*Closed Mon.*

$$–$$$ ✕ **La Fourchette.** *French.* French owner Perig Goulet moves agilely through the petite dining room of this unpretentious bistro. With back-to-back chairs making things cozy (and noisy), this place could be in Paris. Kevin Kelly chooses the wines—predominately French and esoteric, and they befit the authentic fare. Perig boasts of his country pâté, from a recipe handed down from his *grand-mère*. Other favorites include duck salad, scallops sautéed in cognac, and shrimp in a leek sauce. Dieters may be shocked by the golden *frites* fried in duck fat and served with aioli, but they keep putting their hungry hands in the basket. Check the blackboard for fish straight off the boats. ✉*432 King St., Upper King* ☎*843/722–6261* ▭*AE, MC, V* ☉*Closed Sun. No lunch Aug.–Mar.*

$$$– $$$$ ✕ **Magnolias.** *Lowcountry.* The theme here is evident in the vivid paintings of creamy white blossoms that adorn the walls. A visit from Oprah Winfrey revived the reputation of "Mags," a pioneer here of innovative Lowcountry cuisine. (Many locals, particularly the younger ones, prefer its more youthful siblings, Cypress and Blossom.) Executive chef Don Drake refreshes classic dishes like fried green tomatoes with white cheddar grits, caramelized onions, and country ham. Sunday brunch is a more affordable way to sample the fare; the free parking helps defray the cost. ✉*185 E. Bay St., Market area* ☎*843/577–7771* ⌲*Reservations essential* ▭*AE, DC, MC, V.*

$$$$ ✕ **McCrady's.** *American.* Young chef Sean Brock has come
★ of age, turning McCrady's into a superb culinary venture. Passionate about his profession, he spends his nights coming up with innovative pairings that are now working, although he favors meat on the rare side for some tastes. For your

appetizer, try the slow-cooked lobster tail with parsnips, leeks, almond puree, and citrus; follow with a main course such as spice-roasted rack of lamb with eggplant, pine nuts, and golden raisins. The bar area has a centuries-old tavern feel and is frequented by well-heeled downtown residents. The encyclopedia-size wine list includes some wonderful offerings by the glass, as well. The cold soft chocolate with a mascarpone filling is one of the impressive desserts. The sorbet is easily shared: nine tiny cones filled with vivid flavors. ⊠2 *Unity Alley, Market area* ☎843/577–0025 ⌖*Reservations essential* ⊟*AE, MC, V* ⊘*No lunch.*

$$$ ✕**Mercato.** *Italian.* Mercato is the new darling of those in Charleston who like to see and be seen. Placed throughout the two floors are 18th-century antiques and Venetian lighting fixtures juxtaposed with contemporary artwork hung on elaborately plastered walls. Reserve a banquette under the 24-foot-long oil painting inspired by an early Italian circus banner. Music four nights a week, like the incredible gypsy band, is kept low-key until after the normal dinner hour. (There's a late-night menu, too.) Thereafter, the volume goes up, adding fuel to the fiery bar scene. Kudos go to the house-made pastas and raviolis (like duck and wild mushrooms with pine nuts). The beef marsala with wild mushrooms will make any chilly night as warm as Sicily in the summer. Desserts like the *panna cotta* and the warm chocolate cake with vanilla gelato are most agreeable with a small glass of *limoncello.* ⊠*102 N. Market St., Market area* ☎843/722–6393 ⊟*AE, D, DC, MC, V* ⊘*No lunch.*

¢ ✕**Modica.** *Italian.* Known to most for its gelato, Modica often has a line of gelato-lovers in the evenings, especially during Spoleto, after a performance lets out of the Sotille Theater across the street. Less well-known are the fat, sassy, panini and garden-crisp salads like the "picante" salad, which gets heat from the *sopressata* salami and crunch from roasted pistachios. The house soup is a broth made from portobello mushrooms, and on a given day there might also be one made from carrot and sage or creamy Gorgonzola. You can order a decadent gelato cake for a celebration with 24-hours' notice. And Italian patrons say that it has the only true espresso in town—Moak, from Sicily, just like owner Marcello and his cousin Vince. ⊠*41A George St., Lower King* ☎843/723–8868 ⊟*MC, V* ⊘*No dinner Sun.*

$$$ ✕**Muse Restaurant & Wine Bar.** *Mediterranean.* If you want to go to Europe without going through customs or security,

spend the evening at Muse, preferably on Thursday night when there is live piano music. Just off King, on a lovely historic block, many people drop in just to have a drink at its popular Wine Bar (which serves premium liquors and cocktails, too), where a charming bartender will give you a good pour and where more than 100 wines by the glass are offered. Then you can move on to your designated table in one of four dining rooms decorated in the styles of Greece, Italy, France, and Spain. Owner Beth Anne Crane recruited Chef Jason Houser, then the sous-chef at the famed Charleston Grill, to realize her dream. Expect a contemporary take on Mediterranean cuisine, like sumac-rubbed duck breast with dates and pomegranate jus, or pasta with unsweetened cocoa, lemon ricotta, and pesto. ⊠ *82 Society St., Lower King* ☎ *843/577–1102* ⌂ *Reservations essential* ⊟ *AE, MC, V* ⊙ *No lunch.*

$$$$ ✕**Oak Steakhouse.** *Steak.* In a 19th-century bank building, this dining room juxtaposes antique crystal chandeliers with contemporary art. Reserve a table on the third floor for the full effect and the best vistas. It's pricey, but the filet mignon with a foie-gras-black-truffle butter is excellent, and the side dishes, such as creamed spinach, are perfectly executed. Favorite appetizers include beef carpaccio and Gorgonzola fondue. Service is professional and cordial. Chef/owner Brett McKee is nationally known and celebrities like Dennis Hopper fly him out to cook for their dinner parties. On Sunday nights, a reasonably priced, family-friendly prix-fixe Italian supper is now served. An expansion, which will affect the first floor, is being planned at this writing. ⊠ *17 Broad St., Market area* ☎ *843/722–4220* ⊟ *AE, MC, V* ⊙ *No lunch.*

$$$$ ✕**Peninsula Grill.** *Southern.* Eighteenth century–style por-
★ traits hang on walls covered in olive-green velvet in this dining room. You sit beneath black-iron chandeliers feasting on longtime executive chef Robert Carter's imaginative entrées, including rack of lamb with a sesame-seed crust and a coconut-mint pesto. If you start with the foie gras with a duck barbecue biscuit and peach jam—superb—you might want to go simple for your next course. Carter prepares fresh, thick fillets, such as the black grouper, perfectly; all you have to do is to choose your sauce, say, a ginger-lime butter. Palate-cleanse with the homemade sorbet or the signature dessert, a three-way chocolate dessert that comes with a shot of ice-cold milk. The servers, who work in tandem, are pros; the personable sommelier makes

wine selections that truly complement your meal, anything from bubbly to clarets and dessert wines. The atmosphere is animated and convivial. ✉*Planters Inn, 112 N. Market St., Market area* ☎843/723–0700 ⚹*Reservations essential* ▭*AE, D, DC, MC, V* ⊘*No lunch.*

$$ ✕**Pita King.** *Kosher.* The renderings of typical Middle Eastern dishes—falafel, hummus, and *shawarma* (a type of gyro)—are uncommonly good at the city's only fully kosher establishment. The baba ghanoush is excellent, as is the Israeli salad. ✉*437 King St., Upper King* ☎843/722–1977 or 843/224–5100 ▭*AE, D, MC, V* ⊘*Closed Sat. and Sun. No dinner Fri.*

$$$$ ✕**Robert's of Charleston.** *Continental.* Owner Robert Dickson is both a classically trained chef as well as an effusive
★ baritone who belts out show tunes in the intimate dining room. Accompanied by a pianist, he can sing in Italian, too, and even an Italian rendition of "Home on The Range." A Charleston mainstay since the 1970s, the restaurant tends to draw an older crowd, although honeymooners sometimes hold hands across the table while Robert croons to them. It's a popular spot for anniversaries and birthdays. The five-course prix-fixe menu changes and is now one of the most praiseworthy meals in Charleston. It might include scallop mousse with curried lobster sauce, duck with a balsamic fig sauce and creamy polenta, and chateaubriand with a Cabernet demi-glace. Manager Joseph Raya picks the wines to pair with each course. The restaurant is a family-run affair, which puts a warm spin on the experience. Joseph's wife (and Robert's daughter), Maria-Elena, now reigns in the kitchen. ✉*182 E. Bay St., Market area* ☎843/577–7565 ⚹*Reservations essential* ▭*D, MC, V* ⊘*Closed Sun.–Wed. No lunch.*

$–$$ ✕**Sermet's Corner.** *Mediterranean.* Bold artwork by chef/ owner Sermet Aslan decorates the walls of this lively eatery. The dining room's plate-glass windows look out onto the King Street shopping district. Sermet gets artistic in the kitchen, which means the Mediterranean menu is speckled with innovations. The poached pear and salmon salad is a favorite, as is the sautéed calamari with fennel and oranges. The atmosphere is bohemian, and the bar is filled with colorful locals (if you wish, you can even join them and have your meal at the bar). ✉*276 King St., Market area* ☎843/853–7775 ▭*AE, MC, D, V.*

$$$–
$$$$
★ ✕**Slightly North of Broad.** *Southern.* This former warehouse with brick-and-stucco walls has a chef's table that looks directly into the open kitchen. It's a great place to perch if you can "take the heat," as chef Frank Lee, who wears a baseball cap instead of a toque, is one of the city's culinary characters. Known for his talent in preparing game, his venison is exceptional. Many of the items come as small plates, which make them perfect for sharing. The braised lamb shank with a ragout of white beans, arugula and a red demi-glace is divine. Lunch can be as inexpensive as $9.95 for something as memorable as mussels with spinach, grape tomatoes, and smoked bacon. ✉*192 E. Bay St., Market area* ☎*843/723–3424* ▭*AE, D, DC, MC, V* ☼*No lunch weekends.*

$$ ✕**Sticky Fingers.** *Southern.* The sound of blues and the aroma of ribs reach the street—where you may have to wait to get seated. This family-oriented local chain was founded by three Charleston buddies who admired Memphis barbecue. The pulled pork is popular, but the ribs are *it.* You have your choice of five different sauces, including some made with honey or bourbon. ✉*235 Meeting St., Market area* ☎*843/853–7427* ✉*341 Johnnie Dodds Blvd., Mount Pleasant* ☎*843/856–9840* ✉*1200 N. Main St., Summerville* ☎*843/875–7969* ▭*AE, DC, MC, V.*

$$$
★ ✕**39 Rue de Jean.** *French.* In classic French-bistro style— gleaming wood, cozy booths, and white-papered tables— Charleston's trendy set wines and dines until the wee hours on such favorites as steamed mussels in a half-dozen preparations. Order them with *pomme frites,* as the French do. Each night of the week there's a special, such as the bouillabaisse on Sunday. Rabbit with a whole-grain mustard sauce was so popular it jumped to the nightly menu. The duck confit with lentils, braised endive, and blood orange velouté is the most popular new item. If you're seeking quiet, ask for a table in the dining room on the right. It's noisy—but so much fun—at the bar, especially since it has the city's best bartenders. ✉*39 John St., Upper King* ☎*843/722–8881* ⚓*Reservations essential* ▭*AE, D, DC, MC, V.*

★ Fodor'sChoice ✕**Tristan.** *Southern.* Within the French Quarter
$$$–
$$$$
Inn, this fine dining room has a sleek, contemporary style with lots of metal, glass, contemporary art, and fresh flowers. The menu has been purposely tailored to complement the decor: it's ultrachic, innovative, and always evolving. The banquettes that line the wall are sought after, so

ask for one when you reserve. The young talent who has moved up to executive chef, Aaron Deal, has expanded the prix-fixe lunch, consisting of three courses from the dinner menu, for a mere $20—less than that chicken wings place down the block. Imagine sitting down to a lunch of baby beet salad, then lamb ribs with a chocolate barbecue sauce, and moving on to violet crème brûlée. After dark, the prices escalate—it's a status place with a sophisticated bar scene. On Sunday there's a fab brunch with a jazz trio, and residents of the Holy City reserve for after church. ⊠*French Quarter Inn, 55 S. Market St., Market area* ☎*843/534–2155* ☐*AE, D, MC, V.*

$$ ✕**Virginia's on King.** *Southern.* This Charleston newcomer is a tribute to an old Southern tradition: mom's home-cooked Southern family meals. In this case, the mother is Ms. Virginia Bennett, and she has shared her recipes for traditional fare that she still prepares for her extended family. Ms. Virginia makes sure prices here are affordable. Starters are such classics as tomato pie, fried green tomatoes, she-crab soup, okra soup, oyster stew, tomato aspic, and Waldorf salad. Supper might be a creamy chicken and dumplings or country-fried steak with red-eye gravy. And sides? Oh yes—collard greens, grits, sweet potato fries, and more. ⊠*412 King St., Upper King* ☎*843/735–5800* ☐*AE, D, DC, MC, V* ☺ *No lunch Sat. No dinner Sun.*

$$$ ✕**Wentworth Grill.** *Eclectic.* A Continental flair prevails in this dining room with floor-to-ceiling windows, a handsome fireplace, and a mesmerizing pattern in the mosaic-tile floor. The cuisine begins in France with dishes like escargot and leeks sautéed in Pernod and stuffed in a puff pastry, then travels around the Mediterranean with offerings such as grouper with pancetta, arugula, and white beans. It returns to the Lowcountry with the bourbon-mustard barbecued scallops and pecan-dressed mustard greens. On Sunday there's a popular jazz brunch. ⊠*Renaissance Charleston Hotel, 68 Wentworth St., Market area* ☎*843/534–0300* ☐*AE, DC, MC, V.*

SOUTH OF BROAD

$$$– ✕**Carolina's.** *Southern.* On a quiet side street between East
$$$$ Bay Street and Waterfront Park, this longtime favorite occupies a former wharf building. The smartened-up decor includes romantic banquettes. The evolving menu has a strong emphasis on healthful ingredients. (Owner Richard

Stoney also owns Kensington Plantation, where most of the produce is grown.) Lowcountry favorites stand next to original dishes like scallops with roasted cauliflower. Local grouper works amazingly well with a port-wine broth. Ask about the special prix-fixe dinners, including ones with beer pairings. On Sunday and Monday bottles of wine are half-price. The free valet parking is much appreciated. ⊠ *10 Exchange St., South of Broad* ☎ *843/724–3800* ⚓ *Reservations essential* ▭ *D, MC, V* ⊘ *No lunch weekends.*

$ ✕**Gaulart and Maliclet Café.** *French.* Sharing high, family-style tables for breakfast, lunch, or dinner leads to camaraderie at this bustling bistro, aka, Fast 'n' French. Thursday brings a crowd for fondue. The cheese fondue can be disappointing, but the seafood, which you cook yourself in broth, is better. The Bucheron cheese salad is wonderful. Nightly specials, such as bouillabaisse or couscous, are reasonably priced and come with a petite glass of wine. The service is often imperfect, but fun. The subtly sweet chocolate mousse cake is the best. Prices have stayed reasonable, while others downtown have soared. Although not as popular as it once was, the restaurant still has a loyal following. ⊠ *98 Broad St., South of Broad* ☎ *843/577–9797* ▭ *AE, D, MC, V* ⊘ *Closed Sun. No dinner Mon.*

MOUNT PLEASANT & VICINITY

¢ ✕**Boulevard Diner.** *Southern.* This former Dairy Queen is now a no-frills counter-and-booth diner. The service is attentive, but the waitresses don't call you *hon.* The food, soulfully prepared, includes a fried eggplant-and-blue-cheese sandwich, Cajun-style meat loaf, and chili served in a sundae glass with sour cream and a cherry tomato on top. ⊠ *409 W. Coleman Blvd., Mount Pleasant* ☎ *843/216–2611* ▭ *MC, V* ⊘ *Closed Sun.*

$ ✕**Coco's Cafe.** *French.* A nondescript strip mall hosts this bistro, which is now under new ownership. The focus is still on French food with some Southern classics like crab cakes, and it still attracts some French guests. Make the trip over the Ravenel Bridge to Mount Pleasant for freshly-made duck pâté, escargot in garlic butter, rabbit in a red wine and mushroom sauce, and pan-fried flounder in brown butter. Prices are less inflated here than downtown. The $13 prix-fixe lunch includes soup or salad, a main course, *and* a glass of wine. ⊠ *863 Houston Northcutt Blvd., Mount Pleasant* ☎ *843/881–4949* ▭ *AE, MC, V* ⊘ *Closed Sun.*

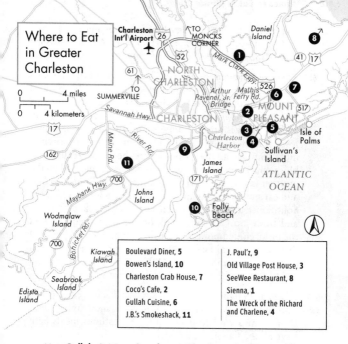

Where to Eat in Greater Charleston

0 ⟷ 4 miles

0 ⟷ 4 kilometers

Boulevard Diner, **5**	J. Paul'z, **9**
Bowen's Island, **10**	Old Village Post House, **3**
Charleston Crab House, **7**	SeeWee Restaurant, **8**
Coco's Cafe, **2**	Sienna, **1**
Gullah Cuisine, **6**	The Wreck of the Richard and Charlene, **4**
J.B.'s Smokeshack, **11**	

$$ ✕**Gullah Cuisine.** *Southern.* Charlotte Jenkins cooks up a
★ mean lunch buffet stocked with fried chicken, collard greens
with ham, crispy okra, and macaroni pie. But it's the Gul-
lah dishes—with roots in African cuisines—that make her
place unique. The Gullah rice—with chicken, sausage,
shrimp, and vegetables—and the fried alligator tails are
both delightful lessons in regional flavors. Dinner options
have expanded to include lobster. ⊠*1717 U.S. 17 N, Mount
Pleasant* ☎*843/881–9076* ▭*AE, MC, V* ⊗*Closed Sun.*

$$$ ✕**Old Village Post House.** *Southern.* If you've been on the road
too long, this circa 1888 inn will provide warmth and sus-
tenance. Many residents of this tree-lined village consider
this their neighborhood tavern. The second, smaller dining room is cozy, and the outdoor space under the market
umbrellas is open and airy. Expect contemporary takes on
Southern favorites like lump crab cakes, shrimp and grits,
and especially the fresh vegetables, like a butter beans
mélange. From the open kitchen, the chefs can perfectly
sautée the catch of the day. Here, pork tenderloin may have
a ginger-peachy glaze. In season, plump soft-shell crabs
are deftly fried. Frank Sinatra serenades as you cleanse

your palate with a tart, key lime pie with a crunchy crust and passion-fruit coulis. ⊠ *101 Pitt St., Mount Pleasant* ☎ *843/388–8935* ▭ *AE, MC, V* ⊘ *No lunch Mon.–Sat.*

$$$ ✕**Seewee Restaurant.** *Southern.* This throwback to the 1950s (or earlier) was once a general store. Some 20 minutes from downtown, it's worth the trip to the country for this Southern-style flashback. You pull open the screen door, and the shelves are still lined with canned goods, with a few tables for four. Outdoors on the screened porch is more seating, and that is also where the bands (really good blues, bluegrass, etc.) set up come Saturday night when the weather is warm. The veteran waitresses will call you *hon* and caringly recommend their favorites, a lot of which are Southern-fried: pickles, green tomatoes, chicken, oysters, and fresh local shrimp. Look on the blackboard to find the more contemporary, less caloric (and more expensive) dishes. For breakfast or lunch, you will love the traditional shrimp and grits. ⊠ *4808 Hwy. 17 N, Awendaw* ☎ *843/928–3609* ▭ *MC, V* ⊘ *No dinner Sun.*

$$$– $$$$ ★ ✕**Sienna.** *Italian.* Ken Vedrinski, who achieved five-star status for The Woodlands, continues to enjoy rave reviews for this, his own laid-back eatery. Sumptuous meals here have all the flavor, complexity, and flair befitting a celebrity chef—but without the pomp. You may taste things here that you have never heard of before, and the menu changes daily according to the seasonal markets. Every day Ken hand-makes his *gnudis* (like a gnocchi but made with cheese instead of potato) or "naked raviolis" with such fillings as morel mushrooms in a Parmesan broth. Four- and seven-course tasting menus are the way to dine, and they can be paired with wine. Well worth the drive over the bridges, it's the best of downtown dining, minus the crowds and paid parking. ⊠ *901 Island Park Dr., Daniel Island* ☎ *843/881–9211* ▭ *AE, MC, V* ⊘ *Closed Sun. No lunch summer and weekends.*

$$ ★ ✕**The Wreck of the Richard & Charlene.** *Seafood.* At first glance the name appears to refer to the waterfront restaurant—a shabby, screened-in porch. In actuality, the *Richard and Charlene* was a trawler that slammed into the building during a hurricane in 1989. Located in the old village of Mount Pleasant, the kitchen serves up Southern tradition on a plate: boiled peanuts, fried shrimp, and stone crab claws. The best deal is the most expensive: the mixed seafood platter with fried flounder, shrimp, oysters, and

scallops. This seafood shack is a hoot. Know that it closes by 8:30 Tuesday through Thursday, and at 9:15 on Friday and Saturday nights. ⊠ *106 Haddrell St., Mount Pleasant* ☎ *843/884–0052* ⚇ *Reservations not accepted* ⊟ *No credit cards* ⊘ *No lunch. Closed Sun. and Mon.*

GREATER CHARLESTON

$$ ✕**Bowen's Island.** *Seafood.* This landmark seafood shack has survived hurricanes, fires, and the trendy restaurant renaissance downtown. Since the original funky restaurant, littered with oyster shells and graffiti, burned down, dinner is served at this writing in the enclosed dockhouse and on the covered deck. Come Spring 2009, a new restaurant should be finished. The menu is the constant: big ol' shrimp, fried or boiled; shrimp and grits; Frogmore stew; hush puppies; and the biggie—all the steamed oysters you can eat for $21.50. No desserts, no cocktails or wine (beer, yes). At this "fishing camp," you might be entertained by Smokin' Weiner or Juke Joint Johnny. It's on an island just before Folly Beach, off Folly Rd., about 15 minutes from downtown; there's a big sign. Go down the dirt road until you see water. ⊠ *1871 Bowen's Island Rd., James Island* ☎ *843/270–7050* ⊟ *No credit cards* ⊘ *No lunch. No dinner Sun. and Mon.*

$$ ✕**Charleston Crab House.** *Seafood.* When you cross over the Wapoo Creek Bridge to James Island, you catch a glimpse of this tiered restaurant, whose decks are splashed by the waters of the intracoastal waterway. Boaters tie up and mingle with the lively crowd. Bus tours do come to the James Island location, however. Crab is the specialty, of course, with she-crab soup a perennial favorite. Owner John Keener keeps the atmosphere inviting and takes pride in the excellent crab cakes and baked oysters. Servers and bartenders are young and fun, but don't expect professional-level service. ⊠ *125A Wappoo Creek Dr., James Island* ☎ *843/795–1963* ⊠ *1101 Stockade La., Mount Pleasant* ☎ *843/884–1617* ⊠ *41 S. Market St., Market area* ☎ *843/853–2900* ⊟ *AE, DC, MC, V.*

$ ✕**J. Paul'z.** *Eclectic.* Just over the Wapoo Creek Bridge, 10 minutes from downtown, this James Island restaurant has survived where many have died. Why? It has established a neighborhood clientele, many of whom work in the food and beverage business and tell the tourists. Everyone prefers the modest prices over those downtown, and the small-plate menu of tapas and sushi. All meld on Wednesdays nights, when there is a jazz combo and the sexy bartendresses shake up drink specials. As contemporary as its sculpture is the plate presentation. Picture crispy red snapper, black rice, shiitake mushrooms, and asparagus with a soy-lime reduction. ✉*1739 Maybank Hwy., Ste. V, James Island* ☎*843/795–6995* ▭*AE, MC, V* ⊘*Closed Sun.*

$ ✕**JB's Smokeshack.** *Southern.* At the sign of the pig (not to mention other rudimentary signs stuck in the ground like CATFISH), this is one of the area's best barbecue joints. A funky find, you will see evidence of the diverse crowd, beat-up pickup trucks to new BMWs—the latter often guests at nearby Kiawah Island. (JB's will deliver out there—for $35.) Most people have the buffet, which includes the barbecue pork, applewood-smoked chicken, and all of the southern veggies—usually including okra gumbo, butter beans, and coleslaw—plus desserts like banana pudding you can eat for one (very) low price. Barbecue connoisseurs know that JB's takes the big prizes at the competitions and that the ribs and the Angus beef brisket are top-shelf. To further flavor the smoky meats, sauces are served on the side. Just come early because dinner is over by 8:30. ✉*3406 Maybank Hwy., John's Island* ☎*843/577–0426* ▭*MC, V* ⊘*Closed Sun.–Tues.*

Where to Stay in Charleston

WORD OF MOUTH

"HarbourView [Inn] is a little notch below Charleston Place for luxury and amenities, but I actually enjoy it more because of the smaller size and more intimacy. Both places are wonderful, and I would not turn down a vacation at either!"

—elsiemoo

By Eileen
Robinson
Smith

CHARLESTON HAS GAINED A REPUTATION, both nationally and internationally, not only as one of the most historic and beautiful cities in our country but also for the quality of its accommodations. It is a city known for its lovingly restored mansions that have been converted into atmospheric bed-and-breakfasts, as well as deluxe inns, all found in the residential blocks of the historic district. Upscale, world-class hotels are in the heart of downtown as well as unique, boutique hotels that provide a one-of-a-kind experience. All are within walking distance of the shops, restaurants, and museums housed within the nearly 800 acres that makes up the historic district.

Chain hotels line the busy, car-trafficked areas (like Meeting Street). In addition, there are chain properties in the nearby areas of West Ashley, Mount Pleasant, and North Charleston, where you'll find plenty of Holiday Inns, Hampton Inns, Marriott Courtyards, and La Quinta Inns. Mount Pleasant is considered the most upscale suburb; North Charleston is the least, but if you need to be close to the airport or are participating in events in its Coliseum, it is probably the cheapest of alternatives.

Overall, Charleston is a lifetime memory, and to know it is to love it. The city's scorecard for repeat visitors is phenomenal. Now Charleston is a port of embarkation for cruise ships, and most cruisers wisely plan on a pre- or post-cruise stay. The premier wedding and honeymoon destination also draws many couples again for their anniversaries.

For condo and house rentals on Seabrook Island, the Isle of Palms, and Wild Dunes, call **Resort Quest** (⊠ *1517 Palm Blvd., Isle of Palms* ☎ *800/344–5105* ⊕ *www.resortquest.com*).

BED & BREAKFAST AGENCIES

As prices escalate, more and more downtown residents are renting out a room or two through the reservation service, **Historic Charleston Bed & Breakfast Association** (☎ *843/722–6606* ⊕ *www.historiccharlestonbedandbreakfast.com*). They can be in up-and-coming revitalized neighborhoods or even on The Battery. Handsomely furnished, these rooms can be less expensive than commercial operations. However, since the owners or families are usually on-site, they may not offer the same level of privacy as more traditional B&Bs or small inns.

PRICES

Charleston's downtown lodgings have three seasons: high season (March to May and September to November); mid-season (June to August); and low season (late November to February). Prices drop significantly during the short low season, except during holidays and special events. High season is summer at the island resorts; rates drop for weekly stays and during off-season. Although prices have gone up at the B&Bs, don't forget that a good breakfast for two is generally included, as well as an evening reception, which can take the place of happy hour and save on your bar bill. You should factor in, however, the cost of downtown parking; *if* a hotel offers free parking, that is a huge plus. In the areas "over the bridges" parking is generally free. Depending on when you arrive—such as a Saturday night, staying Sunday—you can try to find on-street metered parking, as there is no charge at night and on Sundays.

■TIP→ **If you're on a budget, consider lodgings outside the city limits, which tend to be less expensive. Also try booking online, where you can often find good deals and packages. A longer stay sometimes translates to a better per-night price.**

WHAT IT COSTS				
¢	$	$$	$$$	$$$$
HOTELS				
under $100	$100–$150	$151–$200	$201–$250	over $250

Prices are for two people in a standard double room in high season, not including 12.5% tax.

DOWNTOWN CHARLESTON

$$–$$$ ☆**Andrew Pinckney Inn.** The lobby of this boutique inn has a homey ambience that blends South Carolina and the West Indies. The two-story town-house suites, which sleep four, are ideal for longer stays. A heavenly breakfast with fresh-baked pastries and biscuits with sausage gravy is taken on its fourth floor terrace, which overlooks the church spires. It's in the bustling market area, so ask for an interior room. **Pros:** great place if you are looking for quaint Southern charm in the heart of Charleston; afternoon gourmet tea and coffee service with fresh-baked cookies. **Cons:** elevator accesses regular rooms only, not town houses; near the

BEST BETS FOR LODGING

B&Bs: Bed-and-breakfasts conjure up the image of a mom 'n' pop operation with mama at the stove flipping pancakes. In Charleston, the concept has been taken to a higher level; although they may be owned by a couple, most B&Bs also employ a small staff. All are within the Historic District and often were former grand residences, such as the Governors House Inn or the John Rutledge House Inn.

Inns. In this town, a fine line divides true inns from B&Bs. They are usually larger than B&Bs and often have more professional staff, including a concierge (as at the Planters' Inn). The breakfast and evening offerings are often a step above those of B&Bs, and they may even have a restaurant, as in the Wentworth Mansion.

Boutique Hotels: Though small by international hotel standards, Charleston's several boutique hotels offer a pampering staff in a small setting. Those who stay here can dream of the good life by day and at night slumber in a sumptuous bed dressed with Egyptian sheets and cashmere blankets. The Market Pavilion is perhaps the city's best boutique hotel.

Full-Service Hotels: In a city known for its atmospheric B&Bs, there are those visitors who prefer the amenities and privacy of a large, world-class property (Charleston Place) or a well-known American chain hotel (such as the Charleston Marriott). And in a city where the temperatures go on high, particularly during the summer months, a hotel pool may be worth giving up some historic charm.

Island Resorts: The barrier islands surrounding the city of Charleston are the sites for three major, self-contained resorts: Kiawah Island Golf Resort, its neighbor Seabrook Island, and the Wild Dunes Resort on the Isle of Palms. All three have 18-hole golf courses with Kiawah's being the most famous and most costly, and each has excellent tennis facilities. Seabrook has no hotel accommodations (just villas and condos); Wild Dunes is the most casual.

horse stables, which can be smelled. ✉*40 Pinckney St., Market area* ☎*843/937–8800 or 800/505–8983* ⊕*www. andrewpinckneyinn.com* ⤢*41 rooms, 3 town houses, 1 suite* ⚶*In-room: refrigerator (some), Wi-Fi. In-hotel: laundry service, Internet terminal, Wi-Fi, parking (paid), no-smoking rooms* ☰*AE, MC, V* ⚭*BP.*

$$$$ ⚐**Ansonborough Inn.** A shipping warehouse dating from the early 1900s, this building's architectural details have been emphasized by leaving brick walls exposed and designing around the grand, heart-pine beams and wood ceilings. Oil paintings of hunting dogs hang above clubby leather chairs and sofas. You can enjoy evening wine and cheese on a rooftop terrace while you watch the ships sail past. **Pros:** great pub downstairs; large, upscale supermarket with Charleston products across the street; walking distance to the Old Market and Galliard Auditorium. **Cons:** not that close to King Street shops; not luxurious. ⊠*21 Hasell St., Market area* ☎*843/723–1655 or 800/522–2073* ⊕*www.ansonboroughinn.com* ➴*37 suites* ⚿*In-room: safe, refrigerator, Wi-Fi. In-hotel: bar, Wi-Fi, parking (paid), no-smoking rooms* ⊟*AE, MC, V* †⊙†*BP.*

$–$$ ⚐**Broad Street Guesthouse.** Hadassah Rothenberg, an accomplished cook and baker, has realized her dream of opening the city's first kosher B&B. She completely transformed this 1880s frame house, artfully decorating it with a mix of Victorian furnishings, religious art, and vintage family photos. On Friday evening guests can join in traditional prayers and partake in a multicourse Shabbat dinner. Rothenberg's kosher dishes are delicious and fresh, the baked goods delectable. The wholesome breakfast is even better when taken on the terrace. **Pros:** impeccably clean; a fascinating learning experience if you are non-Jewish; decor has a museum quality to it. **Cons:** only three rooms; you cannot bring in foods that are not kosher; innkeeper fussy about noise in the main house. ⊠*133 Broad St., South of Broad* ☎*843/577–5965* ⊕*www.charlestonkosherbedand breakfast.com* ➴*2 suites, 1 cottage* ⚿*In-room: no phone, no TV, kitchen. In-hotel: Wi-Fi, parking (free), no-smoking rooms* ⊟*AE, D, MC, V* †⊙†*BP.*

$$$$ ⚐**Charleston Place.** Even casual passersby enjoy gazing up
★ at the handblown Murano glass chandelier in the hotel's open lobby, clicking across the Italian marble floors, and admiring the antiques from Sotheby's. A gallery of upscale shops completes the ground-floor offerings. Rooms are furnished with period reproductions. The impeccable service is what you would expect from an Orient-Express property, particularly on the Club Level, where rooms carry a $100 surcharge that gets you a breakfast spread, afternoon tea, and cocktails and pastries in the evening. A truly deluxe day spa, with an adjacent fitness room, has an inviting indoor salt- and mineral-water pool with a retractable roof and

Where to Stay in Downtown Charleston

Andrew Pinckney Inn, **11**

Ansonborough Inn, **12**

Broad Street
Guesthouse, **21**

Cannonboro Inn
and Ashley Inn, **1**

Charleston Place, **17**

Doubletree Guest
Suites Historic
Charleston, **19**

1834 Battery Carriage
House Inn, **30**

1837 Bed and Breakfast Tea
Room, **13**

Elliott House Inn, **24**

Embassy Suites
Historic Charleston, **4**

Francis Marion Hotel, **5**

French Quarter Inn, **20**

Governors House Inn, **22**

Hampton Inn—
Historic District, **3**

HarbourView Inn, **27**

Hayne House, **29**

Holiday Inn
Historic District, **6**

Indigo Inn, **10**

Jasmine Inn, **9**

John Rutledge
House Inn, **23**

Market Pavilion Hotel, **26**

Meeting Street Inn, **18**

Mills House Hotel, **25**

Not So Hostel, **2**

Phoebe Pember House, **8**

Planters Inn, **16**

Renaissance Charleston
Hotel Historic District, **7**

Two Meeting
Street, **31**

Vendue Inn, **28**

Victoria House Inn, **15**

Wentworth Mansion, **14**

illuminated skylight for night swimming. **Pros:** two great restaurants; located in the historic district on the best shopping street; pet-friendly. **Cons:** no Wi-Fi; rooms aren't as big as one would expect for the price; much of the business is conference groups in shoulder seasons. ■TIP→ **Even if you aren't staying here, stop by for afternoon tea at the equestrian-themed Thoroughbred Club.** ⊠ *130 Market St., Market area* ☎ *843/722–4900 or 800/611–5545* ⊕ *www.charlestonplace hotel.com* ⬚ *400 rooms, 42 suites* ⌂ *In-room: safe, refrigerator, Internet. In-hotel: 2 restaurants, bars, pool, gym, spa, Internet terminal, parking (paid), some pets allowed, no-smoking rooms* ⊟ *AE, D, DC, MC, V* ⌊⍥⌉ *EP.*

$$–$$$ ⌧ **Doubletree Guest Suites Historic Charleston.** This one-time
⌂ bank wears a restored entrance portico from 1874. Fountains bubble in the three interior garden courtyards. This is not a glamorous property, but it has clean, spacious suites with nice touches like antique reproductions and canopy beds. The efficient and friendly staff dotes on families, even giving out chocolate-chip cookies. Like most, they can arrange babysitting services. **Pros:** located in the Old Market; there's no fee if you have a service animal. **Cons:** no breakfast; Internet is expensive. ⊠ *181 Church St., Market area* ☎ *843/577–2644 or 877/408–8733* ⊕ *www. doubletree.com* ⬚ *47 rooms, 165 suites* ⌂ *In-room: safe (some), refrigerator (some), Internet. In-hotel: bar, laundry facilities, parking (paid), no-smoking rooms* ⊟ *AE, D, DC, MC, V* ⌊⍥⌉ *EP.*

$$$– ⌧ **1834 Battery Carriage House Inn.** Most area residents who
$$$$ don't live South of Broad on the Battery envy those who do and dream of "some day." For visitors, the some day can come without having to sell the farm by just booking into a historic room here, with the enviable presence of the park and the water beyond. Many guests consider White Point Park part of the public space of the inn, which also has a pleasant back courtyard and gardens. The rooms were the carriage house of an antebellum home that now belongs to a lawyer from an old plantation family and his artist wife. You may meet a number of interesting types at the evening wine and cheese receptions. **Pros:** great location that is quiet and romantic at night; high level of service; each room is individually decorated. **Cons:** some rooms are small; not plush with creature comforts; not a full breakfast (light Continental instead). ⊠ *20 S. Battery, South of Broad* ☎ *843/727–3100* ⊕ *www.batterycarriage house.com* ⬚ *11 rooms, 1 suite* ⌂ *In-room: safe, Internet.*

In-hotel: parking (free), no-smoking rooms, no kids under 12 ⊟*AE D, MC, V.*

$$–$$$ ⊡ **1837 Bed & Breakfast/Tea Room.** A hospitable staff helps you get a sense of what it would be like to live in one of Charleston's grand old homes. The owner is delightfully funny. Antique lace-canopy rice beds fill many of the guest rooms, which are in the main house and in the carriage house, each of which is individually decorated. A delicious breakfast includes homemade breads and hot entrées such as sausage pie or ham frittatas. **Pros:** a very good concierge will help you plan your days; nice veranda where guests can relax after touring the town. **Cons:** cell reception not so great in the three carriage house rooms due to the thick walls; off-street parking limited (there are nine rooms but only seven small parking spaces). ⊠*126 Wentworth St., Market area* ☎*843/723–7166 or 877/723–1837* ⊟*843/722–7179* ⊕*www.1837bb.com* ⊸*8 rooms, 1 suite* ⌂*In-room: no phone, refrigerator, Wi-Fi. In-hotel: Wi-Fi* ⊟*AE, DC, MC, V* ⦿*BP.*

$$$–
$$$$ ⊡ **Elliott House Inn.** Listen to the chimes of St. Michael's Episcopal Church as you sip wine in the lovely courtyard of this inn in the heart of the historic district. It is even more fun when you bubble away in the whirlpool tub that can and often does hold a dozen people. You can then retreat to a cozy room with period furniture, including canopied four-posters and Oriental carpets. Some previously loyal guests complain that it has lost some of its personal, homey ambience since it was taken over by a corporate management company; others seem quite pleased with the change. The best are the king-rooms on the second or third floor with courtyard views. **Pros:** convenient location between King and Meeting streets; free bikes and Wi-Fi. **Cons:** ground-floor, street-view rooms can be noisy, small, and dark; a motel-like feel; kids are allowed but there's only one bed in each room. ⊠*78 Queen St., Market area,* ☎*843/723–1855 or 800/729–1855* ⊕*www.elliotthouseinn.com* ⊸*24 rooms* ⌂*In-room: Wi-Fi. In-hotel: bicycles, parking (paid), no-smoking rooms* ⊟*AE, D, MC, V* ⦿*BP.*

$$$–
$$$$ ⊡ **Embassy Suites Historic Charleston.** A courtyard where cadets once marched is now an atrium with skylights, palm trees, and a fountain. The restored brick walls of the breakfast room and some guest rooms in this contemporary hotel contain original gun ports, reminders that the 1822 building was the Old Citadel. Handsome

teak and mahogany furniture and sisal rugs in the common areas recall the British-colonial era. Guest rooms are not nearly as chic, but are clean and serviceable. **Pros:** near Marion Square, where events take place including Saturday's farmers' market; close to newly refurbished Upper King's business and retail district; complementary manager's reception nightly that extends to the courtyard. **Cons:** the suites themselves are chain-hotel standard, not handsome and atmospheric like the lobby; no longer inexpensive. ✉ *337 Meeting St., Upper King* ☎ *843/723–6900 or 800/362-2779* ⊕*www.embassysuites.com* ⇗*153 suites* △*In-room: refrigerator, Wi-Fi. In-hotel: restaurant, pool, gym, laundry facilities, parking (paid), no-smoking rooms* ⊟*AE, D, DC, MC, V* ⧀*BP.*

$$–$$$ ⊞ **Francis Marion Hotel.** Wrought-iron railings, crown moldings, and decorative plasterwork speak of the elegance of 1924, when the Francis Marion was the largest hotel in the Carolinas. Bountiful throw pillows and billowy curtains add flair to the guest rooms, many of which have views of Marion Square. It is the tallest downtown hotel and was once Charleston's showplace; it is still a National Historic Trust Property featuring the original 1924 chandeliers. The hotel divides King Street into its "upper" section. Flavorful Lowcountry cuisine is served at the Swamp Fox. **Pros:** architecturally and historically significant building; marks the start of the newly refurbished business and retail district, yet still near the College of Charleston. **Cons:** rooms are small, as is closet space; on a busy intersection. ✉*387 King St., Upper King* ☎*843/722–0600 or 877/756-2121* ⊕*www. francismarioncharleston.com* ⇗*193 rooms, 34 suites* △*In-room: Wi-Fi. In-hotel: restaurant, gym, spa, parking (paid), no-smoking rooms* ⊟*AE, D, DC, MC, V* ⧀*EP.*

SOMETHING EXTRA. When you book your room, ask about special packages. Extras that are often available include romantic carriage rides, dinners, interesting guided tours, and champagne or other goodies delivered to your room.

$$$$ ⊞ **French Quarter Inn.** The first architectural detail you'll
★   notice in this boutique hotel known for its chic French style is a circular staircase with a wrought-iron banister embellished with iron leaves. Guests appreciate the lavish breakfasts, the afternoon wine and cheese reception, and evening cookies and milk. The pillow menu is a luxury; you can order whatever kind you desire, including big body pil-

lows. Some rooms have fireplaces, others balconies. Among the best are No. 220, a business suite with a corner office niche overlooking the courtyard, and No. 104, with a spacious L-shape design. You'll get champagne at check-in, too. **Pros:** located in the heart of the market area yet is a quiet haven; excellent restaurant (Tristan) on premises. **Cons:** no pool or fitness area; being smack in the busy Market has its downside. ⊠ *166 Church St., Market area* ☎ *843/722–1900 or 866/812–1900* ⊕ *www.fqicharleston.com* ↪ *46 rooms, 4 suites* ⚲ *In-room: safe (some), refrigerator (some), Internet. In-hotel: restaurant, bar, Wi-Fi, parking (paid), no-smoking rooms* ⊟ *AE, MC, V* ⊚*CP.*

$$$$ ⊠ **Governors House Inn.** This quintessential Charleston lodg-
★ ing radiates 18th-century elegance. Its stately architecture typifies the grandeur, romance, and civility of the city's bountiful colonial era. A National Historic Landmark, it's filled with antiques and period reproductions in the public rooms and the high-ceilinged guest rooms, some of which have whirlpool tubs. The best room is the Rutledge Suite, a legacy to the original owner, Governor Edward Rutledge. Nice touches include a proper afternoon tea where wine and cheese are also served. **Pros:** you can take breakfast on the veranda or have it delivered; evening sherry and Godiva chocolates with turndown service. **Cons:** older children are welcome in the former kitchen house rooms, but the main house is not the appropriate environment; no glorious views. ⊠ *117 Broad St., South of Broad* ☎ *843/720–2070 or 800/720–9812* ⊕ *www.governorshouse.com* ↪ *10 rooms, 1 jr. suite* ⚲ *In-room: kitchen (some), Internet, Wi-Fi. In-hotel: Internet terminal, Wi-Fi, parking (free), no-smoking rooms* ⊟ *AE, D, MC, V* ⊚*BP.*

$$$ ⊠ **Hampton Inn–Historic District.** Hardwood floors and a fire-place in the lobby of what was once an 1800s warehouse help elevate this chain hotel a bit above the rest. Spindle posts on the headboards give guest rooms a little personality. Rooms are not large but have little perks like coffeemakers. The location is perfect for exploring downtown. There is always something to eat and drink in the lobby. **Pros:** hot breakfast; located near the business and retail district of Upper King and near a couple of really good restaurants. **Cons:** a long walk to the Market area; rooms are smallish and not atmospheric. ⊠ *373 Meeting St., Upper King* ☎ *843/723–4000 or 800/426–7866* ⊕ *www.hamptoninn. com* ↪ *166 rooms, 5 suites* ⚲ *In-room: refrigerator, Wi-Fi.*

In-hotel: pool, laundry facilities, parking (paid), no-smoking rooms ⊟AE, D, DC, MC, V ⊙BP.

$$$–
$$$$ ▦ **HarbourView Inn.** Ask for a room facing the harbor, and you can gaze down at the landmark pineapple fountain of Waterfront Park. Calming earth tones and rattan soothe and relax; four-poster beds and sea-grass rugs complete the Lowcountry look. Some of the rooms are in a former 19th-century shipping warehouse with exposed brick walls, plantation shutters, and whirlpool tubs. Afternoon wine and cheese and evening milk and cookies are included. **Pros:** Continental breakfast can be delivered to room; service notable; closest hotel to the harbor and Waterfront Park. **Cons:** rooms are off long, modern halls; rooms are not particularly spacious. ⊠*2 Vendue Range, Market area* ☎843/853–8439 or 888/853–8439 ⊕*www.harbourview charleston.com* ⬳*52 rooms* ⚷*In-room: safe, refrigerator, Wi-Fi. In-hotel: Internet terminal, Wi-Fi, parking (paid), no-smoking rooms* ⊟AE, D, DC, MC, V ⊙BP.

$$ ▦ **Holiday Inn Historic District.** Thanks to its staff, this hotel has an outstanding track record for guest satisfaction. And then there's the great location—across from Marion Square and a block from Gaillard Auditorium. It does have a chain-motel feel. Rooms have wooden armoires, headboards, and side tables. On the upside, this former motel was completely gutted in 2000, so its rooms and bathrooms are far more spacious than in some of the older, historic hotels. Breakfast can be the Continental buffet ($5.95) or the feel-good, hot buffet ($11.95). **Pros:** well-respected concierge Kevin McQuade belongs to an international, Italian-based concierge society; self-parking in attached garage. **Cons:** 50% of rooms (along the back of hotel) have no view due to obstruction of other buildings; a long walk (about six blocks) to the Market. ⊠*125 Calhoun St., Upper King,* ☎843/805–7900 or 877/805–7900 ⊕*www. charlestonhotel.com* ⬳*122 rooms, 4 suites* ⚷*In-room: Wi-Fi. In-hotel: restaurant, bar, pool, Internet terminal, Wi-Fi, parking (paid), no-smoking rooms* ⊟AE, D, DC, MC, V ⊙EP.

$$–$$$ ▦ **Indigo Inn.** A former indigo warehouse in Charleston's colonial times is painted an appealing smoky green. The location is convenient to King Street and to the Market, yet it is solidly quiet, with a park-like, inner courtyard. There you can take your complimentary Hunt Breakfast or the wine and hors d'oeuvres that are set out nightly. All-day

beverages, from lemonade to coffee, are available in the petite lobby, which is the meeting ground for guests. The front desk and long-term management of this family-owned hotel are particularly welcoming and helpful; repeat guests are the norm. Rooms are comfy, done in period reproductions, some with four-posters; a couple have desks. The free in-room Wi-Fi is a plus as is the adjacent parking lot, but there is a $10 fee. **Pros:** location, location; mini-bottles of liquor and good bottles of wine can be purchased from front desk; free local calls. **Cons:** rooms are not large and some are dark; opened in 1981, and rooms are a little dated. ⊠*1 Maiden La. Lower King* ☎*843/577–5900* ⊕*www. indigoinn.com* ☜*40 rooms* ♿*In-room: Wi-Fi. In-hotel: Internet terminal, Wi-Fi, parking (paid), some pets allowed, no-smoking rooms* ⊟*AE, D, MC, V* ⌯◎⌯*BP.*

4

$$$–
$$$$ ▥ **Jasmine Inn.** Not as publicized as most downtown properties, this is as close to living in a grand Charleston home as you may ever get without a real estate closing. This 1843 mansion was decorated handsomely when it opened in the 1980s. Walking down the quiet, tree-lined street and coming upon this glorious Greek revival mansion—yellow with white columns—you simply want in. If indeed, you do decide to stay here, it will be like staying in a friend's home. The housekeeper is there by day, but otherwise this inn shares its front desk, phone system, and parking lot with its sister property, Indigo Inn. The main house has royally large rooms; several, including the Canton Room, which opens to the second-story veranda, has an anteroom called a "card room." The separate carriage house "dependency," which looks out to a leafy courtyard, has four cozy rooms of its own. **Pros:** complementary beverages (hot and cold in the kitchen); evening wine and cheese spreads on the sideboard; carriage house rooms were more recently decorated and are aesthetically more appealing. **Cons:** no on-site Internet or Wi-Fi (though guests can use Indigo Inn's next door); bedding could be more plush. ⊠*64 Hassell St., Lower King* ☎*843/577–5900* ⊕*www.jasminehouseinn.com* ☜*10 rooms* ♿*In-hotel: parking (paid), no kids under 18, no-smoking rooms* ⊟*AE, MC, V* ⌯◎⌯*BP.*

$$$$ ▥ **John Rutledge House Inn.** In 1791, George Washington
★   visited this elegant mansion, residence of one of South Carolina's most influential politicians, John Rutledge. This National Historic Landmark has spacious accommodations within the lovingly restored main house (Nos. 6, 8, and 11 are the most appealing). Solid painted walls—in

forest green and buttercream yellow—complement the billowy fabrics on the four-poster beds. Parquet floors sit beneath 14-foot ceilings adorned with plaster moldings. Families gravitate to the privacy and quiet of the two carriage houses overlooking the shaded brick courtyard. A scrumptious afternoon tea is served in the former ballroom. Breakfast—Continental as well as at least one hot item—can be taken in the ballroom or courtyard. **Pros:** at night, when you "go home" and pour a sherry, it's like being a blue-blood Charlestonian; the building has a New Orleans-esque exterior with its wrought iron architectural details; nice, quiet back courtyard. **Cons:** the two carriage houses can cost more than the main and are not nearly as grand; you can hear some street and kitchen noise in the first-floor rooms. ⊠ *116 Broad St., South of Broad* ☎ *843/723–7999 or 800/476–9741* ⊕ *www.charminginns. com* ➫ *16 rooms, 3 suites* ⑁ *In-room: refrigerator, Wi-Fi. In-hotel: Wi-Fi, parking (paid), no-smoking rooms* ⊟ *AE, D, DC, MC, V* ⊠ *BP.*

★ Fodor'sChoice ☆ **Market Pavilion Hotel.** The melee of one of the
$$$$ busiest corners in the city vanishes as soon as the uniformed bellman opens the lobby door to dark, wood-paneled walls, antique furniture, and chandeliers hung from high ceilings. It resembles a European grand hotel from the 19th century, and you feel like visiting royalty. Although management keeps both privacy and security tight, it is a known fact that big-name celebrities and politicos stay here, especially in the presidential suite. You can sometimes hear music coming from the grand piano. Get used to being pampered—smartly attired bellmen and butlers are quick at hand. Rooms are decadent with French-style chaises and magnificent marble baths. One of Charleston's most prestigious fine-dining spots, Grill 225, is here. All guests enjoy delectable refreshments in their respective lounges, with those on the executive fourth floor getting a hot breakfast, afternoon tea, and (good) wine service. **Pros:** opulent furnishings; architecturally impressive, especially the tray ceilings; conveniently located for everything. **Cons:** the building was constructed to withstand hurricane-force winds, which thus far has prohibited Wi-Fi and can limit cell phone reception; those preferring a minimalist decor may find the opulent interior too elaborate. ■ TIP→ **Join sophisticated Charlestonians who do cocktails and apps at the rooftop Pavilion Bar.** ⊠ *225 E. Bay St., Market area* ☎ *843/723–0500 or 877/440–2250* ⊕ *www.marketpavilion.com* ➫ *61 rooms, 9*

suites ♿In-room: Internet. In-hotel: restaurant, bar, pool, Internet terminal, no-smoking rooms ▭AE, D, DC, MC, V ⊙EP.

$$$–
$$$$ ⊠ **Meeting Street Inn.** This 1874 house with second- and third-story porches originally had a tavern on the ground floor; the nightly wine and cheese reception in the lobby, often with live music, is the reincarnation of a more genteel time. Rooms overlook a lovely courtyard with fountains and a garden; many have hardwood floors and hand-woven rugs. Four-poster or canopy beds, chair rails, and patterned wallpaper create a period feel. Despite its good downtown location, the inn has managed to keeps its prices more affordable than some places. **Pros:** all rooms have free Wi-Fi, and more expensive rooms have desks and veranda; within the courtyard is a large heated spa tub. **Cons:** rooms have 19th-century style (reproductions) but could use some updated decor; some employees are excellent while others are somewhat taciturn. *⊠173 Meeting St., Market area ☎843/723–1882 or 800/842–8022 ⊕www.meetingstreet inn.com ⬠56 rooms ♿In-room: refrigerator, Wi-Fi. In-hotel: bar, Wi-Fi, parking (paid), no-smoking rooms ▭AE, D, DC, MC, V ⊙BP.*

$$$–
$$$$ ⊠ **Mills House.** A favorite local landmark, the Mills House is the reconstruction of an 1853 hotel where Robert E. Lee once waved from the wrought-iron balcony. All of the guest rooms have been completely refurbished and have nice touches like antique reproductions and a Charleston motif with Oriental accents. There are some additions to the original design, such as a fitness center and a delightful pool and deck. Lowcountry specialties are served in the Barbados Room, which opens onto the terrace courtyard. **Pros:** convenient to business district, historic district, and art galleries; a popular Sunday brunch spot. **Cons:** staffers are too inexperienced for a hotel of this quality; rooms are small, which is typical of hotels of this time period. *⊠115 Meeting St., Market area ☎843/577–2400 or 800/874–9600 ⊕www.millshouse.com ⬠199 rooms, 16 suites ♿In-room: Wi-Fi. In-hotel: restaurant, bar, pool, gym, parking (paid), no-smoking rooms ▭AE, D, DC, MC, V ⊙EP.*

$$–$$$ ⊠ **Phoebe Pember House.** Named after a maverick female spirit who lived in this Charleston home in 1838, the property is split between a carriage house with two guest rooms and a coach house with three rooms. The decor is tastefully done, and each room has nice touches like lace-covered

canopy beds; bathrooms are artistically tiled. The vibrant artwork is by Charleston artists. Enjoy an organic breakfast in the walled garden shaded by an arbor (yoga classes are held here, too), or you can have silver tray service in your room. This B&B is a unique concept for Charleston: it is holistic, combining history with innovation and stages events, lectures, and retreats with leading-edge writers, thinkers, and spiritual visionaries. **Pros:** the coach house (or carriage house) is more inviting than the other guest rooms, like having your own home and patio entrance; a quiet place with a spirituality about it (guests come here to re-center and restore). **Cons:** spring dates sell out far in advance; don't come with the party-hearty mind-set; wine and cheese reception only on Friday nights. ⊠ *26 Society St., Ansonborough* ☎ *843/722–4186* ⊕ *www.phoebepember house.com* ⋑ *5 rooms* ⅍ *In-room: refrigerator (some), Wi-Fi. In-hotel: parking (free), some pets allowed, no-smoking rooms* ⊟ *MC, V* ⊚ *BP.*

$$$$ ▧ **Planters Inn.** Part of the Relais & Châteaux group, this
★   boutique property is a stately sanctuary amid the bustle of Charleston's Market. Light streams into a front parlor with its velvets and Oriental antiques. It serves as the lobby for this exclusive inn that has both a historic side and a new building wrapped around a two-story piazza and overlooking a tranquil garden courtyard. Rooms all look similar and are beautifully maintained, but the main building has more atmosphere and a more residential feel. Service is genteel and unobtrusive but not stuffy, and the hospitality feels genuine. The best rooms have fireplaces, verandas, and four-poster canopy beds; the "piazza" suites with whirlpool baths and top-tier suites are suitably over the top in terms of comfort. Packages that include either breakfast or dinner at the on-site Peninsula Grill are a good value. **Pros:** triple-pane windows render the rooms soundproof; the same front desk people take your initial reservation and know your name upon arrival; either the Continental or full breakfast is exceptional. **Cons:** no pool; no fitness center; views are not outstanding. ⊠ *112 N. Market St., Market area* ☎ *843/722–2345 or 800/845–7082* ⊕ *www.plantersinn.com* ⋑ *56 rooms, 6 suites* ⅍ *In-room: safe, Wi-Fi. In-hotel: restaurant, Wi-Fi, parking (paid), no-smoking rooms* ⊟ *AE, D, DC, MC, V* ⊚ *EP.*

$$$–   ▧ **Renaissance Charleston Hotel Historic District.** A sense of
$$$$ history prevails in this hotel, one of Charleston's newest upscale properties. Legend has it that British Admiral

George Anson won this neighborhood, now dubbed Ansonborough, in a card game in 1726. (This is why his image is on the playing cards in the library lounge.) The hotel has a delightful courtyard where you can enjoy cocktails. Guest rooms are smallish but have nice touches like period-style bonnet beds. This is one of the few downtown hotels with a pool. The Wentworth Grill serves a mix of French and Lowcountry specialties and is a gem. **Pros:** built in 2000, the rooms were renovated for the first time in 2008, as was the lobby; located in the King Street shopping district. **Cons:** Wi-Fi limited to the lobby; rooms have the feel of a chain hotel. ⊠*68 Wentworth St., Ansonborough* ☎*843/534–0300* ⊕*www.renaissancecharlestonhotel.com* ➴*163 rooms, 3 suites* ⌂*In-room: Internet. In-hotel: restaurant, bar, pool, Wi-Fi, parking (paid), no-smoking rooms* ⊟*AE, D, DC, MC, V* ⦿*EP.*

4

DOGGIE DAY CARE. If you have brought your dog along but don't want to leave him in your room all day, call Charlie Freeman at Dog Daze (⊠*307 Mill St., Mount Pleasant* ☎*843/884–7387 or 843/324–6945*). His services are $20 a day. With advance notice he'll even pick up Rover at your hotel for an additional $10.

$$$– $$$$ ★ ▣**Two Meeting Street.** As pretty as a wedding cake, this Queen Anne mansion has overhanging bays, colonnades, balustrades, and a turret. While rocking on the front porch you can look through soaring arches to White Point Gardens and the Ashley River. Tiffany windows, carved-oak paneling, and a crystal chandelier dress up the public spaces. Some guest rooms have verandas and working fireplaces. Expect to be treated to afternoon high tea as well as a delightful, creative Southern breakfast. **Pros:** 24-hour free on-street parking; community refrigerator on each floor; ringside seat for a Battery view and horse-drawn carriages clipping by. **Cons:** not wheelchair-accessible, some rooms have thick walls and make Wi-Fi spotty; small TVs only get local stations (no cable at all). ⊠*2 Meeting St., South of Broad* ☎*843/723–7322* ⊕*www.twomeetingstreet.com* ➴*9 rooms* ⌂*In-room: no phone, safe, Wi-Fi. In-hotel: no kids under 12, parking (free), no-smoking rooms* ⊟*No credit cards* ⦿*BP.*

$$$$ ▣**Vendue Inn.** Two 19th-century warehouses have been transformed into an inn with a variety of nooks and crannies filled with antiques. This lodging's rooftop restaurant and bar have sweeping views of the nearby waterfront,

but rooms look out at a condo building. Bathrobes hang in the closet, and full buffet breakfast, afternoon wine and hors d'oeuvres, and evening milk and cookies are complimentary. **Pros:** soundproofing is being added to rooms for street noise; pets allowed for a $50 fee; this is a unique, petite inn that still has some comfortable public spaces. **Cons:** popular local hangouts nearby can be noisy; $250 fine for smoking in rooms; larger travelers may find the public spaces too tight. ⊠ *19 Vendue Range, Market area* ☎*843/577–7970 or 800/845–7900* ⊕*www.vendueinn.com* ⋟*31 rooms, 35 suites* ⬚*In-room: safe, Wi-Fi. In-hotel: restaurant, bar, Wi-Fi, parking (no fee), no-smoking rooms* ⊟*AE, D, DC, MC, V* ⦿*BP.*

$$$–
$$$$ ⌧**Victoria House Inn.** Victoria has the unique position of being immediately between its two sister properties, the Fulton Lane Inn and the King's Courtyard Inn. Though each is a separate entity with its own staff and personality, all are connected by stairways and similarly priced. These charming, personable siblings were originally a YMCA in the 1850s. Victoria has the Richardson Romanesque style; its ground floor still houses some King Street retail and antique shops. The inn is a favorite with returnees who appreciate the personal service from caring concierges. Breakfast is served in the namesake courtyard of King's Courtyard Inn (or indoors with air-conditioning), or breakfast can be brought to your room. All guests can use the outdoor Jacuzzi at the King's Courtyard. Wine and cheese service makes every evening a social event. **Pros:** room decor is cozy and feminine with Victorian-style furnishings; some rooms have working fireplaces and whirlpool tubs. **Cons:** rooms on King St. can pick up street noise, so choose an interior room like No. 317; bedding could be finer, but there are new cushy mattresses underneath. ⊠ *208 King St., Lower King* ☎*843/720–2944 or 800/933–5464* ⊕*www.the victoriahouseinn.com* ⋟*27 rooms* ⬚*In-room: refrigerator, Wi-Fi. In-hotel: Internet terminal, Wi-Fi, parking (paid), no-smoking rooms* ⊟*AE, D, MC, V* ⦿*BP.*

★ Fodor'sChoice ⌧**Wentworth Mansion.** Charlestonian Francis
$$$$ Silas Rodgers made his money in cotton. In 1886 he commissioned this four-story mansion with such luxuries as Austrian crystal chandeliers and hand-carved marble mantles. Now guests admire the Second Empire antiques and reproductions, the rich fabrics, inset wood paneling, and original stained-glass windows. In the colder months, the baronial, high-ceilinged guest rooms have the velvet drapes

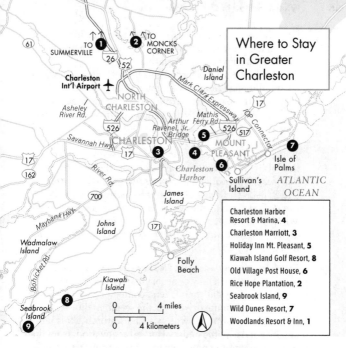

Where to Stay
in Greater
Charleston

Charleston Harbor
Resort & Marina, **4**

Charleston Marriott, **3**

Holiday Inn Mt. Pleasant, **5**

Kiawah Island Golf Resort, **8**

Old Village Post House, **6**

Rice Hope Plantation, **2**

Seabrook Island, **9**

Wild Dunes Resort, **7**

Woodlands Resort & Inn, **1**

drawn and the gas fireplaces lighted. The complimentary evening wine and delectable hors d'oeuvres are now served in the sunny, glass-enclosed porch. Breakfast, with a new expanded hot menu, has been moved to Circa 1886, the inn's laudable restaurant, which shares the former carriage house with the spa. **Pros:** luxury bedding including custom-made mattresses, down pillows, and Italian linens; new carpet and furnishings lend a fresh look. **Cons:** not child-friendly; Second Empire style can strike some people as foreboding; the building has some of the woes of an old building, including loudly creaking staircases. ⊠ *149 Wentworth St., College of Charleston Campus* ☎ *843/853–1886 or 888/466–1886* ⊕ *www.wentworthmansion.com* ⇱ *21 rooms* ☐ *In-room: Internet. In-hotel: restaurant, spa, no-smoking rooms* ☐ *AE, D, DC, MC, V* ⦿ *BP.*

MOUNT PLEASANT

$$$– **☲ Charleston Harbor Resort & Marina.** Mount Pleasant's finest
$$$$ hotel sits on Charleston Harbor, so you can gaze at the city's skyline, yet a water taxi from the marina will get you across the harbor in 10 minutes. A lot goes on here, from splashy

boat shows at the marina to wedding celebrations on the man-made white-sand beach. Ask for one of the renovated rooms with a fireplace and plasma TV. Children can jump into the mini-mariners' program while parents are navigating a sailboat. A number of annual sailing events are held here, and the bar scene is fun. **Pros:** the most accessible hotel to downtown that's not in downtown (approximately 6 mi away); a "trolley" runs to the Old Market from 10–10 daily; renovations have made a huge difference. **Cons:** no gym or spa (both are planned at this writing, however); the lobby and the restaurant are not memorable. ⊠ *20 Patriots Point Rd., Mount Pleasant* ☎*843/856–0028 or 888/856–0028* ⊕*www.charlestonharborresort.com* ☞*160 rooms, 6 suites* ⌂*In-room: safe (some), refrigerator (some), Wi-Fi. In-hotel: restaurant, bar, pool, water sports, children's programs (ages 7–12), parking (free), no-smoking rooms* ⊟*AE, DC, MC, V* ⏣*BP.*

$$–$$$ 🖾 **Holiday Inn Charleston/Mt. Pleasant.** Everything about this place has been tastefully done: big banana trees in the lobby, brass lamps, crystal chandeliers, contemporary furniture. It's just a 10-minute drive over the scenic Arthur Ravenel Jr. Bridge to historic downtown Charleston. At this writing the hotel is in the midst of a total renovation, from the rooms through the public spaces. **Pros:** some resort amenities, including a pool and sauna; for a small property, it has a good business center; some rooms have microwaves. **Cons:** an older property that looks its age (circa 1980s); not downtown nor does it have the atmosphere of a historic B&B; the new Tides condo complex now blocks its bridge view. ⊠ *250 Johnnie Dodds Blvd., Mount Pleasant* ☎*843/884–6000 or 800/290–4004* ⊕*www.ichotelsgroup. com* ☞*158 rooms* ⌂*In-room: refrigerators (some), Wi-Fi. In-hotel: restaurant, room service, bar, pool, gym, laundry facilities, Internet terminal, Wi-Fi, parking (free), some pets allowed, no-smoking rooms* ⊟*AE, D, DC, MC, V.*

$–$$ 🖾 **Old Village Post House.** This white wooden building anchoring Mount Pleasant's historic district is a cozy inn, an excellent restaurant, and a neighborly tavern. Up the high staircase, rooms have hardwood floors and reproduction furnishings that will remind you of Cape Cod. The dark-wood furnishings feel right at home in a building with roots in the 1880s. The food is wonderful, from the pastries at breakfast to the dinners downstairs in the Southern bistro. On Sundays you can order off the brunch menu. Staying in this charming, tree-lined village, you're within walking distance to Charleston Harbor and the nearby fishing community. **Pros:** unique lodging experience in Mount Pleasant; prices are as affordable as some chain motels on the highway; close to Sullivan's Island and Isle of Palm. **Cons:** some minor old building woes including creaky wood floors; not plush and has few cushy creature comforts. ⊠*101 Pitt St., Mount Pleasant* ☎*843/388–8935* ⊕*www.oldvillageposthouse.com* ↪*6 rooms* ⚷*In-room: Wi-Fi. In-hotel: restaurant, bar, Wi-Fi, parking (free), no-smoking rooms* ▤*AE, D, DC, MC, V* ⦿|*BP.*

ELSEWHERE IN CHARLESTON

$$$ ⊡ **Cannonboro Inn.** This B&B is on the edge of the historic district. You can expect a full breakfast served on a wide porch overlooking a garden, tea in the afternoon, and free use of bicycles. Rooms have antiques from the 19th century, when the structure was built. The gray Cannonboro also has one suite with a kitchen. Sister property the pink Ashley Inn is nearby with six rooms, a two-bedroom carriage house, and similar prices. **Pros:** free off-street parking for each room; signature fudge and wine at the afternoon reception; close to the hospitals (MUSC and Roper). **Cons:** not so convenient to the tourist area (approximately eight blocks away); refrigerator and phone are shared. ⊠*184 Ashley Ave., Medical University of South Carolina* ☎*843/723–8572 or 800/235–8039* ⊕*www.charleston-sc-inns.com* ↪*7 rooms, 1 suite* ⚷*In-room: no phone, kitchen (some). In-hotel: bicycles, parking (free), no kids under 10, no-smoking rooms* ▤*AE, D, DC, MC, V* ⦿|*BP.*

$-$$ ⊡ **Charleston Marriott.** This great river-view hotel was completely transformed less than five years ago into a top-notch property. A glamorous glass addition with a cascading waterfall houses the concierge desk. The sunset views from the balconies are better as you go higher and especially good from the classy, rooftop terrace where drinks and tapas are served. The pool area is resort-like, with plenty of palms and a gazebo. The aromas from the brick oven in Saffires are intoxicating, as are the myriad flatbreads it produces. The cuisine is laudable—contemporary dishes with refreshingly flavorful low-calorie options. The new Aqua Terrace, a rooftop lounge, has live jazz nightly. **Pros:** free shuttle to downtown until 10:30 PM; concierge floor is excellent and a real added value; located near The Citadel, MUSC, and marinas. **Cons:** not in the historic district; Wi-Fi available but for a hefty charge; concierge floor does not have breakfast on weekends. ⊠ *170 Lockwood Dr., Charleston* ☎ *843/ 723–3000* ⊕ *www.marriott.com* ⇆ *337 rooms, 3 suites* ⟡ *In-room: safe, refrigerator, Internet, Wi-Fi. In-hotel: restaurant, room service, bar, pool, laundry service, Internet terminal, Wi-Fi, parking (free), no-smoking rooms* ⊟ *AE, DC, MC, V* ⦿ *EP.*

★ Fodor'sChoice ⊞ **Kiawah Island Golf Resort.** Choose from one- to four-bedroom villas and three- to seven-bedroom private homes in two upscale resort villages on 10,000 wooded and oceanfront acres. The decades-old inn complex is no longer open, but a number of the smaller two-bedroom condo-villas are still fairly affordable. Or you can opt to stay at the Sanctuary at Kiawah Island, an amazing 255-room luxury waterfront hotel and spa. Its vast lobby is stunning, with walnut floors covered with hand-woven rugs and a wonderful collection of artworks. When a pianist plays in the lobby lounge it is dreamlike. The West Indies theme is evident in the guest rooms; bedposts are carved with impressionistic pineapple patterns, and plantation-style ceilings with exposed planks are painted white. The Ocean Room has incredible architectural details—wrought-iron gates and sculptures and a stained-glass dome. Its contemporary cuisine is of an international caliber. Along with the 10 mi of island beaches, recreational options include kayak and surfboard rental, nature tours, and arts-and-crafts classes. **Pros:** one of the most prestigious resorts in the country, it is still kid-friendly; the Ocean Room is an ideal venue for an anniversary or a proposal. **Cons:** not all hotel rooms have even an angular view of the ocean; it is pricey and a substantial drive from town. ⊠ *12 Kiawah Beach Dr., Kiawah Island* ☎ *843/768–2121 or 800/654–2924* ⊕ *www. kiawahresort.com* ⇆ *255 rooms, 600 villas and homes* ⟡ *In-room: safe (some), refrigerator, Internet, Wi-Fi. In-hotel: 10 restaurants, golf courses, tennis courts, pools, gym, spa, beachfront, water sports, children's programs (ages 3–12), Internet terminal, Wi-Fi, parking (free), no-smoking rooms* ⊟ *AE, D, DC, MC, V* ⦿ *EP.*

$$$– $$$$

¢ ⊞ **Not So Hostel.** Several 1840s-era buildings were combined to make this hostel. Continental breakfast might be bagels and Nutella, fair-trade coffee, and more. You can sometimes pick organic veggies from the garden and cook them yourself. Nightly prices still put the rest of the city's downtown lodgings to shame. Of course, you need to be able to handle a little peeling paint, a bit of clutter, and a less-than-genteel downtown neighborhood. Linens, a locker, and Internet access are free, and you can borrow DVDs. **Pros:** the price and feeling of camaraderie are right; the historic rooms have character; guests can use the main kitchen. **Cons:** the ambience is not unlike a hippie commune; standards of cleanliness and unapproved sharing can be a problem; communal bathrooms. ✉ *156 Spring St., Medical University of South Carolina* ⊕ *www.notsohostel. com* ⬐ *24 dorm beds, 7 rooms with communal baths* ⌂ *In-room: no phone, kitchen (some), no TV, Wi-Fi. In-hotel: bicycles, laundry facilities, Internet terminal, Wi-Fi, parking (free), no-smoking rooms* ⊟ *AE, D, MC, V* ⦿ *BP.*

$$–$$$ 🖭**Seabrook Island.** The most private of the area's island resorts, Seabrook is endowed with true Lowcountry beauty. Wildlife sightings are common: look for white-tailed deer and even bobcats. Going to the beach is as popular as playing golf or tennis, but erosion has whisked away a lot of the sand. About 200 fully-equipped one- to six-bedroom homes are available, but the smallest units are often priced as cheaply as a hotel room. The Beach Club and Island House are centers for dining and leisure activities, and there is a quality equestrian center that is just inside the gates and open to the public. As each villa is individually owned, the Internet capabilities will vary accordingly. **Pros:** physically beautiful, relatively unspoiled island; the pool complex has ocean views and is immediately adjacent to the clubhouse; great safe haven for kids and biking. **Cons:** beach has eroded despite the seawall in front of the club; accommodations consist only of villas, with no regular hotel rooms. ✉ *3772 Seabrook Island Rd., Seabrook Island* ☎ *843/768–1000 or 800/845–2233* 🖷 *843/768–2361* ⊕ *www.seabrook.com* ⬐ *200 units* ⌂ *In-room: kitchen, Internet (some), Wi-Fi (some). In-hotel: 3 restaurants, bar, golf courses, tennis courts, pools, gym, beachfront, water sports, bicycles, children's programs (ages 4–17), parking (free), no-smoking rooms* ⊟ *AE, D, DC, MC, V* ⦿ *EP.*

$$$$ 🖭**Wild Dunes Resort.** This 1,600-acre island resort has as
★ its focal point the plantation-style Boardwalk Inn. It sits among a cluster of villas that have been painted in pastels to resemble Charleston's Rainbow Row. The guest rooms and suites on the fourth and fifth floors have balconies that overlook the ocean. You can also choose from one- to six-bedroom villas that sit near the sea or the marshes. Guests have a long list of recreational options here including Tom Fazio golf courses and nationally ranked tennis programs; packages including golf and tennis are available. Nearby

is a yacht harbor on the intracoastal waterway. Chef Enzo Steffenelli reigns over the highly-rated Sea Island Grill. A new complex, the Village Condos (135 units) opened next to the inn in 2008 and has a family-friendly restaurant serving three meals daily. In the adjacent plaza, there are music performances, family bingo, and (in the summer) musicians and jugglers. **Pros:** golf courses and marina are appealing; free shuttle runs from 7 AM to 11 PM to wherever you need to go within the complex. **Cons:** in peak summer season, the number of kids in the pool areas and the boardwalk are high; a congested, high-density feel exists in all the main facilities. ⊠*Palm Blvd. at 41st Ave., Isle of Palms* ⌨*Box 20575, Charleston 29413* ☎*843/886–6000 or 888/845–8926* ⊕*www.wilddunes.com* ↪*560 units, 93 rooms* ♿ *In-room: safe, refrigerator (some), Internet, Wi-Fi. In-hotel: 3 restaurants, golf courses, tennis courts, pools, gym, water sports, bicycles, Internet terminal, Wi-Fi, children's programs (ages 3–12), parking (free) no-smoking rooms* ▤*AE, D, DC, MC, V* ⌾*EP.*

Nightlife & the Arts in Charleston

5

WORD OF MOUTH

"The Spoleto and Piccolo Spoleto festivals in Charleston run [from late May through early June]. You might check the Web sites to see if there's anything that intrigues you and your friends. There is a truly amazing selection of all types of performing arts each year."

—dsgmi

By Eileen
Robinson
Smith

FOR A MIDSIZED CITY, Charleston has a surprisingly varied and sophisticated arts scene, though the city really shines during its major annual arts festival, Spoleto Festival USA. Still, throughout the year, there are other opportunities to explore higher culture. Since Charleston is also a college town, its university also offers possibilities.

The nightlife scene is similarly comprehensive, with nocturnal venues for all ages and tastes. The town has a large fun quotient. If your image of Charleston is a proper, mannerly, highbred town, with men in seersucker suits and bow ties, think again. That may been an image of Charlestonians in decades past—and light blue seersucker is still worn on summer nights—but that oldster can probably still out-shag his fraternity son and knock down his share of bourbon along the way. While some of the nightlife can be rowdy and more youth-oriented, there are options for all ages and tastes here, from jazz clubs to techno dance clubs.

THE ARTS

ANNUAL FESTIVALS & EVENTS

Spoleto USA is only the beginning—there are dozens of festivals held throughout the city each year. Some focus on food and wine, whereas others are concerned with gardens and architecture. Charleston is one of the few American cities that can claim a distinctive regional cuisine.

The **BB&T Charleston Food + Wine Festival** (☎843/763–0280 or 866/369–3378 ⊕www.charlestonfoodandwine.com) allows the city to "strut its stuff" at an annual festival, in Marion Square in early March. Some of the most sought-after events sell out early, such as the Restaurant Dine-Around with celebrity chefs, and the Saturday Night Celebration with incredible food stations and live music. Guests can interact with some of the country's top winemakers. Cooking demonstrations under the big tent give guests an opportunity to learn from some of the country's finest chefs.

The **Fall Tours of Homes & Gardens** (☎843/722–4630 ⊕www.preservationsociety.org), sponsored by the Preservation Society of Charleston in September and October, provides an inside look at Charleston's private buildings and gardens.

More than 100 private homes, gardens, and historic churches are open to the public for tours during the **Festival of Houses & Gardens** (☎843/722–3405 ⊕www.historic

charleston.org), held during March and April each year. There are also symphony galas in stately drawing rooms, plantation oyster roasts, and candlelight tours.

The **MOJA Arts Festival** (☎843/724–7305 ⊕*www.mojafestival. com*), which takes place during the last week of September and first week of October, celebrates African heritage and Caribbean influences on African-American culture. It includes theater, dance, and music performances, art shows, films, lectures, and tours of the historic district.

Piccolo Spoleto (☎843/724–7305 ⊕*www.piccolospoleto.org*) is the spirited companion festival of Spoleto Festival USA, showcasing the best in local and regional talent from every artistic discipline. There are hundreds of events—from jazz performances to puppet shows and expansive art shows in Marion Square—from mid-May through early June, and many of the performances are free.

The **Southeastern Wildlife Exposition** (☎843/723–1748 or 800/221–5273 ⊕*www.sewe.com*) in mid-February is one of Charleston's biggest annual events, with fine art by renowned wildlife artists, live animals, an oyster roast, and a gala.

CONCERTS

The **Charleston Symphony Orchestra** (☎843/723–7528 ⊕*www. charlestonsymphony.com*) season runs from October through April, with pops series, chamber series, family-oriented series, and holiday concerts. This symphony is nationally and even internationally renown, as it is also the Spoleto Festival Orchestra. Most performances are in Gaillard Municipal Auditorium.

DANCE

The **Charleston Ballet Theatre** (☎843/723–7334 ⊕*www. charlestonballet.com*) performs everything from classical to contemporary dance. Performances are in a range of venues around town, including Gaillard Municipal Auditorium.

The **Robert Ivey Ballet Company** (☎843/556–1343 ⊕*www. cofc.edu*), a semiprofessional company that includes College of Charleston students, puts on a fall and spring program of jazz, classical, and modern dance at the Sottile Theater.

Spoleto Festival USA

For 17 glorious days in late May and early June, Charleston gets a dose of culture from the **Spoleto Festival USA** (☎843/722-2764 ⊕www.spoletousa.org). This internationally acclaimed performing-arts festival features a mix of distinguished artists and emerging talent from around the world. Performances take place in magical settings, such as beneath a canopy of ancient oaks or inside a centuries-old cathedral.

Well over 100 events—which cost between $10 (for balcony seats) to $130 (good orchestra seats), with most averaging between $25 and $50—include everything from improv to Shakespeare, from rap to chamber music, from ballet to salsa. A mix of formal concerts and casual performances is what Pulitzer Prize–winning composer Gian Carlo Menotti had in mind when, in 1977, he initiated the festival as a complement to his opera-heavy Italian festival. He chose Charleston because of its European look and because its residents love the arts—not to mention any cause for celebration. He wanted the festival to be a "fertile ground for the young" as well as a "dignified home for the masters." Mayor Joseph Riley has diligently worked to renew that Italian connection with the original mother festival in Spoleto, Italy (⊕www.festivaldispoleto.it). In 2008, Spoleto mayor Massimo Brunini came from that Umbrian hill town with a cultural entourage and gave the American festival that kind of inimitable Italian input that had been so missed over the past few years. This reaffirmation of sister-city partnership and the sharing of ideas will encourage Italian influences and increase tourism between the two cities for both festivals and beyond.

The finale is a must-do, particularly for the younger crowd. Staged outdoors at Middleton Place, the plantation house and lush landscaped gardens provide a dramatic backdrop. The inexpensive seating is unreserved and unlimited. The lawn is covered with blankets and chairs, and many cooks prepare lavish spreads. After the Spoleto Festival Orchestra plays a spirited concert of contemporary and classic pieces, spectacular fireworks explode over the Ashley River.

Because events sell out quickly, insiders say you should buy your Spoleto tickets several months in advance. (Tickets to mid-week performances are a bit easier to secure.) Hotels definitely fill up quickly, so book a room at the same time and reserve your tables for the trendy downtown restaurants.

FILM

Palmetto Grande 16 Cinemas (✉*1319 Theater Dr., Mount Pleasant* ☎843/216–8696) is a grand art deco–style multiplex that makes movie-going fun in the traditional style of enjoying popcorn and a soda in a comfortable stadium-style seat.

THEATER

The **Footlight Players** (✉*20 Queen St., Market area* ☎843/722–4487 ⊕*www.footlightplayers.net*) regularly perform fun plays and musicals.

VENUES

Bluegrass, blues, and country musicians step onto this historic stage Of the **Charleston Music Hall** (✉*37 John St., Upper King* ☎843/853–2252 ⊕*www.charlestonmusichall.com*), especially for Piccolo Spoleto performances.

Gaillard Municipal Auditorium (✉*77 Calhoun St., Upper King* ☎843/577–7400) hosts symphony and ballet companies, as well as numerous festival events. The box office is open weekdays from 10 to 6.

Dance, symphony, and theater productions are among those staged at the **North Charleston Performing Art Center** (✉*5001 Coliseum Dr., North Charleston* ☎843/529–5050 ⊕*www.coliseumpac.com*).

Performances by the College of Charleston's theater department and musical recitals are presented during the school year at the **Simons Center for the Arts** (✉*54 St. Phillips St., College of Charleston Campus* ☎843/953–5604).

NIGHTLIFE

You can find it all here, across the board, for Charleston loves a good party. The more mature crowd goes to the sophisticated spots, and there are many: piano bars, wine bars, lounges featuring jazz groups or a guitarist/vocalist, and cigar lounges. Many restaurants have live entertainment on at least one weekend night or every night, and these tend to cater to an older crowd. But Charleston is also a college town, and the College of Charleston students line up to get into the latest in-spot, which is usually located in the Market area. △**A recent city ordinance mandates that** bars must close by 2 AM and that patrons must be out of the establishment and doors locked by that hour.

BARS & BREWERIES

Charleston Beer Works (⊠*468 King St., Upper King* ☎*843/577–5885*) is definitely beverage-friendly and also offers interesting choices of appetizers, small plates, and buffalo wings. Eighty bottled beers and 20 draft selections make this a popular hangout for the college crowd.

Club Habana (⊠*177 Meeting St., Market area* ☎*843/853–5900*) is a chic martini and cognac bar upstairs and a shop for cigar aficionados downstairs. Adjacent rooms of dark hardwood are dimly lit, furnished with sectional sofas in an intimate (at-home) ambience. This is the only establishment in town where you can still smoke inside the club.

Cheap "mystery beers" and billiard tables make **Cumberland's** (⊠*301 King St., Market area* ☎*843/577–9469*) a popular spot for a younger crowd. Throw in some live bluegrass or rhythm and blues, and the joint cranks until 2 AM.

Dunleavy's Pub (⊠*2213 Middle St., Sullivan's Island* ☎*843/883–9646*) is just a block from the beach. This friendly Irish pub is a local favorite, featuring Irish, folk, and blues music. After decades, Bert's Bar, its funky neighbor, finally shut its doors, which has made Dunleavy's all the more popular.

Henry's On The Market (⊠*54 N. Market, Market area* ☎*843/723–4363*) is a Charleston tradition, having evolved over the decades. Once the primary destination for the sophisticated jazz enthusiast, it is now a hot spot for young locals and tourists alike.

King Street Grille (⊠*304 King St., Upper King* ☎*843/723–5464*) offers good food, a fun crowd, and a multitude of TV screens, putting this bar on the "go to" list for many of the city's hard-core sports fans. The beer list includes 100 bottled brews.

Mad River Bar & Grille (⊠*32 N. Market St., Market area* ☎*843/723–0032*) attracts a young, high-energy crowd. It's in the atmospheric Old Seamen's Chapel and serves a wide variety of American cuisine and cold beverages. Several giant TV screens usually show sports, and it's open until 2 AM.

★ **Fodor's**Choice Atop the Market Pavilion Hotel, the outdoor **Pavilion Bar** (✉ *225 E. Bay St., Market area* ☎*843/266–4218*) offers panoramic views of the city and harbor. Sit at the east overlook to appreciate the grand architecture of the Customs House. Enjoy appetizers, delicacies created with lobster and duck and such, with a signature martini. This can be your beginning before dining downstairs at the hotel's famous Grill 225. Or you can make a night of it here, and be soothed by the sounds of the cascading pool. Inevitably, you will meet new sophisticated friends. This is Charleston's best rooftop bar.

At **Rooftop at Vendue** (✉ *23 Vendue Range, Market area* ☎*843/577–7970*) you can have a cocktail and appetizer as you watch the colorful sunset behind the church steeples. The view of the water is not as good as it was before condos were built in front of it; however, you'll find live music every night and a mixed—mostly young—crowd, which means that on Friday nights you may encounter a line to get to the roof.

Social Restaurant & Wine Bar (✉ *188 E. Bay St., Market area* ☎*843/577–5665*) offers 60 wines by the glass, as well as bottles and flights (to better compare and contrast several wines in smaller portions). Light menu choices are available, and there are pizzas and flavorful microbrews, too.

Southend Brewery (✉ *161 E. Bay St., Market area* ☎*843/853–4677*) has a lively bar serving beer brewed on the premises. Try the wood-oven pizzas and the smokehouse barbecue. Thursday is salsa night, Friday showcases a bluegrass band, and Saturday night a guitarist. You can dance if the music moves you; in fact, it is encouraged.

Vickery's Bar & Grill (✉ *139 Calhoun St., Market area* ☎*843/577–5300*) is a fun nightspot with an outdoor patio and good late-night food. Not chichi inside, instead it has well-worn character. A great place for a custom hamburger, also try their famous artichoke appetizer.

DANCE CLUBS

There's a see-and-be-seen crowd at **City Bar** (✉ *5 Faber St., Market area* ☎*843/577–7383*). This club frequently promotes theme parties, special groups, and contests in a fun and creative format.

The throbbing dance beat of DJ Amos draws the crowds at **Club Light** (⊠*213C E. Bay St., Market area* ☎*843/722–1311*), a lively and lighthearted part of downtown's single scene. Only open Thursday through Saturday nights, there is a cover charge after 11 PM. You can stick around 'til last call.

Thursday is Latin Night at the **Trio Club** (⊠*139 Calhoun St., Upper King* ☎*843/965–5333*), where funky 1970s and '80s sounds are perennially popular. This dance club starts late and runs hard until closing. Live music keeps this fashionable clientele moving. Although populated mainly with the young, it is one dance club frequented by all ages, but it's open only from Thursday through Saturday.

DINNER CRUISES

Dine and dance the night away aboard the wide-beamed, motor yacht **Spirit of Carolina** (☎*843/881-7337* ⊕*www.spiritlinecruises.com*). Dinner is generally aged beef tenderloin or crab cakes. The dance band appeals to an older crowd, but for all ages it is nice to be out on the water, hold your partner close, and see the lights of the harbor by night. There's also a cash bar. ■TIP→**Remember that reservations are essential for evening cruises.**

JAZZ CLUBS

★ The elegant **Charleston Grill** (⊠*Charleston Place Hotel, 224 King St., Market area* ☎*843/577–4522*) has live jazz nightly and draws a mature, upscale clientele, hotel guests, and more recently an urbane and somewhat younger crowd. The bartenders could be social directors since they seem to put all manner of customers together until it is like a multigenerational house party. Those who want to stare into each other's eyes choose either a high cocktail table or a comfy chair in the lounge in front of the musicians. Make a reservation for dinner, or you can have something at the classy, sophisticated bar.

At **Mistral** (⊠*99 S. Market St., Market area* ☎*843/722-5709*) live blues and jazz make patrons feel good on Monday, Tuesday, Thursday, and Saturday nights. On Wednesday, two French musicians sing their renditions of pop and folk songs. On Friday, a Dixieland band really animates those who grew up with this music. During Spoleto, fabulous groups, like a Brazilian combo, electrifies the room.

Mistral's French onion soup is fabulous if you want a late-night refuel.

LIVE MUSIC

Best Friend Lounge (⊠*Mills House Hotel, 115 Meeting St., Market area* ☎843/577–2400) has a guitarist playing on weekends. This draws an older crowd of downtown residents and hotel guests. It is sequestered in the front of the hotel behind the drawing room to the right of the entrance, but the bar closes when it slows down in the summer season.

JB Pivot's Beach Club (⊠*1662 Savannah Hwy., West Ashley* ☎843/571–3668) is a no-frills place, with live beach music and shag or swing dancing lessons Tuesday to Thursday.

Mercato (⊠*102 N. Market St., Market area* ☎843/722–6393) is a popular restaurant that has become almost as well known for its entertainment, which begins on Wednesday nights (from 7 to 10), when there is customarily a jazz vocalist. The music usually cranks up from Thursday to Saturday at 8 and goes until 11. At this writing, there's a gypsy swing band on Thursday, a jazz trio on Friday, and a Cuban fusion band on Saturday night. There is no cover, but come early to get a seat at the long, elegant bar. All ages come, though most are youngish.

The Thoroughbred Club (⊠ Charleston Place Hotel, *130 Market St., Market area* ☎843/722–4900) is both fun and classy, with a horse-racing theme and excellent appetizer menu. Go for the impressive afternoon tea (even with alcoholic libations), or sip a cocktail and enjoy the soothing piano being played Monday through Saturday after 1 PM (or Sunday after 5). Each of the pianists has a different repertoire, so depending on the song requests, they can infect the patrons with a wonderful spirit and camaraderie.

Listen to authentic Irish music at **Tommy Condon's** (⊠*15 Beaufain St., Market area* ☎843/577–3818).

The **Windjammer** (⊠*1000 Ocean Blvd., Isle of Palms* ☎843/886–8596) is an oceanfront bar with local and national rock bands playing Thursday through Sunday. Anyone who is ageless goes here, but it is mainly a younger, postcollegiate haunt.

Sports & the Outdoors in Charleston

WORD OF MOUTH

"If you're staying in Charleston and you want to go to the beach, I would go to one of the three that are closest to the city, instead of driving all the way to Kiawah. My personal favorite is Sullivan's Island, but Isle of Palms and Folly Beach are both nice."

—Betsy in KY

By Eileen
Robinson
Smith

CHARLESTON IS A GREAT PLACE TO GET OUTDOORS.
Called the Lowcountry because it is at sea level—and sometimes even below—the city has an array of tidal creeks,
estuaries, and rivers that flow out to the deep blue Atlantic.
The region's beaches are taupe sand, and the Carolina sun
warms them some nine months out of the year. Many are
uncrowded, especially in the spring and fall, and public
beaches are kept clean and well-maintained, mostly by the
staff of the county parks system.

Several barrier islands studded with palm trees and live oaks
festooned with Spanish moss thrive. Even though they are
fairly extensively developed, some still shelter wildlife that
you can frequently see. Charlestonians will tell you (without
bragging) that this is one the most beautiful regions on this
planet. Here you can commune with nature, perhaps like
you haven't in years.

It can be expensive to take part in some of the region's
best outdoor activities, and this may give some pause to
families, especially those who might want to charter a
boat to do some fishing. But dolphin-watching tours on
regularly scheduled group charters are much cheaper on
a per-person basis, and crabbing at low tide is free. You'll
also find an amazing number of low-cost options, from
biking to canoeing and kayaking, and nature walks. Of
course, in the warm weather, the beach is the thing. Those
looking for more of an adrenaline rush can rent a Jet Ski
or surfboard.

Area golf courses are reasonably priced compared to, say,
Hilton Head, the public courses being the least expensive.
The championship courses on the resort islands are the
most beautiful, though they are costly.

Sailing is becoming an increasingly important activity here
in this port city. If you know how to sail, you can rent a
small boat, take a few sailing lessons, or just go out on
crewed charter boats. Among the annual sailing events
held here are the Keel Boat Regatta (mid-April) and the
much-televised Charleston-to-Bermuda Race in late May.
Annually, Charleston's Harbor Fest during the third week
in June, has grown in importance and size, and the parade
of Tall Ships is always a highlight.

BEACHES

The Charleston area's mild climate means you can swim from March through October. Public beaches, operated by the Charleston County Parks & Recreation Commission, generally have lifeguards in season, snack bars, restrooms and dressing areas, outdoor showers, umbrella and chair rental, and large parking lots.

The county park's commission operates three multidimensional family parks, three water parks, and three beach parks. Each offers programming that involves the natural characteristics of each site, but they are careful not to duplicate these leisure services from site to site. There are marinas, fishing piers, dog parks, water parks, campgrounds, cottage rentals, facility and equipment rentals, and boat and kayak landings.

The resorts have all the extras like beach umbrellas, etc. Some will allow you to park on-site and use their facilities for a fee of around $10.

Trees, palmettos, and other natural foliage cover the interior, and there's a river that winds through **Folly Beach County Park** (⊠*1100 W. Ashley Ave., off U.S. 17, Folly Island* ☎*843/588–2426* ⊕*www.ccprc.com* ⊠*$10 per car* ☉*Apr., Sept., and Oct., daily 10–6; May–Aug., daily 9–7; Nov.– Mar., daily 10–5*), 12 mi southwest of Charleston. The Park is more than six football fields long. You may find on-street parking near the Holiday Inn.

Play beach volleyball or rent a raft at the 600-foot-long beach in the **Isle of Palms County Park** (⊠*1 14th Ave., Isle of Palms, Mount Pleasant* ☎*843/886–3863 or 843/768–4386* ⊕*www.ccprc.com* ⊠*$10 per car* ☉ *Apr., Sept., and Oct., daily 10–6; May–Aug., daily 9–7; Nov.– Mar., daily 10–5*).

The public **Kiawah Beachwalker Park** (⊠*Beachwalker Dr., Kiawah Island* ☎*843/768–2395* ⊕*www.ccprc.com* ⊠*$10 per car* ☉*Mar., weekends 10–5; Apr. and Oct., weekends 10–6; May–Aug., daily 10–7; Sept., daily 10–6*), about 28 mi southwest of Charleston, has 500 feet of deep beach.

6

BEST BETS FOR ACTIVITIES

Beaches: Charleston's palm-studded coastline and the beaches of its barrier islands rival those in the Caribbean—and are often less congested, safer, and cleaner. The shoulder seasons of spring and fall are good for beachcombing, while summer is the time for swimming and water sports.

Biking: Charleston's Historic District is particularly biker-friendly, and riding a bike there is a wonderful way to have the wind in your hair and also avoid automobile and parking hassles. You can ride through the various in-town parks, like Francis Marion Square and Waterfront Park, or take the bike path on the colossal Arthur Ravenel Jr. On the island resorts, a bike is the ideal way to get around, especially for parents with older kids.

Boating & Sailing: Charleston's waters offer something for both the blue-water sailor and for those who just want to take a waterborne tour. Fishing is also a top sport here, and a charter is an ex-cellent way to spend the day if you can afford it.

Kayaking: This relatively low-cost activity is one of the best ways to explore the Lowcountry's many waterways. Try paddling to keep up with the schools of dolphins you'll encounter while gliding silently in the Intracoastal Waterway. Middleton Plantation rents kayaks, offering you the opportunity to push your paddle through former rice fields with views of the famous Butterfly Gardens. In Mount Pleasant, you can kayak in Shem Creek, the center of its shrimping industry, and if you are fit, you can paddle all the way to Sullivan's Island.

Golf: The weather is ideal for golf in the spring and fall, or even during the region's relatively mild winter. Summer's strong rays make morning and late afternoon the most popular tee times. Though not quite up to par with the courses of Hilton Head, golf on the nearby island resorts, especially at Kiawah Island Golf Resort, is still quite good.

SPORTS & ACTIVITIES

BASEBALL

The **Charleston Riverdogs** (⊠*Joseph P. Riley, Jr. Stadium, 360 Fishburne St.* ☎*843/577–3647* ⊕*www.riverdogs.com*) play at "The Joe," on the banks of the Ashley River near to The Citadel. Kids love their mascot, Charlie T. Riverdog. After games, fireworks often illuminate the summer sky in honor of this all-American pastime. With "Fun is Good" as their motto, they have theme nights that attract various audiences. The season runs from April through September. Tickets cost a reasonable $7 to $12.

BIKING

The historic district is ideal for bicycling as long as you stay off the busier roads. Many of the city's green spaces, including Colonial Lake and Palmetto Islands County Park, have biking trails. If you want to rent a bike, expect to pay about $15 for a half-day (three hours), and $25 for a full day.

Most of the shops charge the same price, but exceptions are noted. It's one of the best ways to see Charleston, and at your own pace. Those staying at the island resorts, particularly families, almost always rent bikes, especially if they are there for a week.

BTB Bike Rentals (⊠6 *Vendue Range, Market area* ☎*843/853–2453* ⊕*www.bicyclecharleston.com*) can set you up to ride the paths on the spectacular Arthur Ravenel Jr. Bridge. You'll get a map, a self-guided tour booklet, and a free water-taxi ride back. You can also rent comfort bikes, road bikes, tandems for two, unicycles, jogging strollers, and tagalongs.

You can rent bikes at the **Bicycle Shoppe** (⊠*280 Meeting St., Market area* ☎*843/722–8168* ⊠*1539 Johnnie Dodds Blvd., Mount Pleasant* ☎*843/884–7433*).

Carolina Beach Cruisers (⊠*4053 S. Rhett Ave., North Charleston* ☎*843/747–2453*) rents all kinds of bikes, including those with special seats for youngsters. It delivers to all area islands.

Island Bike and Surf Shop (⊠*3665 Bohicket Rd., John's Island* ☎*843/768–1158*) rents island cruisers (beach bikes) for a very moderate weekly rate of $34.95. The shop will even deliver to Kiawah and Seabrook Islands. If you just want a bike for a day or two ($12.90 per day), you have to pick it up and return it.

6

BOATING

Kayak through isolated marsh rivers and estuaries to outlying islands, or explore Cape Romain National Wildlife Refuge. Rates vary of course, depending on location and if you take a guided tour. Typically you can expect to pay $35 a person in a single or double kayak for a two-hour guided tour. Rentals can be $12 a person per hour. Weekly rentals are about $150. The resort islands, especially Kiawah and Wild Dunes, tend to be higher.

The boating options are so varied, from a small "John boat" with an outboard to a chartered sailboat, that it is best to contact these companies for their litany of pricing. Similarly, small sailboat lessons can be arranged.

If you want a sailing or motor yacht charter, perhaps a beach barbecue, an ecotour, or just to go offshore fishing, contact **AquaSafaris** (⊠*Patriots Point Marina, Mount Pleasant* ☎*843/886–8133* ⊕*www.aqua-safaris.com*). Check the company's Web site because prices vary depending on vessel size, be it the catamaran or an offshore fishing trip.

Outings for individuals, families, and groups are provided by **Coastal Expeditions** (⊠*514B Mill St., Mount Pleasant* ☎*843/884–7684*).

Island Bike & Surf Shop (⊠*3665 Bohicket Rd., John's Island* ☎*843/768–1158*) rents surfboards and kayaks and will deliver to the resort islands. Boards cost $15 a day.

You can rent kayaks from **Middleton Place Plantation** (⊠*4300 Ashley River Rd., West Ashley* ☎*843/556–6020* ⊕*www. theinnatmiddletonplace.com*) and glide along the Ashley River. You need to call ahead for reservations.

Take your family sailing, be at the helm, and learn how to command your own 26-foot sailboat on Charleston's beautiful harbor with the guidance of an instructor at **Ocean Sailing Academy** (⊠*24 Patriots Point Rd., Mount Pleasant* ☎*843/971–0700* ⊕*osasailing.com*).

FISHING

★ FodorsChoice For inshore (saltwater) fly-fishing, guides generally charge $350 (for two people) for a half-day, $450 for an hour more. Deep-sea fishing charters cost about $1,400 for 12 hours for a boatload of anglers.

Anglers can rent gear for $8 to $12 (with a $25 deposit) and cast a line at the 1,000-foot fishing pier at **Folly Beach County Park** (⊠*101 E. Arctic Ave., Folly Beach* ☎*843/588–3474*). Baby sharks are commonly on the end of your line. You'll pay $5 for a fishing pass, or just $3 if you're a non-fisher.

Bohicket Marina (⊠*1880 Andell Bluff Blvd., John's Island* ☎*843/768–1280* ⊕*www.bohicket.com*) has half- and full-day charters on 24- to 48-foot boats. Small boat rentals are also available, as well as dolphin-watching and dinner cruises. This marina is the closest to Kiawah and Seabrook, and this charter company has a long-standing reputation. For inshore fishing, expect to pay about $395 for three hours minimum (four to six people), including bait, tackle, and licenses.

Saltwater fly-fishers looking for an Orvis-endorsed guide do best by calling **Captain Richard Stuhr** (⊠*547 Sanders Farm La., North Charleston* ☎*843/881–3179* ⊕*www.capt stuhr.com*), who has been fishing the waters of Charleston, Kiawah and Isle of Palms since 1991; he'll haul his boat, a 19-foot Action Craft, to you.

Palmetto Charters (⊠*224 Patriots Point Rd., Mount Pleasant* ☎*843/849–6004*) has guided trips that take you out in the ocean or stay close to shore. They also handle power yacht charters, crewed sailboat charters, and bareboats, both locally and in the Caribbean. There is a litany of prices, from the luxury category on down.

GOLF

With fewer golfers than in Hilton Head, the courses around Charleston have more choice starting times available. Nonguests can play at private island resorts, such as Kiawah Island, Seabrook Island, and Wild Dunes. There you will find breathtaking ocean views within a pristine setting. They offer enchantment and escape from the stresses of the workaday world. Don't be surprised if a white-tailed deer is grazing a green or if there is a gator drinking from the water holes. For the top courses like Kiawah's Ocean Course, nonguests can expect to pay $240 to $350 (peak season spring and early fall). Municipal golf courses are a golfing bargain, from $29 to $37 for 18 holes. Somewhere in between are the Shadowmoss Golf Club, West of the Ashley, for $45 to $86, and The Links at Stono Ferry in Hollywood for $45 to $86.

To find out about golf vacation packages in the area, contact the **Charleston Area Golf Guide** (☎*800/774–4444* ⊕*www. charlestongolfinc.com*).

The public **Charleston Municipal Golf Course** (⊠*2110 Maybank Hwy., James Island* ☎*843/795–6517*) is a walker-friendly course. Green fees run $29 to $37.

Charleston National Country Club (⊠*1360 National Dr., Mount Pleasant* ☎*843/884–7799*) is well maintained and tends to be quiet on weekdays. Green fees are $25 to $88.

The **Dunes West Golf Club** (⊠*3535 Wando Plantation Way, Mount Pleasant* ☎*843/856–9000*) has great marshland views and lots of modulation on the greens. Green fees are $45 to $92.

Of the three championship courses at **Kiawah Island Resort** (⊠*12 Kiawah Beach Dr., Kiawah Island* ☎*800/576–1570*), Gary Player designed Cougar Point (originally named Marsh Point); Tom Fazio was the architect for Osprey Point; and Jack Nicklaus designed Turtle Point. All three charge the same green fees: $175 for resort guests, $219 for nonguests. Turtle Point is one of Nicklaus's earliest designs and the longest course on the island. Osprey Point has a world-class layout (a par-72) and a large and elegant clubhouse. In the middle of the island, Cougar Point has one of the most dramatic vistas on Kiawah. Its front nine are along the Kiawah River. Also owned by Kiawah is the 18-hole course Oak Point, one mile off the island, with free shuttle service. A par-72 course, Oak Point was redesigned by Clyde Johnston in 2004 and has some superb marsh views, particularly at sunset, and a comfortable, Lowcountry clubhouse with a grill restaurant and a bar. It is the most affordable, at $106 for resort guests, $133 for nonguests.

Links at Stono Ferry (⊠*4812 Stono Links Dr., Hollywood* ☎*843/763–1817*) is a popular public course with reasonable rates. Green fees are $45 to $86.

★ **Fodor'sChoice** The prestigious **Ocean Course** (⊠*1000 Ocean Course Dr., Kiawah Island* ☎*843/266-4670*), designed by Pete Dye, was the site of the 1991 Ryder Cup. This is the best golf in the immediate Charleston area; to do better, you have to travel down to Hilton Head. The course starred in Robert Redford's *The Legend of Bagger Vance* in 2000, which really made it known. It has more seaside holes than any other course in the northern hemisphere.

Unfortunately, its fame translates to green fees of $298 for resort guests, $350 for nonguests. (It is a walking-only facility until noon.)

Patriots Point (⊠*1 Patriots Point Rd., Mount Pleasant* ☎*843/881–0042*) has a partly covered driving range and spectacular harbor views. Green fees are $75 to $100.

Seabrook Island Resort (⊠*Seabrook Island Rd., Seabrook Island* ☎*843/768–2529*) has two championship courses: Crooked Oaks, by Robert Trent Jones Sr., and Ocean Winds, by Willard Byrd. Green fees are $95 to $150.

Shadowmoss Golf Club (⊠*20 Dunvegan Dr., West Ashley* ☎*843/556–8251*) is a well-marked, forgiving course with one of the best finishing holes in the area. Green fees are $28 to $52.

Tom Fazio designed the Links and the Harbor courses at **Wild Dunes Resort** (⊠*10001 Back Bay Dr., Isle of Palms* ☎*843/886–2180* ⊠*5881 Palmetto Dr., Isle of Palms* ☎*843/886–2301*), where green fees for 18 holes will run you $140 to $165.

HORSEBACK RIDING

★ Put your foot in the stirrup and get a leg up! You will love seeing the beaches, maritime forests, marshlands, and former rice fields from horseback. Several good stables in the area offer trail rides, and there are also equestrian centers, lessons, and jumping rings which you can also enjoy. Trail rides average from $40 for wooded terrain to $85 for an advanced beach ride; they go out for about an hour.

Middleton Equestrian Center (⊠*4280 Ashley River Rd., West Ashley* ☎*843/556–8137* ⊕*www.middletonplace.org*) is a long-established stable that specializes in English riding lessons. It now offers trail rides through wooded and open terrain and former rice fields. All experience levels are welcome, and headgear is provided. The price is $40 for the trail, but only children 10 and older can ride. This is the home stable for Middleton Place Hounds, and in the fall visitors can watch them depart ceremoniously on Wednesday and Sunday for their fox hunts.

Seabrook Island Equestrian Center (⊠*Seabrook Island Rd., Seabrook Island* ☎*843/768–7541* ⊕*www.discover seabrook.com*) is open to the public. The center, 24 mi south of Charleston, has trail rides through the maritime forests for $65 (children must be eight years old and up) and beach rides for advanced riders for $85, for 45 minutes to an hour. This is a classy operation that hosts annual equestrian events and notable hunter/jumper shows.

About 7 mi south of Charleston, **Stono River Stables & Farms** (✉2962 Hut Rd., John's Island ☎843/559–0773 ⊕www.stonoriverstable.com) is a well-established and caring school/stable that offers trail rides through 300 acres of maritime forests, with excellent instructors and guides. It employs the only farm manager in the state who is a member of Phi Beta Kappa. Rides must be arranged in advance, and it is $55 an hour; mainly English saddles are used. It is about 7 mi from Kiawah and Seabrook Islands. Non-riders can walk the nature trails for $15 a day.

SCUBA DIVING

Experienced divers can explore the Cooper River Underwater Heritage Diving Trail, upriver from Charleston. The 2-mi-long trail has six submerged sites, including ships that date to the Revolutionary War. Charters will run you out to the starting point. Expect to pay $95 to $145 a trip. Equipment rentals average $10 for a tank.

Charleston Scuba (✉335 Savannah Hwy., West Ashley ☎843/763–3483 ⊕www.charlestonscuba.com) has maps, equipment rentals (Monday through Saturday, 10 AM–6:30 PM), and charter trips to the Cooper River Trail. They frequent a total of eight sites, and prices range from $45–$65. Equipment can be rented, too.

SOCCER

Charleston Battery (✉Blackbaud Stadium, 1990 Daniel Island Dr., Daniel Island ☎843/971–4625 ⊕www.charlestonbattery.com) is the first privately-funded soccer-specific facility in the U.S. Games are played from April through September and feature fun-filled giveaways and promotions. The faithful team supporters of the Charleston Battery are referred to as "The Regiment," and after the games, fans retreat to the clubby English pub. The seating capacity is 5,100.

TENNIS

Whether your interest in tennis is casual or serious, the Charleston area, especially its resort islands, offers tennis options for every skill level. Spring and fall are simply ideal for play. You can play for free at neighborhood courts, including several near Colonial Lake and at the Isle of Palms Recreation Center. If you want the privilege of playing where stars like the Williams sisters compete, at the Family Circle Tennis Center, the cost is $15 per hour for a clay court, and $10 per hour for a hard court. The resort islands are the most costly, depending on whether or not you are a guest.

Charleston Tennis Center (✉ *19 Farmfield Ave., West Ashley* ☎ *843/724–7402*) is a city facility with lots of courts and locker rooms.

Maybank Tennis Center (✉ *1880 Houghton Dr., James Island* ☎ *843/406–8814*) has lights on its six courts.

The women's tennis Family Circle Cup is hosted each April at the **Family Circle Tennis Center** (✉ *161 Seven Farms Dr., Daniel Island* ☎ *843/534–2400* ⊕ *www.familycirclecup. com*). The 17 lighted courts (13 clay, four hard) are open to the public. A signature event for women's tennis, this annual tourney has brought in the sport's top names.

WATER SPORTS

Although the ocean waters are warm and inviting, you'll also find some surf and waves at some beaches, notably at Folly and Kiawah Island. Surfboards can be rented from McKelvin's for as little as $5 per hour to $25 for 24 hours (or $75 for a week); instruction is an additional $40 and includes board use. Out on John's Island, near Kiawah and Seabrook Islands, instruction is $15 a day. Jet Skis are now available at Folly Beach for $50 a half-hour, $85 an hour, and a second rider pays just $10.

Island Bike and Surf Shop (✉ *3665 Bohicket Rd., John's Island* ☎ *843/768–1158*) rents surfboards, shredders, and kayaks and will deliver to the resort islands. Boards cost $15 a day.

The pros at **McKevlin's Surf Shop** (✉ *8 Center St., Folly Beach* ☎ *843/588–2247*) can teach you what you need to know about surfing at Folly Beach County Park. Surfboard rentals and instruction can be arranged.

Sun & Ski (⊠*1 Cedar St., Folly Beach* ☎*843/588–0033*) rents Jet Skis off the beach, just to the left of the fishing pier. You can also rent a chair and umbrella here for five hours for $20.

SPAS

Charleston Place Spa (⊠*130 Market St., Market area* ☎*843/722–4900* ⊕*www.charlestonplacespa.com*), a truly deluxe day spa, has nine treatment rooms and a wet room where seaweed body wraps and other treatments are administered. Four-handed massages for couples are a popular option. Locker rooms for men and women have showers and saunas; men also have a steam room. Adjacent is a fitness room, an indoor pool with skylights, and a spacious hot tub.

In a historic Charleston "single house," **Stella Nova** (⊠*78 Society St., Lower King* ☎*843/723–0909* ⊕*www.stella-nova.com*) is just off King Street. It's serious about all of its treatments, from waxing to salt scrubs. For couples, there are aromatherapy massages and men's services, too. Enjoy refreshments on the breezy verandas. The spa is open daily, even on Sunday when street parking is easier to find.

Shopping in Charleston

7

WORD OF MOUTH

"[N]o way you can shop on King Street for only two hours. Start at Berlin's and head up King Street. Also, there are some wonderful shops on East Bay where Charleston Cooks! is located."

—GoTravel

By Eileen
Robinson
Smith

THE SHOPPING SCENE THAT EXISTS TODAY IS A FAR CRY—more like a shout for joy—from what existed here in the 1980s. In the not-so-distant past, King Street was still lined with retail shops with 1950s facades, which sold merchandise that was not much more current. When the Charleston Place (then the Omni) first opened its gallery of upscale shops in 1986, a spark was ignited that has continued to fire up a whole new generation of shops.

One-of-a-kind, locally-owned boutiques, where the hottest trends in fashion hang on the racks, make up an important part of the contemporary Charleston shopping experience. Long-established, Christian Michi anchors the corner of Market and King across from Saks Fifth Avenue; its window displays are like artworks, while its innovative and European designs are treasured by well-heeled, more mature clients. New to the scene is Hampden Clothing, where you will find hip fashions from young designers like Alexander Wang; Hampden appeals mostly to a younger clientele. More mature shoppers are pleased to find such high-end shops that sell either their own designer fashions or carry names that are found in Paris, New York, and South Beach.

High-end shoe stores comprise a category that tends to draw repeat visitors. The number and quality of shoe stores on King Street are surprising for the city's size. And the menfolk will find something to like as well. Rangoni Shoes is a longtime, classic Italian shop here; the shoe department at Saks is exceptional. However, such family-owned shops as Bob Ellis and Pete Banis are also worth a look. Pete Banis in particular will appeal to a younger crowd, offering trendy American and European brands. Newer is Farushga, which is turning heads with its emphasis on handmade, cutting-edge Italian leather shoes; you'll often see boots and accessories there that can be found only in Europe.

The Upper King Design District is full of home decor shops and art galleries interspersed between the clothing boutiques and restaurants. These locally owned, one-of-a-kind shops give the personal service that has always been a hallmark of existing King Street merchants in this area, like Morris Sokol Furniture. The revival of this neighborhood has sparked a new wave of home fashion stores; long-term antique hunters, accustomed to buying on Lower King, have been lured uptown as well. Haute Design is one of the most tasteful of these shops, offering a wide selection of antiques, particularly lighting, imported from France and Italy.

Charleston has more than 25 fine art galleries, making it one of the top art towns in America. Local Lowcountry art, which includes both traditional landscapes of the region as well as more contemporary takes, is among the most prevalent styles here. Such innovative artists as Betty Smith and Fred Jamar, a Belgian known for his whimsical cityscapes, can give you a piece of Charleston to keep close until your next visit. But collectors will find high-end nationally and internationally renowned work in such exquisite galleries as Ann Long Fine Art and the more contemporary Martin Gallery.

Tourists, too, will also find classy gift shops with Charleston-themed collectibles as well as jewelry stores with costume and precious gems.

To give an idea as to just how seriously in style Charleston has become, look no further than the city's newest annual event: **Charleston Fashion Week** (⊕*www.charlestonfashionweek.com*). The first was in 2007 and the weeklong event under a big tent was a huge success. Area fashion designers, store owners, hair and makeup artists, and models put on quite a show for the big turnout. The local version of Bryant Park in NYC is Marion Square, which is transformed for the entire week in late March. Take a seat each night with other fashionistas at the catwalk and learn what is up-and-coming in the fashion world. The Silver VIP tickets get you great seats and open bar and hors d'oeuvres—definitely worth it. Each night, an after-party is held at a local hot nightspot. The Red Carpet Finale is a big celebration.

SHOPPING DISTRICTS

The Market area is a cluster of shops and restaurants centered around the **Old City Market** (⊠*E. Bay and Market Sts., Market area*). Sweetgrass basket weavers work here and you can buy the resulting wares, although these artisan-crafts have become expensive. The shops run the gamut, from inexpensive stores selling T-shirts and souvenirs to upscale boutiques catering to the sophisticated tourist. In the covered, open-air market vendors have stalls with everything from jewelry to dresses and purses.

Freshfields Village (⊠*Kiawah Island Pkwy., John's Island* ☎843/768–6491), at the crossroads of Kiawah and Seabrook Islands, includes a variety of homegrown stores. In addition to the gourmet Freshfields market, there's a French restaurant and stores selling upscale merchandise and apparel. It was a welcome addition to the island area since the islands have been distant from all shopping options for decades.

★ Fodor'sChoice **King Street** is the major shopping street in town. Lower King (from Broad to Market streets) is lined with high-end antiques dealers. Middle King (from Market to Calhoun streets) is a mix of national chains like Banana Republic and Pottery Barn. Upper King (from Calhoun Street to Cannon Street) is the up-and-coming area where fashionistas like the alternative shops such as Putumayo. That area has been dubbed the Design District as well, for the furniture and interior design stores selling home fashion. Some are minimalist contemporary, others carry Euro-antiques, and they all will ship.

SPECIALTY STORES

ANTIQUES

Birlant & Co. (⊠191 King St., Lower King ☎843/722–3842) mostly carries 18th- and 19th-century English antiques, but keep your eye out for a Charleston Battery bench, for which they are famous.

English Rose Antiques (⊠436 King St., Upper King ☎843/722–7939) has country-style accessories at some of the best prices on the Peninsula.

Haute Design (⊠489 King St., Upper King ☎843/577–9886) sells antiques, chandeliers, and French and Italian furniture, as well as custom-designed pieces like tables and mirrors. Belgian linen and hand-screen-printed fabrics are a specialty, and available accessories include Vinnini blown glass and "antique" pillows. Interior design services are available. If you don't live locally, they will ship your treasures.

In Mount Pleasant, **Hungryneck Mall** (⊠401 Johnnie Dodds Blvd., Mount Pleasant ☎843/849–1744) has more than 60 antiques dealers hawking sterling silver, oak and mahogany furnishings, rugs, keepsakes from the past decades, and Civil War memorabilia.

The **King Street Antique Mall** (⊠495 King St., Upper King ☎843/723–2211) is part flea market, part antique store.

Livingstons' Antiques (✉*2137 Savannah Hwy., West Ashley* ☎*843/556–6162*) deals in 18th- and 19th-century English and Continental furnishings, clocks, and bric-a-brac.

Page's Thieves Market (✉*1460 Ben Sawyer Blvd., Mount Pleasant* ☎*843/884–9672*) specializes in furniture, especially medium- to large-scale pieces such as tables, desks, chests, and headboards. The market occasionally hosts auctions on the weekends.

ART GALLERIES

The downtown neighborhood known as the French Quarter, named after the founding French Huguenots, has become a destination for art lovers. The French Quarter Gallery Association consists of roughly 30 art galleries within the original walled city. Galleries here host a delightful art walk, with wine and some refreshments, from 5 to 8 PM on the first Friday in March, May, October, and December.

Serious art collectors head to **Ann Long Fine Art** (✉*12 State St., Market area* ☎*843/577–0447*) for neoclassical and modern works.

Charles II Gallery (✉*2 Queen St., Market area* ☎*843/577–7101*) is a contemporary gallery featuring international and regional artists. It holds the city's exclusive outlet for the work of Belgian artist Fred Jamar, known for his "bubble-tree" Charleston cityscapes.

The **Charleston Renaissance Gallery** (✉*103 Church St., South of Broad* ☎*843/723–0025*) carries museum-quality Southern art.

The **Corrigan Gallery** (✉*62 Queen St., Market area* ☎*843/722–9868*) displays the paintings of owner Lese Corrigan, as well as rotating shows from other painters and photographers.

Ellis-Nicholson Gallery (✉*1½ Broad St., South of Broad* ☎*843/722–5353*) showcases artists and sculptors who span many levels, from emerging artists to those with international recognition. It has a premier selection of oils, acrylics, mixed media, bronze, clay, glass, and handcrafted jewelry.

★ The **Eva Carter Gallery** (✉*132 E. Bay St., Market area* ☎*843/722–0506*) displays the most recognized abstract paintings in the area of owner Eva Carter, and abstract works by the late William Halsey.

Horton Hayes Fine Art (✉*30 State St., Market area* ☎*843/958–0014*) carries the sought-after Lowcountry paintings depicting coastal life by Mark Kelvin Horton, who also paints architectural and figurative works. Shannon Rundquist is among the other Lowcountry artists shown; she has a fun, whimsical way of painting local life and is known for her blue crab art.

★ Fodor'sChoice The **Martin Gallery** (✉*18 Broad St., South of Broad* ☎*843/723–7378*), in a former bank building, is the city's most impressive gallery, selling art by nationally and internationally acclaimed artists, sculptors, and photographers. The gallery is known especially for its bronzes and large wooden sculptures, as well as glass sculpture and custom-designed jewelry.

Smith-Killian Fine Art (✉*9 Queen St., Market area* ☎*843/853–0708*) exhibits contemporary paintings and Lowcountry-scapes by Betty Smith and her talented triplets Jennifer, Shannon, and Tripp. Her son is a nature photographer specializing in black-and-white images.

Wells Gallery (✉*125 Meeting St., Market area* ☎*843/853–3233*) has relocated to a new, larger location. Stop by to see the glass floor panel that reveals an underground cistern found during the renovation of the building. Wells showcases the talents of many fine artists, their Lowcountry-scapes, still lifes, black-and-white photographs, and handblown glass vases.

BOOKS

Look for out-of-print and rare books, including hardcover classics, at **Boomer's Books & Collectibles** (✉*420 King St., Upper King* ☎*843/722–2666*).

The **Preservation Society of Charleston** (✉*King and Queen Sts., Market area* ☎*843/722–4630*) carries books and tapes of historic and local interest, as well as sweetgrass baskets, prints, and posters.

CLOTHING

Charleston's own **Ben Silver** (✉*149 King St., Lower King* ☎*843/577–4556*), premier purveyor of blazer buttons, has more than 800 designs, including college and British regimental motifs. He also sells British neckties, embroidered polo shirts, and blazers.

Need a ball gown? **Berlins** (⊠*114 King St., Lower King* ☎*843/723–5591*) is the place for designer outfits.

Christian Michi (⊠*220 King St., Market area* ☎*843/723–0575*) carries chichi women's clothing and accessories. Designers from Italy, such as Piazza Sempione Bella Harrari, are represented. High-end fragrances add to the luxurious air.

Shop **Copper Penny** (⊠*311 King St., Market area* ☎*843/723–2999*) for trendy dresses and names like Trina Turk and Nanette Lepore.

Everything But Water (⊠*130 Market St., Lower King* ☎*843/722–5884*), in The Shops at Charleston Place, has one of the town's largest and finest collections of swimwear for all ages. Calvin Klein, La Blanca, and Ralph Lauren are among the designers and brands carried.

Boutique favorite **Finicky Filly** (⊠*303 King St., Lower King* ☎*843/534–0203*) carries exceptional women's apparel and accessories by such designers as Lela Rose, Molly B., and Etro.

Hampden Clothing (⊠*357 King St., Lower King* ☎*843/724–6373*) is one of the city's trendiest new boutiques with the young and well-heeled, who come here for an edgier style. The shop's sophisticated sensitivity and hot new designers such as Thread Social, Vena Cava, Alexander Wang, and Jenni Kayne help make it a premier destination for the latest in fashion. Even a more mature client may want to consider adding some of these cutting-edge pieces to her classic wardrobe.

Lula Kate (⊠*231 King St., Lower King* ☎*843/723–5885*) offers unique designs for the fun and flirtatious of all ages. You'll find just a few offerings in each size, so they are sure to retain their originality.

Nancy's (⊠*342 King St., Lower King* ☎*843/722-1272*) offers unique, one-of-a-kind fashions for the traveler and fun-lover in you. Offerings are not trendy but lean toward a timeless and very sexy style.

Nula (⊠*320 King St., Market area* ☎*843/853–6566*) sells hipster wear.

The Trunk Show (⊠*281 Meeting St., Market area* ☎*843/722–0442*) is an upscale consignment shop selling designer dresses, handbags and shoes, and vintage apparel. The back room is all about interior design. The shop has

Sweetgrass Baskets

The purchase of a handwoven Charleston sweetgrass basket is proof to your friends that you've been here. For centuries, African-American (Gullah) artisans have been weaving and selling these baskets in the Old City Market, where they sit busily in their chairs and place their wares on the sidewalk around them. Other places where they are known to set up are beside the downtown Post Office on Meeting and Broad streets, and on the right side of Highway 17N past Mount Pleasant (where you'll find the best prices). Prices range from about $60 for a small basket, but up into the hundreds for the larger sizes. Many buyers display these treasures in their homes like artwork or sculptures. Please be respectful of the renowned presence of the "basket ladies" in this city. Before taking their photograph, ask permission and offer a tip to show your appreciation.

become known for its estate jewelry and also custom-made jewelry from semiprecious stones. It has an excellent selection of gowns and evening wear. Many items now come in new from other shops.

CLOTHING FOR CHILDREN

Having traveled the world and countless fashion centers, the owners of **Kids on King** (⊠*195 King St., Lower King* ☎*843/720–8647*) bring you the finest in children's apparel and accessories from everywhere. Be transported to other lands with handcrafted unique designs just for your kids.

FOODSTUFFS

Bull Street Gourmet (⊠*60 Bull St., College of Charleston Campus* ☎*843/720–8992*) sells upscale picnic fare made fresh daily. It has great deals on wine and sponsors friendly tastings.

Caviar and Bananas (⊠*51 George St., Lower King* ☎*843/577–7757*) is an upscale specialty market and café featuring not-so-ordinary supermarket items like epicurean prepared foods and artisanal cheeses. Made-to-order sushi and fine wines are also offered. If you need help, the expert staff can make recommendations. A full espresso/tea bar invites you into this up-and-coming market atmosphere.

Charleston Candy Kitchen (✉32A N. Market St., Market area ☎843/723–4626) sells freshly made fudge, Charleston chews, and sesame-seed wafers.

The 24-hour **Harris Teeter** (✉290 E. Bay St., Market area ☎843/722–6821) is one of the best local supermarkets, and it carries Charleston foodstuffs.

Kennedy's Bakery and Market (✉60 Calhoun St., Upper King ☎843/723–2026) sells wine and cheeses, as well as freshly baked breads, muffins, and scones.

Make time to stop at **Market Street Sweets** (✉100 N. Market St., Market area ☎843/722–1397) for the melt-in-your-mouth pralines and fudge.

O'Hara & Flynn (✉225 Meeting St., Market area ☎843/534–1916) is one of Charleston's most well-known wine shops. It also has a wine bar open Monday through Saturday until 10 PM. If you buy a bottle of wine at retail price, you can drink it at the tables or right at the wine bar for just a $5 corkage fee. Cheeses, meats (including imported sausage and salami), and fresh olive oil are sold here, and you can order some as small appetizer plates. There's live jazz on Friday and Saturday evenings.

Ted's Butcherblock (✉334 East Bay St., Ansonborough ☎843/577–0094) sells gourmet meals to go. Light fare includes deli sandwiches, panini, and regional specialties from around the globe. You can also buy wines, cheeses, cold meats, and olive oil, or attend one of the frequent wine tastings.

FURNITURE

Carolina Lanterns (✉917 Houston Northcutt Blvd., Mount Pleasant ☎843/881–4170 ⊕www.carolinalanterns.com) sells gas lanterns based on designs from downtown's historic district.

Historic Charleston Reproductions (✉105 Broad St., South of Broad ☎843/723–8292) has superb replicas of Charleston furniture and accessories, all authorized by the Historic Charleston Foundation. Royalties from sales contribute to restoration projects.

At the **Old Charleston Joggling Board Co.** (✉652 King St., Upper King ☎843/723–4331), these Lowcountry oddities (on which people bounce) are for sale.

GIFTS

Charleston Cooks/ Maverick Kitchen Store (⊠*194 E. Bay St., Market area* ☎*843/722–1212*) carries just about any gourmet kitchen tool or accessory you can think of. Regional food, cookbooks, and culinary gifts abound. And you can also enjoy cooking classes and demonstrations. If you want to learn to cook, the store focuses on Lowcountry cuisine by day and has a litany of other classes in the evening. You get to taste what is prepared, with wine as a complement. Gift certificates are offered, too.

ESD (⊠*314 King St., Lower King* ☎*843/577–6272*) is a top local interior-design firm, and the company's King Street shop sells coffee-table books, jewelry, and pillows.

Indigo (⊠*4 Vendue Range, Market area* ☎*843/723–2983*) stocks funky home and garden accessories.

The Smoking Lamp (⊠*189 E. Bay St., Market area* ☎*843/577–7339*) is Charleston's oldest smoke shop, selling cigars, pipes, and accessories.

Artsy and hip baby gear, housewarming gifts, jewelry, books, and even office supplies make the mundane fun at **Worthwhile** (⊠*268 King St., Market area* ☎*843/723–4418*).

JEWELRY

Dixie Dunbar Jewelry (⊠*192 King St., Lower King* ☎*843/722–0006*) deals in artistic, unique jewelry. The handmade pieces here can be delightfully unpredictable.

Geiss & Sons Jewelers (⊠*116 E. Bay St., South of Broad* ☎*843/577–4497*) has been a family tradition for almost 90 years and is a member of the American Gem Society. The shop features the work of couture jewelry designers as well as high-end timepieces by Rolex and some custom designs.

SHOES & ACCESSORIES

Bob Ellis (⊠*332 King St., Lower King* ☎*843/722–2515*) sells shoes from Dolce & Gabbana, Prada, and Manolo Blahnik, among other high-end designers.

Dona Hay Store (⊠*160 E. Bay St., Market area* ☎*843/723–1400*) is a must-see store for the handbag connoisseur and the most-visited destination in the city for high-end bags. With something for any and every occasion to complement every fashion, Italian leather bags are a specialty.

Farushga (⊠*337-A King St., Lower King* ☎*843/722–3131*) sells high-quality, cutting-edge Italian shoes for both men and women, from chic daytime looks to pulling-out-all-of-the-stops evening glamour. But the real beauty of Farushga is that you will not find the same fine brands sold at every other upscale Italian shoe stores. Husband and wife team Massimo and Eva specialize in those sold mainly in Europe, and thanks to their Italian connections, their prices are much lower than one would expect for handmade Italian shoes. Be warned, this boutique carries only one pair per size for every style, so if you see something you like, you may want to buy it on the spot.

Gucci (⊠*132 Market St., Lower King* ☎*843/722–3788)*, in the Shops at Charleston Place, carries a full line of hand-bags, luggage, beautiful designer jewelry, and even a dress or two.

Magar Hatworks (⊠*57 Cannon St., Upper King* ☎*843/577–7740*) sells handcrafted headgear. This young designer/milliner has withstood the test of some time now and has introduced her love of hats to the young and fashionable. Her wholesale business includes sales to Barneys New York, and she has received national attention. She has relocated into a single house in a residential neighborhood and will be hosting tea parties, too.

Mary Norton's (⊠*316 King St., Lower King* ☎*843/534–2233*), formerly Moo Roo, has now gone big-time. This young Charleston mother has started handcrafting purses in her home. She also sells celebrity-made handbags and shoes to complement them, as well as a line of jewelry and scarves.

Pete Banis (⊠*375 King St., Lower King* ☎*843/577–0950*) sells some of the trendiest footwear in town from such designers as Luichiny, BCBC Girls, and Steve Madden.

Hilton Head & the Lowcountry

WORD OF MOUTH

"Fripp [Island], especially at its south end, has a wide beach. During high tide north beach disappears. Fripp can be traversed on foot in about 30 minutes, if the marsh deer get out of your way. They're everywhere. Enjoy."

—Lex1

"[A] visit to Beaufort would . . . be a really nice addition to your stay. It's smaller and really manageable but quite lovely."

—cpdl

By Eileen
Robinson
Smith

THE ACTION-PACKED ISLAND OF HILTON HEAD anchors the southern tip of South Carolina's coastline and attracts 2.5 million visitors each year. Although historically it has drawn an upscale clientele, and it still does, you'll find that the crowd here is much more diverse than you might think. Although it has more than its fair share of millionaires (you might run into director Ron Howard at the Starbucks, for instance), it also attracts families in search of a good beach.

This half-tame, half-wild island is home to more than 25 world-class golf courses and even more resorts, hotels, and top restaurants. Still, it's managed development thanks to building restrictions that aim to marry progress with environmental protection. North of Hilton Head, the coastal landscape is peppered with quiet small towns and flanked by rural sea islands. Beaufort is a cultural treasure, a graceful antebellum town with a compact historic district and waterfront promenade. Several of the 18th- and 19th-century mansions have been converted to bed-and-breakfasts.

The stretch of coastline between Hilton Head and Charleston is one of the most scenic parts of the state, and is still a mostly rural blend of small towns, winding country roads, and semitropical wilderness that turns into pristine beachfront before ending at the Atlantic. Here, especially along U.S. 17, look for roadside stands that sell boiled peanuts and homemade jams, and small-time shrimpers selling their catch out of coolers. Listen, too, for Gullahtinged accents among the African-American natives—the sound is musical.

Continuing north, midway between Beaufort and Charleston is Edisto Island, where you can comb the beach for shells and camp out on the mostly barren Edisto Beach State Park, or rent the modest waterfront cottages that have been in the same families for generations. Ocean Ridge, the one resort property there, formerly a Fairfield resort, is now a Wyndham.

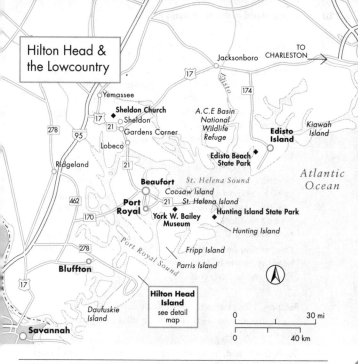

Hilton Head &
the Lowcountry

ORIENTATION & PLANNING

GETTING ORIENTED

Hilton Head is just north of South Carolina's border with Georgia. It's so close to Savannah that they share an airport. This part of the state is best explored by car, as its points of interest spread over a flat coastal plain that is a mix of wooded areas, marshes, and sea islands, the latter of which are sometimes accessible only by boat or ferry. Take U.S. 170 and 17 to get from one key spot (Hilton Head, Beaufort, and Edisto) to another. It's a pretty drive that winds through small towns and over old bridges. Charleston, the Queen Belle of the South, is at the northern end of the region.

Hilton Head Island. One of the southeast coast's most popular tourist destinations, Hilton Head is known for its golf courses and tennis courts. It's a magnet for time-share owners and retirees.

LOWCOUNTRY BEST BETS

Beaufort: A small antebellum town that has offers large doses of heritage and culture; nearly everything you might want to see is within its downtown historic district.

Beachcombing: Hilton Head has 12 mi of beaches. You can swim, soak up the sun, or walk along the sand. The differential between the tides leaves a multitude of shells, sand dollars, and starfish.

Challenging Golf: Hilton Head's nickname is "Golf Island," and its many challenging courses have an international reputation.

Serving up Tennis: One of the nation's top tennis destinations, with academies run by legends like Stan Smith, former Wimbledon champion.

Staying Put: This semitropical island has been a resort destination for decades and it has all of the desired amenities for visitors: a vast array of lodgings, an endless supply of restaurants, and excellent shopping.

Beaufort. This charming town just inland from Hilton Head is a destination in its own right, with a lively dining scene and cute B&Bs.

Daufuskie Island. A scenic ferry ride from Hilton Head, Daufuskie is now much more developed than it was during the days when Pat Conroy wrote *The Water is Wide,* but it's still a beautiful island to explore, even on a day-trip. You can also stay for a few days at a deluxe resort with good golf and tennis.

Edisto Island. More down-home than the other coastal islands, Edisto has one time-share resort as well as several vacation homes for rent, and a lovely state park, where you can rent bare-bones cabins.

WHEN TO GO

The high season follows typical beach-town cycles, with June through August and holidays year-round being the busiest and most costly. Mid-April, during the annual Verizon Heritage Golf Classic, is when rates tend to be highest. Thanks to the Lowcountry's mostly moderate year-round temperatures, tourists are ever-present. Spring is the best time to visit, when the weather is ideal for tennis and golf. Autumn is almost as active for the same reason. Because the island is a popular destination for corporate meetings, business during the shoulder seasons and winter can still be brisk.

To get a good deal, it's imperative that you plan ahead. The choicest locations can be booked six months to a year in advance, but booking agencies can help you make room reservations and get good deals during the winter season, when the crowds fall off. Villa rental companies often offer snowbird rates for monthly stays during the winter season. Parking is always free at the major hotels, but valet parking can cost from $10 to $15; the smaller properties have free parking, too, but no valet service.

GETTING HERE & AROUND

You can fly into Savannah's airport, which is about an hour from Hilton Head, but then you absolutely must have a car to get around.

BY AIR

Hilton Head Island Airport is served by US Airways Express. Most travelers use the Savannah/Hilton Head International Airport, less than an hour from Hilton Head, which is served by American Eagle, Continental Express, Delta, Northwest, United Express, and US Airways.

Contacts **Hilton Head Island Airport** (⊠ *120 Beach City Rd., Hilton Head, SC* ☎ *843/689-5400* ⊕ *www.hiltonheadairport.com*). **Savannah/Hilton Head International Airport** (⊠ *400 Airways Ave., Savannah, GA* ☎ *912/964-0514* ⊕ *www.savannahairport.com*).

BY BOAT & FERRY

Hilton Head is accessible via the intracoastal waterway, with docking available at Harbour Town Yacht Basin, Hilton Head Boathouse, and Shelter Cove Harbour.

Contacts **Harbour Yacht Basin** (☎ *843/671-2704*). **Hilton Head Boathouse** (☎ *843/681-2628*). **Shelter Cove Harbor** (☎ *843/842-7001*).

BY BUS

Greyhound Bus connects Beaufort with other destinations in the area. The Lowcountry Regional Transportation Authority has a bus that leaves Beaufort in the morning for Hilton Head that costs $2.50. Exact change is required. This same company has a van that, with 24-hour notice, will pick you up at your hotel and drop you off at your destination for $3. You can request a ride weekdays 7 AM to 10 AM or 12:30 PM to 3 PM.

8

Contacts **Greyhound** (✉ *3659 Trask Pkwy., Beaufort* ☎ *843/524–4646 or 800/231–2222* ⊕ *www.greyhound.com*). **The Lowcountry Regional Transportation Authority** (☎ *843/757–5782* ⊕ *www. gotohhi.com/bus*).

BY TAXI

At Your Service and Gray Line Lowcountry Adventures are good options in Hilton Head.

Contacts **At Your Service** (☎ *843/837–3783*). **Gray Line Lowcountry Adventures** (☎ *843/681–8212*).

BY TRAIN

Amtrak gets you as close as Savannah or Yemassee. Gray Line Lowcountry Adventures will send a limo to pick you up at a cost of $66 per hour.

Contacts **Savannah Amtrak Station** (✉ *2611 Seaboard Coastline Dr., Savannah* ☎ *912/234–2611 or 800/872–7245* ⊕ *www.amtrak. com*). **Gray Line Lowcountry Adventures** (☎ *843/681–8212*).

TOURS

Hilton Head's Adventure Cruises hosts dinner, sightseeing, and murder-mystery cruises. Several companies, including H2O Sports and Lowcountry Nature Tours in Hilton Head, run dolphin sightseeing, shark fishing, and delightful environmental trips. Carolina Buggy Tours show you Beaufort's historic district by horse-drawn carriage.

Gullah Heritage Trail Tours gives a wealth of history about slavery and the Union takeover of the island during the Civil War; tours leave from the Discovery Museum of Hilton Head and cost $35. Gullah 'n' Geechie Mahn Tours leads groups throughout Beaufort with a focus on African-American culture. Costumed guides sing and act out history during walking tours by the tour group, Spirit of Old Beaufort.

Contacts **Adventure Cruises** (✉ *Shelter Cove Marina, 9 Shelter Cove Lane, Mid-Island, Hilton Head Island* ☎ *843/785–4558* ⊕ *www.hiltonheadisland.com*). **Carolina Buggy Tours** (✉ *901 Port Republic St., Beaufort* ☎ *843/525–1300*). **Gullah Heritage Trail Tours** (✉ *Hilton Head* ☎ *843/681–7066* ⊕ *www.gullaheritage.com*). **Gullah 'n' Geechie Mahn Tours** (✉ *671 Sea Island Pkwy., Beaufort* ☎ *843/838–7516* ⊕ *www.gullahngeechietours.net*). **H2O Sports** (✉ *Harbour Town Marina, 149 Lighthouse Rd., South End, Hilton Head Island* ☎ *843/363–2628* ⊕ *www.h2osportsonline.com*). **Low Country Nature Tours** (✉ *Shelter Cover Marina, Shelter Cove Lane, Mid-Island, Hilton Head Island* ☎ *843/683–0187* ⊕ *www.lowcountry-*

naturetours.com). **Spirit of Old Beaufort** (⊠ *103 West St., Beaufort* ☎ *843/525–0459* ⊕ *www.thespiritofoldbeaufort.com*).

ABOUT THE RESTAURANTS

Given the proximity to the Atlantic and small farms on the mainland, most locally owned restaurants are still heavily influenced by the catch of the day and seasonal field harvests. There are numerous national chain and fast-food restaurants within commercial complexes or malls. Although hard to fathom, relatively few restaurants on Hilton Head are on the water or even have a water view. Although you will find more high-end options, there are still holes-in-the-wall that serve good-tasting fare and are frequented by locals.

Most restaurants open at 11 and don't close until 9 or 10, but some take a break between 2:30 and 6. Most of the more expensive restaurants have an early dining menu aimed at seniors, and this is a popular time to dine. During the height of the summer season, reservations are essential at all times, though in the off-season you may need them only on weekends (still, more and more of the better restaurants require them).

ABOUT THE HOTELS

Hilton Head is known as one of the best vacation spots on the East Coast, and its hotels are a testimony to the reputation. The island is awash in regular hotels and resorts that are called plantations, not to mention beachfront or golf-course-view villas, cottages, and mansions. Here and on private islands you can expect the most modern conveniences and world-class service at the priciest places. Clean, updated rooms and friendly staff are everywhere, even at lower-cost hotels—this is the South, after all. Many international employees add a cosmopolitan atmosphere. Staying in cooler months, for extended periods of time, or commuting from nearby Bluffton, where there are some new limited-service properties, chains like Hampton Inn, can mean better deals.

PLANNING YOUR TIME

Three days in the Hilton Head area will give you enough time to enjoy some outdoor fun, shopping, and a history lesson or two. No matter where you stay, spend your first day relaxing on the beach or hitting the links. After that, you'll have time to visit some of the area attractions, including the Coastal Discovery Museum or the Sea Pines Resort. Bluffton is a quaint 1850s town with many quirky, locally owned shops, or you can also visit one of the many outlet malls. If you have a few more days, you should really visit Beaufort or even spend the night there. The ride along U.S. 17 or 170 from Hilton Head is a pretty one, so don't rush. The heart of this town is its historic district; if you have a week or more, spend a couple of nights here in an antebellum B&B. With a full week, you would also have time to visit Edisto or Daufuski Island.

WHAT IT COSTS				
¢	$	$$	$$$	$$$$
RESTAURANTS				
under $10	$10–$14	$15–$19	$20–$24	over $24
HOTELS				
under $100	$100–$150	$151–$200	$201–$250	over $250

Restaurant prices are for a main course at dinner. Hotel prices are for two people in a standard double room in high season. Tax of rooms is 12%; restaurant tax is 7.5% for food, and 8.5% for alcohol.

HILTON HEAD ISLAND

No matter how many golf courses pepper its landscape, Hilton Head will always be a semitropical barrier island. That means the 12 mi of beaches are lined with towering pines, palmetto trees, and wind-sculpted live oaks; the interior is a blend of oak and pine woodlands and meandering lagoons. Rental villas, lavish private houses, and luxury hotels line the coast as well.

Since the 1950s, resorts like Sea Pines, Palmetto Dunes, and Port Royal have sprung up all over. Although the gated resorts, called "plantations," are private residential communities, all have public restaurants, marinas, shopping areas, and recreational facilities. All are secured, and cannot be toured unless arrangements are made at the visitor office near the main gate of each plantation. Hilton Head prides itself on strict laws that keep light pollution to a minimum. ■TIP→ **The lack of streetlights makes it difficult to find your way at night, so be sure to get good directions.**

EXPLORING HILTON HEAD & VICINITY

Driving Hilton Head by car or tour bus is the only way to get around. Off Interstate 95, take Exit 8 onto U.S. 278, which leads you through Bluffton and then onto Hilton Head proper. A 5¾-mi Cross Island Parkway toll bridge ($1) is just off 278, and makes it easy to bypass traffic and reach the south end of the island, where most of the resort areas and hotels are. Know that U.S. 278 can slow to a standstill at rush hour and during holiday weekends, and the signs are so discreet that it's easy to get lost without explicit directions. ⚠**Be careful of putting the pedal to the metal, particularly on the Cross Island Parkway. The speed limits change dramatically.**

GETTING HERE & AROUND

Hilton Head Island is 19 mi east of I–95. Take Exit 8 off I–95 South and then Hwy. 278 directly to the bridge. If you're heading to the southern end of the island, your best bet to save time and avoid traffic is to take the Toll Expressway. The cost is $1 each way.

Visitor Information **Welcome Center of Hilton Head (**✉*100 William Hilton Pkwy.* ☎*843/689–6302 or 800/523–3373* ⊕*www. hiltonheadisland.org.*

AROUND IN CIRCLES. **Locals call the island's many traffic circles the "tourist's nemesis." So they won't be your undoing, get very precise directions. And if you miss a turn, don't brake violently, just go around again.**

WHAT TO SEE

Audubon-Newhall Preserve, in the south, is 50 acres of pristine forest, where native plant life is tagged and identified. There are trails, a self-guided tour, and seasonal walks. ✉*Palmetto Bay Rd., near southern base of Cross Island Pkwy., South End* ☎*843/842–9246* ⊕*www.hiltonhead audubon.org* ✉*Free* ☉*Daily dawn–dusk.*

★ **Bluffton.** Tucked away from the resorts, charming Bluffton has several old homes and churches, a growing artists' colony, several good restaurants (including Truffles Cafe), and oak-lined streets dripping with Spanish moss. You could grab Southern-style picnic food and head to the boat dock at the end of Pritchard Street for great views. There are interesting little shops and galleries and some limited-service B&Bs that provide a nearby alternative to Hilton Head's higher prices. This town and surrounding area are

Hilton Head Island

Port Royal Sound

HILTON HEAD PLANTATION

Seabrook Landing

Pickney Island

Country Club of Hilton Head

PALMETTO HALL PLANTATION

Old South Golf Links

Arthur Hills at Palmetto Hall

Beach City Road

Bluffton

Welcome Center of Hilton Head

Hilton Head Island Airport

NORTH END

Main Street

TO SAVANNAH, GEORGIA

Matthews Dr.

Folly Field Rd.

May River Golf Club

Coastal Discovery Museum

Port Royal Plantation

Cross Island Pkwy.

MID-ISLAND

Seabrook Drive

Waterway

Golden Bear at Indigo Run

Marshland Rd.

Broad Creek

Bull Island

Shelter Cove Lane

Shelter Cove

Palmetto Dunes Resort

Harbourside Lane

Shelter Cove Marina

Palmetto Bay Rd.

SOUTH END

Robert Trent Jones at Palmetto Dunes

Audubon-Newhall Preserve

Shipyard Golf Club

Intracoastal

Sea Pines Forest Preserve

Pope Ave.

North Forest Beach Drive

Lighthouse Road

Sea Pines Resort

Greenwood Dr.

Cordillo Pkwy.

Daufuskie Island Club & Resort

Harbour Town

Plantation Dr.

South Forest Beach Drive

Cooper River Landing

Harbour Town Golf Links

Sea Pines Dr.

OCEANSIDE

Daufuskie Island

South Beach Marina

SOUTH BEACH

South Beach Marina

Atlantic Ocean

0   1/2 mi

0   1/2 km

Fodor's First Person: John Jakes, Writer, on Hilton Head

If you happened to be in Hilton Head in April 2008 and saw lines snaking out of Jump & Phil's Restaurant, it's probably because the famous historical novelist John Jakes was having a book signing for his latest novel *The Gods of Newport*. Jakes and his wife, Rachel, will celebrate their 30th anniversary of living on Hilton Head in 2009.

He writes about his island: "Hilton Head is always good for a visit despite the clutter of advancing 'development' between the island and I-95. Town organizers wisely kept the commercial buildings mostly low-rise—no towering oceanside condos here. Sugar-white beaches and Civil War ruins in Port Royal Plantation. In 1861, the island was captured by a Union fleet. A false-front town of some 15,000 civilians—cardsharps, floozies et al—supplemented the military garrison until 1865. I'm told they even presented amateur theatricals."

experiencing some rapid growth since Hilton Head has little remaining undeveloped land. Much of the area's work force, especially its young, Latin, and international employees, live here. ⊠*Route 46, 8 mi northwest on U.S. 278.*

★ **Fodor's Choice Coastal Discovery Museum.** The museum has relocated to what was the Horn Plantation, and it's an all-new and wonderful Lowcountry learning experience, especially for visitors with children. Although a small museum, its interpretive panels and exhibits have been done in with a contemporary mind-set. Kids, for example, can dress up in the clothing of centuries past. The museum's mission is to develop an understanding and appreciation for the cultural heritage and natural history of the Lowcountry. Visitors will learn about the early development of Hilton Head as an island resort from the Civil War to the 1930s. Admission is free, and its litany of lectures and tours on subjects both historical and natural range from $3 and up. The terrace and grounds are such that it is simply a comfortable, stress-free green landscape just off the Cross Island Parkway entrance ramp, though it feels a century away. The gift shop remains in its original location, within the Visitors Center at 100 William Hilton Pkwy. ⊠*Hwy. 278 at Gumtree Rd., North End* ☎*843/689–6767* ⊕*www.coastaldiscovery.org* ⊡*Free* ⊗*Mon.–Sat. 9–5, Sun. 10–3.*

Palmetto Dunes Resort. This complex is home to the renowned Rod Laver Tennis Center, a good stretch of beach, three golf courses, a golf academy and several oceanfront villa complexes. The oceanfront Hilton Head Marriott Beach & Golf Resort and the Hilton Oceanfront Resort are also within this plantation, as are villa-condo complexes with large inventories of rental units. ✉*Queens Folly Rd. at U.S. 278, Mid-Island* ☎*800/845–8160* ⊕*www.palmetto dunesresort.com.*

Port Royal Plantation. The main draws here are the posh Westin Resort, which is on the beach, three PGA-championship golf courses, and the Port Royal racquet club, with 16 tennis courts. ✉*2 Grasslawn Ave., Mid-Island* ☎*843/681–4000* ⊕*www.portroyalplantation.com.*

Sea Pines Forest Preserve. At this 605-acre public wilderness tract, walking trails take you past a stocked fishing pond, waterfowl pond, and a 3,400-year-old Indian shell ring. Pick up the extensive activity guide at the Sea Pines Welcome Center to take advantage of goings-on—moonlight hayrides, storytelling around campfires, and alligator- and bird-watching boat tours. The preserve is part of the grounds at Sea Pines Resort. ✉*Off U.S. 278, Sea Pines Resort, South End* ☎*843/363–4530* ⊕*www.seapines.com* ⊡*$5 per car* ☉*Daily dawn–dusk.*

★ Fodor'sChoice **Sea Pines Resort.** The oldest and best known of Hilton Head's developments, this resort occupies 4,500 thickly wooded acres with three golf courses, tennis clubs, stables, a fine beach, and shopping plazas. The focus of Sea Pines is **Harbour Town,** a charming marina with a luxury boutique hotel, shops, restaurants, condominiums and vacation rental homes, and the landmark, candy-striped Hilton Head Lighthouse. A free "trolley" shuttles visitors around the resort. There is a $5 per charge per car for parking (nonguests only). ✉*Off U.S. 278, South End* ☎*843/363–4530* ⊕*www.seapines.com* ⊡*$5 per car.*

WHERE TO EAT

$$$– ✕**Aqua Grille & Lounge.** *Seafood.* A great deal of effort was
$$$$ expended to create the ambience here—a waterfall on the first level, a fireplace lounge adjacent to the second-story dining room. The food—particularly the shellfish—and portions are commendable, the wine list up with the latest trends, the servers savvy. Grazing is the way to go: the oysters with champagne mignonette or chili-lime remou-

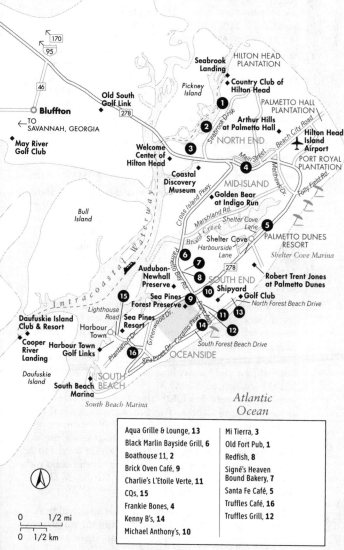

Where to Eat on Hilton Head Island

KEY

Beach

Ferry

Port Royal Sound

Bluffton

TO SAVANNAH, GEORGIA

May River Golf Club

Old South Golf Link

Welcome Center of Hilton Head

Coastal Discovery Museum

Bull Island

Seabrook Landing

Pickney Island

Country Club of Hilton Head

Arthur Hills at Palmetto Hall

HILTON HEAD PLANTATION

PALMETTO HALL PLANTATION

NORTH END

Main Street

Hilton Head Island Airport

Beach City Road

PORT ROYAL PLANTATION

MID-ISLAND

Golden Bear at Indigo Run

Marshland Rd.

Shelter Cove Lane

Shelter Cove

Harbourside Lane

PALMETTO DUNES RESORT

Shelter Cove Marina

Audubon-Newhall Preserve

Sea Pines Forest Preserve

SOUTH END

Shipyard

Golf Club

North Forest Beach Drive

Robert Trent Jones at Palmetto Dunes

Daufuskie Island Club & Resort

Cooper River Landing

Harbour Town Golf Links

Lighthouse Road

Harbour Town

Sea Pines Resort

OCEANSIDE

South Forest Beach Drive

Daufuskie Island

South Beach Marina

SOUTH BEACH

South Beach Marina

Atlantic Ocean

0   1/2 mi

0   1/2 km

Aqua Grille & Lounge, **13**

Black Marlin Bayside Grill, **6**

Boathouse 11, **2**

Brick Oven Café, **9**

Charlie's L'Etoile Verte, **11**

CQs, **15**

Frankie Bones, **4**

Kenny B's, **14**

Michael Anthony's, **10**

Mi Tierra, **3**

Old Fort Pub, **1**

Redfish, **8**

Signé's Heaven Bound Bakery, **7**

Santa Fe Café, **5**

Truffles Café, **16**

Truffles Grill, **12**

Shrimp Boats Forever

The sunset sight of shrimp trawlers coming into home port, with mighty nets raised and an entourage of hungry seagulls, is a cherished Lowcountry tradition. The shrimping industry has been an integral staple of the South Carolina economy for nearly a century. (Remember Bubba Gump?) It was booming in the 1980s. But alas, cheap, farm-raised shrimp from foreign markets and now the cost of diesel fuel are decimating the shrimpers' numbers.

The season for fresh-caught shrimp is May to December. Lowcountry residents support the freelance fishermen by buying only certified, local wild shrimp in restaurants and in area fish markets and supermarkets. If you wish to follow this "When in Rome" mentality, visitors can follow suit by patronizing local restaurants and markets that display the logo that reads: CERTIFIED WILD AMERICAN SHRIMP. Or you can simply ask before you eat.

lade; the delicious sashimi; the bibb and red-leaf salad with macadamias dressed with orange-miso vinaigrette. (Forget the spring rolls.) The more sought after main courses are tuna, blackened mahimahi, and pecan-crusted sea bass, with the filet mignon the best steak. A late-night menu is served from 10 to midnight. Happy Hour is a must. ⊠ *10 N. Forest Beach Dr., South End* ☎ *843/341–3331* ⊟ *AE, MC, V* ⊘ *No lunch.*

$$$ ✕ **Black Marlin Bayside Grill.** *Seafood.* If you want to dine in the marina with a view of the "blue," then head to this new player, the latest creation of a seasoned local restaurant group. Attracting local boat people and also business lunchers, there's a steady stream of customers most days, but Saturday and Sunday brunch are the highlights (check out the well-priced Bloody Marys) for eggs Benedict and live entertainment. For lunch, the best bets include one of the seafood sandwiches or Baja fish tacos; there are always two or three items under $10. Prices go up for dinner, and the buzz calms. The bar is fun and promulgates a gentrified Key West ambience, especially at happy hour from 4 to 7. There's an early dining menu, but the kitchen cranks out entrees until 10 every night. ⊠ *Palmetto Marina, 86 Helmsman Way, South End* ☎ *843/785–4950* ⊟ *AE, MC, V.*

$$$ ✕ **Boathouse 11.** *Seafood.* Boathouse 11 is an actual waterfront restaurant; although hard to fathom, waterfront dining is difficult to find on this island. To soak in the

salty atmosphere, reserve an outdoor table on the partially covered patio or grab a seat at the bar that looks out on the charter fishing pier. This is one fun place, and the simple fare is well-prepared. Fish and shellfish are the best choices here; for lunch you can order a perfect oyster po'boy. Yes, there are a few landlubber main courses, too. Want chicken instead? Ask for the teriyaki sandwich named after a local DJ. Distinguished by quality, fresh produce, this casual place also has a surprisingly admirable wine list with reasonably-priced glasses and a number of bottles in the $30-something range. Brunch is a Sunday happening and quite popular. ⊠ *397 Squire Pope Rd., North End* ☎ *843/681–3663* ⊟ *AE, D, MC, V.*

$$–$$$ ✕ **Brick Oven Café.** *American.* Velvet drapes, dramatic chandeliers, and 1940s-era lounge-style entertainment—on top of good, reasonably priced food served late—make this an *in* place. It's a refreshingly quirky joint on an island that is more luxe than funky, and the menu is equally eclectic. Appetizers include sweet-potato and lobster cakes, and shrimp and pork spring rolls; among the best entrées are wood-fired pizzas, roasted veggie sandwiches, and veal meat loaf. Check out the new grazing menu called Tappatizers (appetizer-size small plates that can still make up a meal), as well as the pastas. The wine list has a good range and pricing. ⊠ *Park Plaza, 224 Greenwood Dr., South End* ☎ *843/686–2233* ⊸ *Reservations essential* ⊟ *AE, D, DC, MC, V* ⊘ *No lunch.*

$$$$ ✕ **Charlie's L'Etoile Verte.** *French.* This family-owned culinary landmark has oozed personality for a quarter-century. Originally one tiny room, its popularity with locals and repeat visitors sparked the move to these new spacious digs. As you first step in the door, you'll be wowed by the eclectic, country French decor and the homey ambience. Unusual for Hilton Head, the blackboard menu is handwritten daily according to market availability. The menu is just as homespun and cozy, primarily French classics. Certain items are constants, like the perfectly perfect curried shrimp salad at lunch. Come nightfall, out comes the *pâté maison* and veal tenderloin with wild mushroom sauce. The wine list is distinguished. ⊠ *8 Orleans Rd., Mid-Island* ☎ *843/785–9277* ⊸ *Reservations essential* ⊟ *AE, MC, V* ⊘ *Closed Sun. No lunch Mon.*

★ Fodor's Choice ✕ **CQs.** *Eclectic.* If you heard that all island res-
$$$$ taurants are in shopping centers and lack atmosphere,

then you need to experience CQs. Its rustic ambience—heart-pine floors, sepia-toned island photos, and a lovely second-story dining room—coupled with stellar cuisine, a personable staff, live piano music, and a feel-good spirit put most of the island's other restaurants to shame. Chef Eric Sayer's imaginative, original creations are divine. Imagine a lobster triumvirate as an appetizer, with an incredible lobster cheesecake the standout. Imagine a golden brown Alaskan halibut afloat in a crab cream sauce. Manager Drew can pair your wine perfectly from an impeccable list. You will awake next morning thinking about it all. The gate pass for Sea Pines ($5) will be reimbursed with purchase of one main course or more. ⊠*Harbour Town, 140 Lighthouse La., South End* ☎*843/671–2779* ⚞*Reservations essential* ⊟*AE, MC, V* ⊙*No lunch.*

$$–$$$ ✕**Frankie Bones.** *Italian.* Since this restaurant is dedicated to the loving memory of Frank Sinatra, you might assume that its name is also one of the handles of "ole blue eyes." But no, "Bones" was a Chicago gangster before Prohibition. This place has a strong appeal to an older set of regulars who like the traditional parmesagnas and marsalas on the early-dining menu. But during happy hour, the bar and tall cocktail tables are populated with younger patrons who order flat-bread pizzas and small portions of pasta. It's especially popular with guys who prefer the substantial and familiar, but some dishes have more innovative twists, including a 16-ounce rib eye with a sweetened coffee rub. Be an honorary Italian and just drink your dessert, something Amaretto-based such as a Godfather or a Burnt Almond. ⊠*1301 Main St., North End* ☎*843/682–4455* ⚞*Reservations essential* ⊟*AE, D, MC, V* ⊙*Closed Sun. No lunch.*

WORD OF MOUTH. "Not the 'country club' you might expect, Harold's Country Club & Grill is a sprawling, remodeled gas station in the little town of Yemassee, a short way east of I–95, south of Charleston. Cheerful ladies slap a steak on your plate (or whatever the featured entrée is that evening), then you proceed past an array of sides and find a place in one of the large, kitschy dining rooms. Karaoke begins in the bar at 8 pm on weekends; good-natured local people throng in to sing or watch."—John Jakes.

¢–$ ✕**Kenny B's French Quarter Café.** *Cajun-Creole.* Surrounded by Mardi Gras memorabilia, Kenny himself cooks up jam-

Cooking Italian Style in Hilton Head

You can "get naked" in a hands-on cooking class with Chef Michael Cirafesi, the talented chef of Michael Anthony's, one of the island's best restaurant experiences. Held on the restaurant's second floor, where he has his chef's table, too, you can also attend demonstration classes, wine tastings, and spouse programs for visiting corporate groups.

You get to sample what is cooked with wine that will complement it and add to the camaraderie. Since there is a high demand for these classes, not to mention limited availability, check the schedule and reserve your place as far in advance as possible on the Michael Anthony Web site (⊕ *www.michael-anthonys.com*).

---

balaya, gumbo, and muffaletta sandwiches. His wife runs the dining room, serving hungry working folks golden-fried oyster po'boys topped with real remoulade sauce. Go for the Sunday buffet brunch: there's chicory coffee, perfect beignets, spicy omelets, and various eggs Benedicts. A local haunt for nearly 10 years, this place in a shopping center is open from morning until 9 PM. ⊠*Bi-Lo Circle, 70 Pope Ave., Mid-Island* ☎*843/785–3315* ▭*AE, D, MC, V* ⊙*No dinner Sun.*

★ Fodor'sChoice ✕**Michael Anthony's.** *Italian.* This throwback goes
$$$– back to the days when the most exotic, ethnic restaurant
$$$$ in a town was a family-owned Italian spot, where professional waiters would received your rapt attention as they described the nightly specials. This is that kind of place, but contemporized and more upscale, with fresh, top-quality ingredients, simple yet elegant sauces, and waiters who know and care about the food they serve. Owned by a talented, charismatic Philadelphia family, the restaurant has a convivial spirit, and its innovative pairings and plate presentations are au courant. Locals file in for the early-dining menu, which includes three courses and a glass of wine; this is a superior value for about $20. But you can order off the à la carte menu, and after homemade gnocchi or a succulent veal chop with wild mushroom sauce, you can finish happily with a sambuca and panna cotta. Then sing *Volare!* ⊠*Orleans Plaza, 37 New Orleans Rd., Ste. L, South End* ☎*843/785–6272* ☖*Reservations essential* ▭*AE, D, MC, V* ⊙*Closed Sun. No lunch.*

8

$ ✕ **Mi Tierra.** *Tex-Mex.* At this friendly Mexican restaurant, freshness is the key to tasty fare like fried-fish tacos. You can also grab take-out from Baja Tacos—next door, run by the same people—a simple taco stand with counter service, café tables, and a condiments bar with fresh salsas and relishes. Down a *cerveza* (beer) as you watch Mexican *telenovelas* (soap operas). ⊠ *160 Fairfield Sq., North End* ☎ *843/342-3409* ▭ *MC, V.*

$$$– ✕ **Old Fort Pub.** *Continental.* Overlooking the sweeping
$$$$ marshlands of Skull Creek, this romantic restaurant has
★ almost panoramic views. It offers one of the island's best overall dining experiences: the building is old enough to have some personality, and the professional waiters do their duty. More important, the kitchen serves flavorful food, including a great appetizer of roasted calamari with sun-dried tomatoes and olives. Entrées like duck confit in rhubarb sauce and filet mignon with shiitake mushrooms hit the spot. The wine list is extensive, and there's outdoor seating plus a third-floor porch for toasting the sunset. Sunday brunch is celebratory and includes a mimosa. "Pub Hour" downstairs from Monday through Friday offers discounted drinks and an interesting crowd to drink with (it lasts from 5 to 6:30). ⊠ *65 Skull Creek Dr., North End* ☎ *843/681-2386* ▭ *AE, D, DC, MC, V* ⊘ *No lunch.*

$$$– ✕ **Redfish.** *Caribbean.* The "naked" catch of the day—sea-
$$$$ food grilled with olive oil, lime, and garlic—is a low-cal, heart-healthy specialty that many diners opt for; it's a welcome change from the fried fare at many other local spots. Caribbean and Cuban flavors pervade the rest of the menu in dishes such as red trout with Boursin-cheese grits; spicy tasso ham in a cream sauce spiked with Amaretto, Tabasco, and Worcestershire; and Dominican braised pork, roasted with bananas, chilies, and coconut. The restaurant's wine cellar is full with some 1,000 bottles, and there's also a retail wine shop. Although this commercial strip location isn't inspired, the lively crowd sitting amid candlelight, subdued artwork, dark furniture, and white linens more than makes up for this typical island shortcoming. The increasingly innovative cooking is a draw for chic tourists; locals don't frequent as they once did since menu prices have gone up. ⊠ *8 Archer Rd., corner Palmetto Bay Rd., South End* ☎ *843/686-3388* ▭ *AE, D, MC, V* ⊘ *No lunch Sun.*

¢ ✕ **Signe's Heaven Bound Bakery & Café.** *American.* Every morning locals roll in for the deep-dish French toast, crispy polenta, and whole-wheat waffles. Since 1974, European-born Signe has been feeding islanders her delicious soups (the chilled cucumber has pureed watermelon, green apples, and mint), curried chicken salad, and loaded hot and cold sandwiches. The beach bag ($10 for a cold sandwich, pasta or fresh fruit, chips, a beverage, and cookie) is a great deal. The key-lime bread pudding is amazing, as are the melt-in-your mouth cakes and the rave-worthy breads, especially the Italian *ciabatta*. Wedding cakes are a specialty—Signe decorates more than 300 a year, and she'll provide other special-occasion cakes, too. If you want to become part of the Hilton Head scene, you need to know Signe. ⊠*93 Arrow Rd., South End* ☎*843/785–9118* ▤*AE, D, MC, V* ⊘*Closed Sun. No dinner.*

$$$– ✕ **Santa Fe Café.** *Southwestern.* The Southwest has been
$$$$ convincingly re-created here in South Carolina. Guests are greeted by the sights, sounds, and aromas of New Mexico: native American rugs, Mexican ballads, steer skulls and horns, and the pungent smells of chilies and mesquite on the grill. The restaurant is perhaps best experienced on a rainy, chilly night when the adobe fireplaces are cranked up. Go for the rush of spicy food chased with an icy Mexican cerveza or one of the island's best margaritas (order one up, with top-shelf tequila, and let the fiesta begin). A party for the senses, after the fiery and artistic Painted Desert soup (a thick puree of red pepper and chilies in chicken stock), you can chill with the Yucatan *ceviche* made from a mix of fish and shellfish. Forgo the Tex-Mex standards like burritos or the appetizer sampler and experience instead the better Southwestern dishes like mesquite lamb with cranberry-chipotle sauce. Plan on listening to *guitara* music in the rooftop cantina on Wednesday through Saturday nights. ⊠*700 Plantation Center, Mid-Island* ☎*843/785–3838* ⊴*Reservations essentials* ▤*AE, MC, V* ⊘*No lunch Sat. and Sun.*

8

$$–$$$ ✕ **Truffles Cafe.** *American.* When a restaurant survives here for more than 20 years, there's a reason. This place has personable, hands-on owners, prices low enough to keep the islanders coming all year, and food that is fresh and flavorful. There are none of the namesake truffles, but there's grilled salmon with a mango-barbecue glaze and—if you're gonna be bad—barbecued baby back ribs. This is a favorite for families because of its kid-friendly environment. Check out the wildly creative gift shop. ⊠*Sea Pines Center, 71 Lighthouse Rd.* ☎*843/671–6136* ▤*AE, D, MC, V.*

$$$–
$$$$ ✕**Truffles Grill.** *American.* The latest entrant in the island's Truffles trilogy is also the best for those who like contemporary takes on American food. The decor, including giant-sized black-and-white, island-themed photos, is striking; the lighting is also trendy. All five appetizers are outstanding, with the famous Tee-time cheese ring a great item to share. The Oriental Napa salad with tuna is big enough to be a main course. If you're on a budget, choose a specialty like the Kobe burger with pimento cheese. If you're not, then venture to pricey yet juicy, center-cut steaks. You will need to order sides, too. As always with Price Beall's restaurants, the quality of the ingredients is super-fresh and wholesome, so you can devour a scrumptious blondie for dessert without guilt. Speaking of naughty, martinis are full-sized, with a creative twist or straight-on up, for a moderate price; you can also get excellent wines by the glass. ⊠ *8 Executive Park Rd., off Pope Ave., South End* ☎*843/785–3663* ⌖*Reservations essential* ▤*AE, D, MC, V* ⊗*Closed Sun. No lunch.*

WHERE TO STAY

$$$–
$$$$ ☷**Crowne Plaza Hilton Head Island Beach Resort.** Decorated in a classy nautical theme and set in a luxuriant garden, the Crowne Plaza is appropriately resplendent. It's the centerpiece of Shipyard Plantation, which means guests have access to all its amenities. It also has one of the more elegant lobbies and public spaces; however, this resort has the fewest oceanfront rooms of the majors and is the farthest from the water. Its latticed bridge and beach pavilion have seen many an island wedding. **Pros:** it is the closest hotel to all the restaurants and nightlife in Coligny Plaza and Park Plaza; parking is free, although valet parking costs $10. **Cons:** Wi-Fi and cell service problematic due to low-rise, older concrete structures; large and sometimes impersonal. ⊠ *Shipyard Plantation, 130 Shipyard Dr., Mid-Island* ☎*843/842–2400 or 800/334–1881* ⊕*www.ichotels group.com* ⇌*331 rooms, 9 suites* ⌖*In-room: refrigerator, Internet. In-hotel: 3 restaurants, golf courses, pools, gym, bicycles, Wi-Fi, children's programs (ages 3–12), parking (free), no-smoking rooms* ▤*AE, D, DC, MC, V* ⊙*EP.*

$$$$ ☷**Disney's Hilton Head Island Resort.** Disney's typical cheery
☾ colors and whimsical designs create a look that's part South-
★ ern beach resort, part Adirondack hideaway. The villas here have fully furnished dining, living, and sleeping areas, as well as porches with rocking chairs and picnic tables. It's

The International Connection

When guests pull up to the grand entrance of a Hilton Head resort and a dark-skinned bellman greets them with a smile, extending a welcome in a lilting accent, visitors assume he is of local African-American decent, known in the Lowcountry as a "Gullah."

Although that is possible—some of the Gullahs have been employed in the hotel industry here for more 25 years—chances are that the man is Jamaican. Since 2002, the island's resorts have been importing thousands of Jamaicans during peak season to fill service openings that they have trouble staffing locally. These willing workers come on annual visas that can be renewed after a return trip to Jamaica for several months. All went well until 2008, when South Carolina politicians voted to stop issuing these visas. Those who

had already obtained green cards were able to stay on, and repeat guests to Hilton Head are pleased to see them.

Another plan had to be implemented especially for the outlying resorts, like the Daufuskie Island Club. These resorts tapped into agencies that handle staffing for ski resorts and were able to fill their quotas. The Marriott, for example, has an extensive international intern program, with trainees eventually being able to transfer to other Marriott properties and to move into management positions. Under a staffer's name badge you will see his country of origin: Turkey, the Philippines, Australia, Brazil, etc. At the Inn at Harbour Town, where the bellmen traditionally wear Scottish kilts, the young man parking your car may have a Russian accent.

8

on a little islet in Broad Creek; many units have marsh or marina views. The smallest villa is a studio; the largest has three bedrooms, four baths, and space to sleep a dozen. The resort has a fishing pier and a lively beach club a mile from the accommodations (shuttle service provided). Kids are kept happy and busy, be it crabbing or roasting marshmallows. Surprisingly, it's popular with couples unaccompanied by children. **Pros:** it is all about kids; young and friendly staffers. **Cons:** many guests actually think that there is a theme park here and are disappointed; it is a time-share property; not inexpensive. ⊠*22 Harbourside La., Mid-Island* ☎*843/341–4100 or 407/939–7540* ⊕*www. dvcmagic.com* ⊐*102 units* ⌂*In-room: kitchen (some), Internet. In-hotel: 2 restaurants, pools, gym, water sports,*

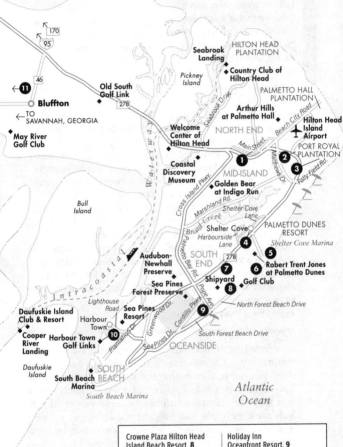

Where to Stay on Hilton Head Island

KEY

⚓ Beach

⛴ Ferry

Port Royal Sound

→ 170
→ 95

← 46
⑪ **Bluffton**

← TO SAVANNAH, GEORGIA

May River Golf Club

Old South Golf Link

278

HILTON HEAD PLANTATION

Seabrook Landing

Pickney Island

Country Club of Hilton Head

PALMETTO HALL PLANTATION

Arthur Hills at Palmetto Hall

Beach City Road

Hilton Head Island Airport

Welcome Center of Hilton Head

NORTH END

Seabrook Dr.

Main Street

Matthews Dr.

PORT ROYAL PLANTATION

① ②

③

Folly Field Rd.

Coastal Discovery Museum

MID-ISLAND

Cross Island Pkwy.

Golden Bear at Indigo Run

Marshland Rd.

Shelter Cove Lane

PALMETTO DUNES RESORT

Bull Island

Broad Creek

Shelter Cove

Harbourside Lane

Shelter Cove Marina

④

⑤

Palmetto Bay Rd.

Audubon-Newhall Preserve

SOUTH END

278

Robert Trent Jones at Palmetto Dunes

⑦

⑥

Intracoastal

Sea Pines Forest Preserve

Shipyard

Golf Club

⑧

Pope Ave.

North Forest Beach Drive

Daufuskie Island Club & Resort

Lighthouse Road

Sea Pines Resort

Greenwood Dr.

Cordillo Pkwy.

⑨

Cooper River Landing

Harbour Town

⑩

South Forest Beach Drive

Harbour Town Golf Links

Plantation Dr.

Sea Pines Dr.

OCEANSIDE

Daufuskie Island

South Beach Marina

SOUTH BEACH

Atlantic Ocean

South Beach Marina

0   1/2 mi

0   1/2 km

Crowne Plaza Hilton Head Island Beach Resort, **8**

Disney's Hilton Head Island Resort, **4**

Hampton Inn on Hilton Head Island, **2**

Hilton Head Marriott Resort & Spa, **5**

Hilton Oceanfront Resort, **6**

Holiday Inn Oceanfront Resort, **9**

The Inn at Harbour Town, **10**

The Inn at Palmetto Bluff, **11**

Main St. Inn & Spa, **1**

Park Lane Hotel & Suites, **7**

Westin Hilton Head Island Resort & Spa, **3**

bicycles, children's programs (ages 3–16), laundry service, no-smoking rooms ⊟*AE, MC, V* ⊺◯|*EP.*

$ ⊞ **Hampton Inn on Hilton Head Island.** Tree-shaded, this hotel, which is sheltered from the noise and traffic, is a good choice if you have kids. The two-bedroom family suites are surprisingly upscale; the parents' rooms are tastefully appointed, and the kids' rooms are cool enough to have foosball tables. King-size studios with sleeper sofas are another alternative for families. Breakfast is as Southern as country gravy and biscuits or as European as Belgian waffles. Major renovations throughout the buildings included the replacement of carpets, bedspreads, and other fabrics. Corporate and business travelers favor this moderately-priced option, too. **Pros:** good customer service; clean; eight different breakfast menus. **Cons:** not on a beach (the closest is Folly Field, 2 mi away); grounds are not memorable, and your view is often the parking lot. ⊠*1 Dillon Rd., Mid-Island* ☎*843/681–7900* ⊕*www.hampton-inn. com* ⟿*115 rooms, 7 suites* &*In-room: Internet. In-hotel: pool, Wi-Fi, parking (free), no-smoking rooms* ⊟*AE, D, DC, MC, V* ⊺◯|*BP.*

$$$$ ⊞ **Hilton Head Marriott Resort & Spa.** Marriott's standard
☾ rooms get a tropical twist at this palm-enveloped resort:
★ sunny yellow-and-green floral fabrics and cheery furnishings are part of the peppy decor. All guest rooms have private balconies (spring for an oceanfront room), writing desks, and down comforters. The tallest granddaddy of the island's resorts, it's looking good after a major renovation in 2008 that includes revamped pool areas and restaurants, notably Conroy's. To take in the sea views, you can lounge by the pool or lunch at the fun, outdoor snack bar. On rainy days and at dusk, the indoor pool under a glass dome is a great alternative. Kids love Dive-in Theater nights and the real sand castle in the lobby. Hammocks have been added to the sandy knoll adjacent to the pool area, and while you swing yourself gently into a siesta, you think, "Ahh, this is the life." A new spa is also a must-do. **Pros:** the multicultural staff has a great spirit; a full-service Marriott, it is one of the best-run operations on the island. **Cons:** rooms could be larger; in the summer kids are everywhere; in-room Wi-Fi costs $9.95 a day. ⊠*1 Hotel Circle, Palmetto Dunes, Mid-Island* ☎*843/686–8400 or 888/511–5086* ☒*843/686–8450* ⊕*www.hiltonheadmarriott.com* ⟿*476 rooms, 36 suites* &*In-room: safe, kitchen (some), Wi-Fi. In-hotel: restaurant, bar, golf courses, tennis courts, pools,*

8

gym, spa, beachfront, water sports, bicycles, Wi-Fi, children's programs (ages 3–12), no-smoking rooms ▭*AE, D, DC, MC, V* |O|*EP.*

\$\$–\$\$\$ 🏨**Hilton Oceanfront Resort.** Unquestionably, there's a Caribbean sensibility to this five-story chain hotel; the grounds are beautifully landscaped with deciduous and evergreen bushes, and palms run along the beach. This is not what you think of when you think Hilton, which usually denotes a high-rise property; rather, this resort is far more casual, laid back, and more family- than business-friendly. The smallest accommodations are large, commodious studios with a kitchenette; they go on up to two-bedroom suites. Many rooms face the ocean, and all are decorated with elegant wood furnishings, such as hand-carved armoires. A new, urbane lounge called the XO is a happening nightspot. HH Prime is the steak house, and the excellent deli/breakfast restaurant is being expanded at this writing. The resort has three pools, one strictly for little children, another for families, and an adults-only pool overlooking the ocean. Prices span a long range; online deals can be the best, with outdoor cabana massages, breakfast, and a bottle of wine included in some packages. **Pros:** competes more with condos than hotels because of the size of its accommodations; lots of outdoor dining options. **Cons:** boisterous wedding parties can be too noisy; problems with cell reception; minimum stay is two nights during summer. ✉*23 Ocean La. Palmetto Dunes, Mid-Island* ✆*Box 6165, 29938* ☎*843/842–8000 or 800/845–8001* ⊕*www.hiltonheadhilton.com* ⇆*303 studios, 20 suites* ♿*In-room: kitchen, Internet. In-hotel: restaurants, golf courses, pools, gym, water sports, bicycles, Wi-Fi, children's programs (ages 5–12), no-smoking rooms* ▭*AE, D, DC, MC, V* |O|*EP.*

\$\$\$– 🏨**Holiday Inn Oceanfront Resort.** This high-rise on one of **\$\$\$\$** the island's busiest beaches is within walking distance of major South End shops and restaurants. Standard rooms are spacious and furnished in a contemporary style, recently renovated in bright and bold color schemes. It attracts a diverse crowd: budget-minded vacationers, mainly families, corporate travelers and meeting groups, and those liking the fun, social aspects of the beach scene. Golf and tennis packages are available, and rates with breakfast included are the better deal. A resort fee is charged, \$8.95 a day that includes Wi-Fi and parking. The two-bedroom suites with ocean views usually have to be booked a month in advance, particularly in summer. The outdoor Tiki Hut lounge, a poolside bar, is hugely popular at one of the island's most populated beaches. Pets are allowed, but not during peak season. **Pros:** the price is a good value for Hilton Head, particularly for families; strong professional management and corporate standards; microwaves in rooms. **Cons:** if you are looking for posh, it is not; in summer, the number of kids raises the noise volume; small front desk can back up. ✉ *S. Forest Beach Dr., South End* ☐ *Box 5728, 29938* ☎ *843/785–5126 or 800/423–9897* 🖷 *843/785–6678* ⊕ *www.hihiltonhead.com* ⇨ *201 rooms* ☐ *In-room: refrigerator, Internet, Wi-Fi. In-hotel: restaurant, bar, pool, gym, bicycles, Wi-Fi, children's programs (ages 3–12), no-smoking rooms* ⊟ *AE, D, DC, MC, V* ⊙ *EP.*

$$$ ⊡ **The Inn at Harbour Town.** The most buzz-worthy of Hilton Head's properties is this European-style boutique hotel. A proper staff, clad in kilts, pampers you with British service and a dose of Southern charm. Butlers are on hand any time of the day or night, and the kitchen delivers around the clock. The spacious guest rooms, decorated with neutral palettes, have luxurious touches like Frette bed linens, which are turned down for you each night. The back patio with its upscale furnishings, landscaping, and brickwork is enviable and runs right up to the greens of the fairways of the Harbour Town course. The lobby isn't a lobby per se; it just has a concierge desk for check-in. There are three additional seating areas, each with a different high-end decor. The Harbour Town Grill serves some of the best steaks on the island. Parking is free and easy, and valet service only costs $10. **Pros:** a service-oriented property, it is a centrally located Sea Pines address; unique, it is one of the finest hotel operations on island; complimentary parking. **Cons:** some concierges give you too much information to digest; no water views; golf-view rooms are $20 extra. ✉ *Lighthouse La., off U.S. 278, Sea Pines South End* ☎ *843/363–8100 or 888/807–6873* ⊕ *www.seapines.com* ⇨ *60 rooms* ☐ *In-room: refrigerator, Wi-Fi. In-hotel: restaurant, golf courses, tennis courts, bicycles, laundry service, Wi-Fi, parking (free), no-smoking rooms* ⊟ *AE, D, DC, MC, V* ⊙ *EP.*

★ Fodor'sChoice ⊡ **The Inn at Palmetto Bluff.** Fifteen minutes from $$$$ Hilton Head and a member of the Leading Small Hotels of the World, this is the Lowcountry's most luxurious resort. This 22,000-acre property has been transformed into a perfect replica of a small island town, complete with its own clapboard church. As a chauffeured golf cart takes you to your cottages, you'll pass the clubhouse, which resembles a mighty antebellum great house. All of the cottages are generously sized—even the one-bedrooms have more than 1,100 square feet of space. The decor is coastal chic, with sumptuous bedding, gas fireplaces, surround-sound home theaters, and marvelous bathroom suites with steam showers. Your screened-in porch puts you immediately in touch with nature. Rental homes (four bedrooms) with chic interiors are also available. New is the Canoe Club with its restaurant, family pool, and bar. The spa puts you close to heaven with its pampering treatments. Dinner at its River House Restaurant is definitely worth an excursion from Hilton Head even if you do not stay here. **Pros:** the tennis/boccie/croquet complex has an atmospheric, impressive retail shop; the river adds both ambience and boat excursions; pillared ruins dotting the grounds are like sculpture. **Cons:** the mock Southern town is not the real thing; not that close to the amenities of Hilton Head. ⊠*476 Mount Pelia Rd., Bluffton* ☎*843/706–6500 or 866/706–6565* ⊕*www.palmettobluffresort.com* ⚲*50 cottages* ⌂*In-room: safe, refrigerator, Wi-Fi. In-hotel: 4 restaurants, bars, golf course, pools, water sports, bicycles, Internet terminal, Wi-Fi, no-smoking rooms* ⊟*AE, MC, V* ⌶*EP.*

★ Fodor'sChoice ⊠ **Main Street Inn & Spa.** This Italianate villa has
$$–$$$ stucco facades ornamented with lions' heads, elaborate ironwork, and shuttered doors. Staying here is like being a guest at a rich friend's estate. Guest rooms have velvet and silk brocade linens, feather duvets, and porcelain and brass sinks. An ample breakfast buffet is served in a petite, sunny dining room. In the afternoon there's complimentary wine at cocktail hour; before that, you can get gourmet coffee and homemade cookies which can be taken into the formal garden. Wi-Fi is free. The spa offers treatments ranging from traditional Swedish massages to Indian Kyria massages. Four king-size junior suites overlook the pool and gardens and are the inn's largest. Some rooms have balconies and fireplaces. **Pros:** when someone plays the piano while you are having your wine, it's super-atmospheric; the lion's head fountains and other Euro-architectural details. **Cons:** weddings can overwhelm the resort, especially on weekends and throughout June; regular rooms are small. ⊠*2200 Main St., North End* ☎*843/681–3001 or 800/471–3001* ⊕*www.mainstreetinn.com* ⚲*29 room, 4 jr. suites* ⌂*In-room: refrigerator, Wi-Fi. In-hotel: pool, spa, Internet terminal, Wi-Fi, no-smoking rooms* ⊟*AE, D, MC, V* ⌶*BP.*

\$\$ ▦ **Park Lane Hotel & Suites.** The island's only all-suites property has a friendly feel, since many guests stay for weeks. Each suite has a full kitchen, so there's no need to eat out for every meal. Pet-friendly, the hotel is definitely geared to families, though retirees also favor it and represent most of the long-term guests. You can cool off in the pool after heating up on the tennis courts, but the public beach is 2 mi away. You will be close to Sea Pines Resort and its facilities in Harbour Town. A free shuttle runs hourly to Caligny Beach. Both parking and Wi-Fi are free. **Pros:** this is one of the island's most reasonably priced lodgings; the bigger the unit, the nicer the condition and decor; flat-screen TVs. **Cons:** not high-end; more kids mean more noise, especially around the pool area; rooms need to be renovated (a total renovation was just beginning at this writing and was expected to finish by March 2009). ⊠ *12 Park Lane, South End* ☎ *843/686–5700* ⊕ *www.hiltonheadparklanehotel.com* ⌂ *156 suites* &*In-room: kitchen, Wi-Fi. In-hotel: tennis court, pool, bicycles, Internet terminal, Wi-Fi, no-smoking rooms.* ▤ *AE, D, MC, V* ⍥ *BP.*

★ **Fodor's**Choice ▦ **Westin Hilton Head Island Resort & Spa.** A circular
\$\$\$\$ drive winds around a metal sculpture of long-legged marsh
☯ birds as you approach this luxury resort. The lush landscape lies on the island's quietest, least inhabited stretch of sand. Guest rooms, most with ocean views from the balconies, have homey touches, crown molding, and contemporary furnishings. If you need space to spread out, there are two- and three-bedroom villas. The service is generally efficient and caring. A new spa opened in 2007 and has become the big buzz on the island. This continues to be one of the top resorts on Hilton Head, particularly for honeymooners. **Pros:** the number and diversity of children's activities is amazing; a good destination wedding hotel, ceremonies are performed on the beach and other atmospheric, outdoor venues; the beach here is absolutely gorgeous. **Cons:** in the off-seasons, the majority of its clientele are large groups; the hotel's phone service can bog down; difficult to get cell phone reception indoors. ⊠ *2 Grass Lawn Ave., North End* ☎ *843/681–4000 or 800/228–3000* ⊕ *www.westin. com* ⌂ *412 rooms, 29 suites* &*In-room: Internet, Wi-Fi. In-hotel: 3 restaurants, golf courses, tennis courts, pools, gym, beachfront, bicycles, children's programs (ages 4–12), no-smoking rooms.* ▤ *AE, D, DC, MC, V* ⍥ *EP.*

8

How to Talk to a Hilton Head Insider

Hilton Head is known as a place where people come to start a new life, or to happily live out their golden years. It is politically incorrect to immediately ask someone you just met, "Where did you come from?" or "What brought you here?" or "What did you do in your former life?" Residents are asked these questions all the time, and it gets old, especially if they moved here decades ago. Their reluctance to tell all does not mean that they necessarily have skeletons in their closets. Now, conversely, they are allowed to ask *you* where you are from—not to mention how long you are staying—or they may be considered unwelcoming. But do let them tell you about themselves in time, or over a cocktail. You may learn that your golfing partner was the CEO of a big national corporation, or the guy next to you at the bar is a best-selling author, or the friendly fellow in line at the store is a billionaire entrepreneur who might even be a household name.

PRIVATE VILLA RENTALS

Hilton Head has some 6,000 villas, condos, and private homes for rent, almost double the island's available hotel rooms. Villas and condos seem to work particularly well for families with children, especially if they want to avoid the extra costs of staying in a resort. Often these vacation homes cost less per diem than hotels of the same quality. Guests on a budget can further economize by cooking some meals at the house, and most villas have laundry facilities; some even have private pools. Villas and condos are primarily rented by the week, Saturday to Saturday.

RENTAL AGENTS

ResortQuest (☎*843/686–8144 or 800/448–3408* ⊕*www. resortquesthiltonhead.com*) boasts that it has the most comprehensive selection of accommodations (500-plus) on Hilton Head, from oceanfront to golf views, all in premier locations. A quality rating helps prospective guests know the type of decor their accommodation will have. Guests receive an exclusive ResortQuest Recommends card that gives discounts to shops, restaurants, and island activities. Generally, guests renting from this company can play tennis for free and get preferred golf rates at the most prestigious courses. Departure cleaning is not included in the quoted rates, but ResortQuest does offer optional cleaning services from a daily towel and trash service to a mid-week "full clean."

Resort Rentals of Hilton Head Island (☎*843/686–6008 or 800/845–7017* ⊕*www.hhivacations.com*) represents some 300 homes and villas island-wide from the gated communities of Sea Pines, Palmetto Dunes and Shipyard to some of the older non-gated areas that have the newest homes such as North and South Forest Beach and the Folly Field, Singleton Beach area. Stays are generally Saturday to Saturday during the peak summer season; three- or four-night stays may be possible off-season. Most of the properties are privately owned, so decor and amenities can vary. In addition to the rental fee, you'll pay 11% tax, a $60 reservation fee, and a 4% administration fee. Linens and departure cleaning are included in the quoted rates, but daily maid service or additional cleaning is not.

Sea Pines Resort (☎*843/842–1496* ⊕*www.seapines.com*) operates in its own little world, a microcosm on the far south end of the island. The vast majority of the overnight guests rent one of the 500 suites, villas, and beach houses. In addition to quoted rates, expect to pay an additional 19.5% to cover the combined taxes and resort fees. Minimum rental periods are one-week in summer, three nights otherwise. All houses have landlines and most have Wi-Fi. In general, housekeeping throughout the week is additional, and price depends on the size of the villa, but departure cleaning is included. A special racquet club privilege is two hours a day of free tennis per rental unit. Sea Pines has its own security force that patrols the community.

$$$$ ☒**Hot Tin Roof.** Now this is a beach house! Smack on North Forest Beach with sweeping views of the Atlantic Ocean, this elevated, two-story home (circa 2001) is breathtaking. From the time you enter the spacious, open living area, the ocean commands your attention. The kitchen brings out the gourmet in guests, and cooks can watch the view while they work. At least two couples can enjoy one of the two master suites; there is one downstairs, one up. Upstairs a large living area functions as a media room with a wet bar, commodious sofas, and a game table. This is a great choice for double families, *Big Chill* reunions, and incentive groups. **Pros:** handsomely furnished with several plasma and flat-screen TVs and upscale contemporary furnishings; oceanfront pool deck is outfitted with a whirlpool tub, bar, shower, gas grill, and high-end outdoor furniture. **Cons:**

8

pool is small and half under the deck; house does not have a traditional warm and fuzzy feeling; the elevator is off-limits to renters. ✉*North Forest Beach, 129 Dune Lane, South End* ☎*843/686–6008 or 800/845–7017* ⊕*www.hhivacations.com* ⌑*7 bedrooms, 7.5 bathrooms* ⌂*Dishwasher, DVD, Internet, Wi-Fi, pool, beachfront, laundry facilities, no–smoking* ⊟*AE, D, MC, V.*

$$$$ 🖫**Hunt Club Three.** This remarkable home is a great value
★ for the money. Tall, coffered ceilings, an open layout with wide arches, and exquisite details like a downstairs powder room with black floral wallpaper and an oversized leather mirror make it special. An African motif takes in tiger wallpaper and various leopard-skin prints, yet it is not overdone; the whole feel is elegant yet tropical. In the den, a white life preserver emblazoned with: WELCOME TO THE BEACH hangs on a fieldstone fireplace, but guests aren't allowed to light a fire. An oversized gas grill overlooks the atmospheric pool area with tiered palms and a mature live oak. **Pros:** real Euro tiles, even in the pool, which is surrounded by lush tropical vegetation; the jazz/media room with its 50-inch plasma TV; an eat-in gourmet kitchen is great for vacationing families. **Cons:** some older TVs; not very close to the beach; no water views. ✉*Palmetto Dunes, 3 Hunt Club Dr., Mid-Island* ☎*843/785–2248* ⊕*www.resortquesthiltonhead.com* ⌑*6 bedrooms, 6.5 bathrooms* ⌂*Dishwasher, DVD, VCR, Wi-Fi, pool, laundry facilities, no-smoking* ⊟ *AE, E, MC, V.*

★ **Fodor's**Choice 🖫**The Manor.** A modern-day mansion, with
$$$$ shades of *The Great Gatsby,* this very large home was built in 2007 with top-of-the-line materials. From the front entrance you admire the interior pillars in the living room, the high ceilings and ornate fireplace, and the Brazilian cherry and maple hardwood floors. A chef's dream kitchen has exquisite marble countertops. (Most guests hire the chef and butler.) There's a wine-storage room as well as a formal dining room. Take the elevator up to the media room, which has a phenomenal sound system and leather recliners. The billiards room has its own bar and balcony. Commodious bedrooms are carpeted; some have French doors, espresso machines, and mini-fridges. It's a perfect wedding venue or a place for a corporate retreat. **Pros:** all fireplaces are working; beautiful saltwater infinity pool and waterfall with a hot tub and even a screened, outdoor living area with fireplace; separate guesthouse with two bedrooms and two baths. **Cons:** no ocean view; a walk

or bike ride to the beach. ✉*Sea Pines Resort, 206 N. Sea Pines Dr., South End* ⊕*www.seapines.com* ➾*7 bedrooms, 8.5 bathrooms* ⌂*Dishwasher, DVD, Wi-Fi, daily maid service, hot tub, pool, gym, laundry facilities, no-smoking* ▤*AE, MC, V.*

$$$$ ▦**Saint Andrews Place 1.** This is one of Hilton Head's early contemporary homes, which has been painstakingly remodeled. It has strong appeal to multigenerational families. The upscale but traditional decor and one-level design suit seniors. Located within a swing of the second tee of The Harbour Town Links Course, the house has a strong draw for golfers; it is in demand for the Heritage Golf Tourney. Another major enticement is a private pool, the deck equipped with a giant gas grill and stylish outdoor furnishings. Prep can be done in the gourmet kitchen, while dinner is served in the formal dining room. **Pros:** screened-in porch and large windows bring the outdoors in; preferred golf rates to guests; an office/media room has a plasma TV and premier channels. **Cons:** no water views; you have to bike or drive to a beach. ✉ *Sea Pines Resort, Saint Andrews Place 1, South End* ☎*843/363–2115* ⊕*www. resortquesthiltonhead.com* ➾*4 bedrooms, 4.5 bathrooms* ⌂ *Dishwasher, DVD, VCR, Wi-Fi, pool, laundry facilities, no-smoking* ▤ *AE, D, MC, V.*

$$$$ ▦**Sound Villa 1458.** Sound Villas is the oldest condominium cluster on the island (some 25 years old) and were developed by founder Charles Frazer, yet these villas are not inexpensive. Smack on South Beach Marina, this is a prime location. You can just sit on the deck and watch the boats go by. The well-appointed, tri-level town house is also very special inside, with an urbane sophistication and excellent details: gorgeous, ochre-and-brown granite countertops; a wine cooler; wainscoting on doors; an aged pine dining-room table; hardwood floors; leather furniture; plasma TVs; a fieldstone fireplace; an outdoor shower; a large barbecue grill; and expensive outdoor furniture. **Pros:** the water view is of Calibogue Sound meeting the Atlantic; small but exquisite garden and landscaping with impressive interior/exterior design. **Cons:** the 1970s faux-stucco facade could be on a downscale apartment complex; the tiny front porch, with two wicker chairs, looks down on two a/c units; it's only 100 yards to the beach, but you may need transportation if you have kids or a lot of stuff to carry. ✉*Sea Pines, 253 South Sea Pines Drive, South End* ☎*843/785–1171* ⊕*www.resortquesthiltonhead.com*

8

⌐5 bedrooms, 5 bathrooms ⌂Dishwasher, DVD, Wi-Fi, laundry facilities, no-smoking ▤AE, D, MC, V.

$$$$ ▦**10 Singleton Shores.** New and unblemished (the home was built in 2008), this three-story 5,000 square-foot home is an exceptional value for the price. It's not within one of the established plantations; instead, it's in one of the newer, upscale residential enclaves with views across the wetlands to the ocean, notably from the balcony of the third-floor master suite but also from the back porch. There are 1,800 square-feet of verandas; one has a large barbecue grill. With a gourmet kitchen and a butler's pantry on the second and third floors, it is ideal for a family reunion, a wedding group, or a two-family vacation. There are even two laundry rooms. No worries about stair climbing for senior members; the hardwood-paneled elevator is just a push-button away. **Pros:** gorgeous Brazilian hardwood floors and granite countertops; oversized bathrooms and closets; stereo system throughout and media room great for kids. **Cons:** not in a plantation; it's a long trip to the beach; although the furnishings are handsome, the decor doesn't quite gel. ⊠*10 Singleton Shores, Mid Island* ☎*843/686–2361* ⊕*www.resortquesthiltonhead.com* ⌐*7 bedrooms, 7.5 bathrooms* ⌂*Dishwasher, DVD, Wi-Fi, pool, laundry facilities, no-smoking* ▤*AE, MC, V.*

$$$–$$$$ ▦**1024 Caravel Court.** This villa is smack on Harbour Town Marina. Like many of the Sea Pines condo complexes built on choice waterfront property, this one dates from the early 1970s. And like most of them, this unit has been well-maintained and nicely updated. Golfers like the location and price, and corporate groups book during shoulder season, as the conference centers are a quick walk away. Seniors like the compact size and first-floor location, as well as the homey, traditional furnishings. Everyone likes the price. The kitchen is adequate for the limited cooking that you might do. Guests happily enjoy their cocktails on the spacious balcony overlooking the action of the yacht basin as colorful parasailers float by. **Pros:** handsome granite counter tops; it's a short walk to Harbour Town Golf Links and the resort's amenities. **Cons:** public areas are reminiscent of a mediocre apartment complex; a bike ride or drive to the beach; not terribly spacious. ⊠*Sea Pines Resort, 1024 Caravel Court, South End* ⊕*www.seapines. com* ⌐*2 bedrooms, 2 bathrooms* ⌂*DVD, Wi-Fi, laundry facilities, no-smoking* ▤*AE, MC, V.*

$$$$ ⌂ **13 Mizzenmast Court.** A view of the 18th hole of the Harbour Town Golf Links is a great tease for golfers. A view of the lagoon and even Calibogue Sound are more eye candy. This well-appointed home has a special quality with such details as a first-floor kitchen with two skylights, Charles Frazer–style. Constructed during Frazer's heyday, it has been considerably updated. It's a great retreat during big island golf events, especially because it has another kitchen and bar on the second floor, with the adjacent deck a good vantage point for watching the play. During the spring this charmer can be had for as little as $300 a night. Come peak wedding season, this is one of the most popular villas. **Pros:** the contemporary spiral staircase; the coziness will appeal to those who like traditional interiors; several fireplaces, a small plunge pool, and a hot tub. **Cons:** some undersized TVs with wires too obvious; master bedroom is three flights up; it's one mile from the beach club. ✉*Sea Pines Resort, 13 Mizzenmast Court, South End* ⊕*www.seapines.com* ↝*3 bedrooms, 2.5 bathrooms* ⚒*Dishwasher, DVD, Wi-Fi, pool, hot tub, laundry facilities, no-smoking* ▤*AE, MC, V.*

$–$$ ⌂ **Turnberry 251.** This is a perennial favorite condo for golf and tennis retreats, and the price is certainly right. Alas, it is not in a waterfront complex. However, golfers will appreciate that both the George Fazio and Robert Trent Jones courses are within walking distance. It's popular for girls' getaways and family trips, too, perhaps because of the complex's playground, oversized pool, children's wading pool, and open-air pavilion. The condo is quite spacious, simple in its furnishings, but attractive and with a private deck. The kitchen opens into the dining area. The beach is close, but you'll still need to take a bike or golf cart. **Pros:** free daily tennis and preferred golf rates; in sports-oriented shoulder seasons, it is a real value; not as large as a home but substantially larger than a good hotel room and less expensive. **Cons:** the exterior is not so attractive; as a condo, it lacks the privacy of a villa. ✉*Palmetto Dunes, 59 Carnoustie, Mid-Island* ☎*843/842–2093* ⊕*www.resortquesthiltonhead.com* ↝*2 bedrooms, 2 bathrooms* ⚒*Dishwasher, DVD, Internet, laundry facilities, no-smoking* ▤*AE, D, MC, V.*

$$$$ ⌂ **Villamare 1402.** This condo is in a complex near the Marriott, and its oceanfront location and extensive beachfront, with many family-oriented amenities, is why it is priced higher than the typical two-bedroom. Moms love the fully-

equipped kitchen and indoor and outdoor pools, the elevator, and the convenience of it all. Active guests will love the
fitness center and outdoor grilling area; plus, these condos
offer free tennis and golf discounts for ResortQuest guests.
This fourth-floor unit has a unique decor, which you will
either love or not. The tiled bar is boldly creative; the sofa
has red seat pillows and head pillows with a dramatic print.
The furniture is mostly blonde, Scandinavian-design. The
master bathroom has a whirlpool tub and two freestand-
ing, black bowl sinks. **Pros:** beachfront location with its
own beach walk; next door to the Marriott. **Cons:** con-
crete building and facades look like a modest apartment
complex; although Villamare has always been one of the
most requested complexes in Palmetto Dunes, it may not
be worth the high-end price tag; not so spacious, especially
for the price. ⊠*Palmetto Dunes, 1 Ocean Lane, Mid-Island
29928* ☎*843/785–1316* ⊕*www.resortquesthiltonhead.
com* ⏦*2 bedrooms, 2 bathrooms* ⚲*Dishwasher, DVD,
Wi-Fi, beachfront, laundry facilities, no-smoking* ▤*AE,
D, MC, V.*

$$$ ▣**Windsor 2219.** Windsor is in a secluded, villa condo com-
plex that is oceanfront in Palmetto Dunes. This unit is on
the second floor and has water views from the living/dining
area and two of the bedrooms. With a spacious kitchen (for
a condo), it lends itself to families. The master and second
bedrooms have ocean views; the third bedroom is simplis-
tic, with twin beds (better suited for kids). The building is
elevated, offering a covered, complimentary parking area.
Amenities in the complex include an oceanfront swimming
pool, children's play pool, hot tub, a large deck, and covered
gazebo with a grill. A private boardwalk leads directly to
the ocean. **Pros:** excellent location; with an elevator and
communal amenities, it is convenient for parents with small
children; a library offers several DVDs to watch. **Cons:**
the building is getting old and is not memorable; not as
commodious and appealing as a private home; decor has
that packaged look. ⊠*Palmetto Dunes, 2219 Windsor 11,
Mid-Island* ☎*843/686–6008 or 800/845–7017* ⊕*www.
hhivacations.com* ⏦ *3 bedrooms, 3 bathrooms* ⚲*Dish-
washer, DVD, Wi-Fi, pools, beachfront, laundry facilities,
no-smoking* ▤*AE, D, MC, V.*

SPORTS & THE OUTDOORS

BEACHES

Although resort beach access is reserved for guests and residents, there are four public entrances to Hilton Head's 12 mi of ocean beach. The two main parking spots are off U.S. 278 at Coligny Circle in the South End, near the Holiday Inn, and on Folly Field Road, Mid-Island. Both have changing facilities. South of Folly Field Road, Mid-Island along U.S. 278, Bradley Beach Road and Singleton Road lead to beaches where parking is limited. ■TIP→**A delightful stroll on the beach can end with an unpleasant surprise if you don't put your towels, shoes, and other earthly possessions way up on the sand. Tides here can fluctuate as much as 7 feet. Check the tide chart at your hotel.**

BIKING

There are more than 40 mi of public paths that crisscross Hilton Head Island, and pedaling is popular along the firmly packed beach. The island keeps adding more to the "boardwalk" network as visitors are utilizing it and it is such a safe alternative for kids. Keep in mind when crossing streets that in South Carolina, vehicles have the right-of-way. ■TIP→**Bikes with wide tires are a must if you want to ride on the beach. They can save you a spill should you hit loose sand on the trails.**

Bicycles can be rented at most hotels and resorts. You can also rent bicycles from the **Hilton Head Bicycle Company** (⊠*112 Arrow Rd., South End* ☎*843/686–6888* ⊕*www. hiltonheadbicycle.com*).

Pedals Bicycles. (⊠*71 Pope Ave., South End* ☎*843/842–5522*).

South Beach Cycles (⊠*Sea Pines Resort, off U.S. 278, South End* ☎*843/671–2453* ⊕*www.southbeachracquetclub.com*) rents bikes, helmets, tandems, and adult tricycles.

HOT WHEELS. **An amazing array of bicycles can be hired, from beach cruisers to mountain bikes to bicycles built for two. Many can be delivered to your hotel, along with helmets, baskets, locks, child carriers, and whatever else you might need. There are 40 mi of trails, as well as 12 mi of hard-packed beach, so the possibilities are endless.**

CANOEING & KAYAKING

This is one of the most delightful ways to commune with nature on this commercial but physically beautiful island. You paddle through the creeks and estuaries and try to keep up with the dolphins!

★ **Outside Hilton Head** (⊠*Sea Pines Resort, off U.S. 278, South End* ⊠*Shelter Cove Lane at U.S. 278, Mid-Island* ☎*843/686–6996 or 800/686–6996* ⊕*www.outsidehilton head.com*) is an ecologically sensitive company that rents canoes and kayaks; it also runs nature tours and dolphin-watching excursions.

FISHING

Captain Jim of **The Stray Cat** (⊠*The Docks at Charlie's Crab, 3 Hudson La., North End* ☎*843/683–5427* ⊕*www. straycatcharter.com*) will help you decide whether you want to fish "in-shore" or go offshore into the deep blue. You can go for four, six, or eight hours, and the price is $120 an hour; bait and tackle are provided, but you must bring your own lunch. If his 27-foot power catamaran is booked for the day, Jim will set you up with one of the other seven boats that call this pier home. All of the charter boats here have to enjoy a good reputation and maintain it.

GOLF

Hilton Head is nicknamed "Golf Island" for good reason: the island itself has 25 championship courses (most semi-private), and the outlying area has 16 more. Each offers its own packages, some of which are great deals. Almost all charge the highest green fees in the morning and lower the rates as the day goes on. Some offer lower rates in the hot summer months. It's essential to book tee times in advance, especially in the busy summer season; resort guests and club members get first choices. Most courses can be described as casual-classy, so you will have to adhere to certain rules of the greens. ■TIP→ **The dress code on island golf courses does not permit blue jeans, gym shorts, or jogging shorts. Men's shirts must have collars.**

The most internationally famed golf event in Hilton Head is The Heritage, now named the annual **Verizon Heritage PGA Golf Tournament** (⊕*www.seapines.com/golf*), which is held mid-April.

GOLF SCHOOLS

The Academy at Robert Trent Jones (⊠*Palmetto Dunes Resort, 7 Trent Jones La., Mid-Island* ☎*843/785–1138* ⊕*www.*

Susan Yeager, Writer, on Golf Schools

It was a mildly windy Tuesday afternoon in May when Doug Weaver, a Top instructor (according to *Golf Digest*), and Lindsey Letzig, an LPGA golf instructor, gave me an hour lesson at the Arthur Hills Golf Course in Leamington (a subdivision of Palmetto Dunes). They are part of a team of professional instructors for the Academy at Robert Trent Jones, another golf course located in Palmetto Dunes Resort.

Doug noticed my problems from the very first swing and jumped in with enthusiasm. I improved immediately with his instructions. He has a unique way of teaching golf. His artful approach is from a personal as well as a scientific perspective: while he identifies what type of personality one has by his golf swing, he sees his attitude towards the game, and applies the science of the swing. Doug's golf science included how to lighten one's grip on the club and how to use less effort in the swing. I also liked that he videotaped

my swing, because when do we ever get to see our own selves swinging a club? There are no vanity mirrors out there!

After much improvement from a private lesson with these two professionals, it was suggested that I come out the next morning for Lindsey's group, a ladies clinic. And that I awaited with anticipatory delight.

I found that the ladies clinic (my first) was the best way to learn how to hit the ball from every lie on the course. In 3½ hours, Lindsey covered the most important shots of the game, with individual attention and such professionalism and gentleness. I now feel confident enough to play golf with my colleagues and look as respectable as they do. The golf course is a great place to network. Now I have one less worry: I can keep up!

I have never walked away from lessons feeling so learned and fulfilled. These pros know their game and now I am more confident with mine.

palmettodunes.com) offers one-hour lessons, daily clinics, one- to three-day schools, family clinics, ladies programs, instructional videos, and free demonstrations at 4 PM each Monday from Doug Weaver, former PGA tour pro and Director of Instruction for the academy.

The TOUR Academy of Palmetto Hall Plantation (✉ *Palmetto Hall Plantation, 108 Fort Hollow Dr., North End* ☎*843/681–1516* ⊕*www.palmettohallgolf.com*) is the only golf school on the island affiliated with the PGA and is one of only six in the country. This academy is known for its teaching technologies that include video analysis, which compares one's swing on a split-screen with the best golfers in the world. Students can chose from a one-hour private lesson to up to five days of golf instruction to include a round of golf with an instructor. There are two pristine 18-hole courses at the school, one designed by Arthur Hills and the other, Robert Cupp.

GOLF COURSES

Arthur Hills at Palmetto Hall (✉ *Palmetto Hall, 108 Fort Howell Dr., North End* ☎*843/689–9205* ⊕*www.palmettohallgolf.com* ⚐*18 holes. 6,918 yds. Par 72. Green Fee: $60–$104*) is a player favorite from the renowned designer Arthur Hills; this course has his trademark: undulating fairways. The course, punctuated with lakes, gently flows across the island's rolling hills, winding around moss-draped oaks and towering pines. The clubhouse is a replica of an antebellum great house. This course is managed by Heritage Golf Group.

Although it's part of a country club, the course at **Country Club of Hilton Head** (✉*70 Skull Creek Dr., North End* ☎*843/681–4653 or 888/465–3475* ⊕*www.golfisland.com* ⚓*Reservations essential* ⚐*18 holes. 6,919 yds. Par 72. Green Fee: $50–$119*) is open for public play. A well-kept secret, it's never overcrowded. This 18-hole Rees Jones–designed course is a more casual environment than many of the others.

On an island renowned for its exceptional golf, Jack Nicklaus, the golf legend and course designer, has created **Golden Bear Golf Club at Indigo Run** ✉*Indigo Run, 72 Golden Bear Way, North End* ☎*843/689–2200* ⊕*www.goldenbearindigorun.com* ⚐*18 holes. 6,643 yds. Par 72. Greens fee: $85–$109*), another must-play course for Hilton Head. Located in the upscale Indigo Run community, it's in a natural woodlands setting and offers easygoing rounds. It is a course that requires more thought than muscle, yet you will have to earn every par you make. Though fairways are generous, you may end up with a lagoon looming smack ahead of the green on the approach shot. And there are the fine points—the color GPS monitor on every cart and women-friendly tees. After an honest, traditional test of golf, most golfers finish up at the plush clubhouse and with some food and drink at Just Jack's Grille.

★ Fodors Choice **Harbour Town Golf Links** (⊠*Sea Pines Resort,
11 Lighthouse La., South End* ☎*843/842–8484 or
800/955–8337* ⊕*www.golfisland.com* ↖*18 holes. 6,973
yds. Par 71. Green Fee: $153–$295*) is considered by many
golfers to be one of those must-play-before-you-die courses.
It's extremely well known because it has hosted The Heritage every spring for the last three decades. Designed by
Pete Dye, the layout is reminiscent of Scottish courses of
old. The Golf Academy is ranked among the top 10 in
the country.

The May River Golf Club (⊠*Palmetto Bluffs, 476 Mt. Pelia
Rd., Bluffton* ☎*843/706–6500* ⊕*www.palmettobluffre-
sort.com/golf* ↖*18 holes. 7,171 yds. Par 72. Green Fee:
$90–$260*), an 18-hole Jack Nicklaus course, has several
holes along the banks of the scenic May River and will
challenge all skill levels. The greens are covered by Pas-
palum, the latest eco-friendly turf. A distinction of this
classy operation is that caddy service is always required,
even if you choose to rent a golf cart, and then no carts are
allowed earlier than 9 AM. This is to encourage walking so
golfers will enjoy the beauty of the course.

Old South Golf Links (⊠*50 Buckingham Plant Dr., Bluffton*
☎*843/785–5353* ⊕*www.golfisland.com* ↖*18 holes. 6,772
yds. Par 72. Green Fee: $75–$85*) has scenic holes with
marshland and views of the intracoastal waterway. A recent
Internet poll had golfers preferring it over the famous Harbour Town Golf Links and Robert Trent Jones.

Robert Trent Jones at Palmetto Dunes (⊠*7 Robert Trent Jones
Way, North End* ☎*843/785–1138* ⊕*www.palmettodunes.
com* ↖*18 holes. 7,005 yds. Par 72. Green Fee: $125–$165*)
is one of the island's most popular layouts. Its beauty and
character are accentuated by the par-5, 10th hole, which
offers a panoramic view of the ocean. It's one of only two
oceanfront holes on Hilton Head.

HORSEBACK RIDING

☾ **Lawton Stables** (⊠*Sea Pines Resort, Plantation, off U.S.
★ 278, South End* ☎*843/671–2586*) gives riding lessons and
pony rides, in addition to having horseback tours through
the Sea Pines Forest Preserve. The latter can be troop
movements, with many participants. It is a safe ride, if
not adrenaline-racing.

CLOSE UP

The World of Gullah

In the Lowcountry, Gullah refers to several things: a language, a people, and a culture. Gullah (the word itself is believed to be derived from *Angola*), an English-based dialect rooted in African languages, is the unique language of the African-Americans of the Sea Islands of South Carolina and Georgia, more than 300 years old. Most locally born African-Americans of the area can understand, if not speak, Gullah.

Descended from thousands of slaves who were imported by planters in the Carolinas during the 18th century, the Gullah people have maintained not only their dialect but also their heritage. Much of Gullah culture traces back to the African rice-coast culture and survives today in the art forms and skills, including sweetgrass basket-making, of Sea Islanders. During the colonial period, when rice was king, Africans from the West African rice kingdoms drew high premiums as slaves. Those with basket-making skills were extremely valuable because baskets were needed for agricultural and household use. Made by hand, sweetgrass baskets are intricate coils of marsh grass with a sweet, haylike aroma.

Nowhere is Gullah culture more evident than in the foods of the region. Rice appears at nearly every meal—Africans taught planters how to grow rice and how to cook and serve it as well. Lowcountry dishes use okra, peanuts, *benne* (the African word for sesame seeds), field peas, and hot peppers. Gullah food reflects the bounty of the islands: shrimp, crabs, oysters, fish, and such vegetables as greens, tomatoes, and corn. Many dishes are prepared in one pot, a method similar to the stew-pot cooking of West Africa.

On St. Helena Island, near Beaufort, Penn Center is the unofficial Gullah headquarters, preserving the culture and developing opportunities for Gullahs. In 1852 the first school for freed slaves was established at Penn Center. You can delve into the culture further at the York W. Bailey Museum.

On St. Helena, many Gullahs still go shrimping with hand-tied nets, harvest oysters, and grow their own vegetables. Nearby on Daufuskie Island, as well as on Edisto, Wadmalaw, and Johns islands near Charleston, you can find Gullah communities. A famous Gullah proverb says: *If oonuh ent kno weh oonuh dah gwine, oonuh should kno weh oonuh come f'um.* Translation: If you don't know where you're going, you should know where you come from.

SPAS

Spa visits have become a recognized activity on the island, and for some people they are as popular as golf and tennis. In fact, spas have become one of the top leisure-time destinations, particularly for golf "widows." And this popularity extends to the men as well; previously spa-shy guys have come around, enticed by couples massage, deep-tissue sports massage, and even the pleasures of the manicure and pedicure. One landmark spa, Faces, has a men's night.

There are East Indian–influenced therapies, hot-stone massage, Hungarian organic facials—the treatments span the globe. Do your research, go online, and call or stop by the various spas and ask the locals their favorites. The quality of therapists island-wide is noteworthy—their training, certifications, and expertise. In the words of Jack Barakitis, premier therapist at Main Street Inn & Spa and one of the island's most respected instructors: "Body therapies strengthen more positive perceptions on your daily outlook of life. Spa services are intended to simply have you feeling better when you finish than when you started."

The low-key **Faces** (⊠*The Village at Wexford, 1000 William Hilton Pkwy., North End* ☎*843/785–3075* ⊕*www. facesdayspa.com*) has been pampering loyal clients for 20 years, with body therapists and cosmetologists who do what they do well. It has a fine line of cosmetics and does makeovers or evening makeups. Open seven days a week, Monday night is for the guys.

★ Fodors Choice **Heavenly Spa by Westin** (⊠*Westin Resort Hilton Head Island, Port Royal Plantation, 2 Grasslawn Ave., North End* ☎*843/681–4000 Ext. 7519*) is a new facility at the Westin resort offering the quintessential sensorial spa experience. Known internationally for its innovation and latest in therapies and decor, Westin's Heavenly spa brand also brings the treatments home. Prior to a treatment, clients are told to put their worries in a Gullah (a sweetgrass burden-basket); de-stressing is a major component here. Unique is a collection of treatments based on the energy from the color indigo, once a cash crop in the Lowcountry. The full-service salon, the relax room with its teas and healthy snacks, and the adjacent retail area with products like sweetgrass scents are heavenly, too.

The **Spa at Main Street Inn** (⊠*2200 Main St., North End* ☎*843/681–3001* ⊕*www.mainstreetinn.com*) has holistic massages that will put you in another zone. A petite facility, it offers deep muscle therapy, couples massage, hydrother-apy soaks and outdoor courtyard massages. Jack Barakatis instructs both his students and his own clients in the art of de-stressing, with a significant dose of spirituality.

The **Spa at Palmetto Bluffs** (⊠*476 Mount Pelia Rd., Blufton* ☎*843/706–6500* ⊕*www.palmettobluffresort.com*) has been dubbed the "celebrity spa" by locals, for this two-story facility is the ultimate pamper palace. It is as creative in its names that often have a Southern accent, as it is in its treatments. There are Amazing Grace and High Cotton bodyworks and massages, sensual soaks and couples mas-sage, special treatments for gentlemen/golfers, and Belles and Brides packages as this is a premier wedding destina-tion. Nonguests are welcome.

Spa Soleil (⊠*Marriott Hilton Head Resort & Spa, Palmetto Dunes, 1 Hotel Circle, Mid-Island* ☎*843/686–8400* ⊕*www.csspagroup.com*) is one of the newest spas on island; this $7-million facility has the atmosphere and professionalism, the therapies, and litany of massages found in the country's finest spas. Since the facility is all new, everything is still quite pristine. The colors, aromas, teas, and snacks make your treatment a soothing, therapeutic experience.

TENNIS

There are more than 300 courts on Hilton Head. Tennis comes in at a close second as the island's premier sport after golf. It is recognized as one of the nation's best tennis destinations. Hilton Head has a large international orga-nization of coaches. Spring and Fall are the peak seasons for cooler play with numerous tennis packages available at the resorts and through the schools.

Palmetto Dunes Tennis Center (⊠*6 Trent Jones La., Mid-Island* ☎*843/785–1152* ⊕*www.palmettodunes.com*) welcomes nonguests.

Port Royal (⊠*15 Wimbledon Ct., North End* ☎*843/686–8803* ⊕*www.heritagegolfgroup.com*) has 16 courts, including two grass.

★ **Sea Pines Racquet Club** (⊠*Sea Pines Resort, off U.S. 278, 32 Greenwood Dr., South End* ☎*843/363–4495*) has 23 courts, instructional programs, and a pro shop.

★ FodorsChoice Highly rated **Van der Meer Tennis Center/Ship-yard Racquet Club** (⊠*Shipyard Plantation, 19 de Allyon Rd., Mid-Island* ☎*843/686–8804* ⊕*www.vandermeertennis.com*)

is recognized for tennis instruction. Four of its 28 courts are covered.

NIGHTLIFE & THE ARTS

THE ARTS

In warm weather, free outdoor concerts are held at Harbour Town and Shelter Cove Harbour; at the latter fireworks light up the night every Tuesday from June to August. Guitarist Gregg Russell has been playing for children under Harbour Town's mighty Liberty Oak tree for decades. He begins strumming nightly at 8, except on Saturday.

The **Arts Center of Coastal Carolina** (✉*Shelter Cove La., Mid-Island* ☎*843/686–3945* ⊕*www.artscenter-hhi.org*) has a gallery and a theater with programs for young people. The Hallelujah Singers, Gullah performers, appear regularly.

The **Native Islander Gullah Celebration** (☎*843/689–9314* ⊕*www.gullahcelebration.com*) takes place in February and showcases Gullah life through arts, music, and theater.

NIGHTLIFE

Hilton Head has always been a party place, and that's true now more than ever. Bars, like everything else in Hilton Head, are often in strip malls. A fair number of clubs (often restaurants that crank up the music after dinner) cater to younger visitors, others to an older crowd, and still others that are "ageless" and are patronized by all generations. Some places are hangouts frequented by locals, and others get a good mix of both locals and tourists. As a general rule, the local haunts tend to be on the north end of the island. Why? There is more affordable housing there, and it is where the large contingent of young people live—there and over the bridge in Bluffton.

BARS

Reggae bands play at **Big Bamboo** (✉*Coligny Plaza, N. Forest Beach Dr., South End* ☎*843/686–3443*), a bar with a South Pacific theme.

Boathouse 11 (✉*397 Squire Pope Rd., North End* ☎*843/681–3663*), a popular waterfront restaurant, has two buzzing bars; in season, there's nightly entertainment (mainly vocalist/guitarists) seven nights a week. This is one of those restaurants where a lot of the locals "hang," boating types in particular.

The **Hilton Head Brewing Co.** (⊠*Hilton Head Plaza, Greenwood Dr., South End* ☎*843/785–2739*) lets you shake your groove thing to 1970s-era disco on Wednesday. There's live music on Friday and karaoke on Saturday.

Jazz Corner (⊠*The Village at Wexford, C-1, South End* ☎*843/842–8620*) will always be known and remembered for its live music and fun, New Orleans–style atmosphere. Each Friday and Saturday night, entertainers are brought in who are quite well known for their jazz, swing, Broadway, blues, or Motown performances. On Sunday through Thursday, co-owner and horn player Bob "Jazz" Masteller is the leader of his band, and he has a strong following, mainly an older crowd. The restaurant has a newly updated menu, so to assure yourself of a seat on busy nights, make reservations for dinner.

Jump & Phil's Bar & Grill (⊠*3 Hilton Head Plaza, South End* ☎*843/785–9070*) is a happening scene, especially for locals, and you could pass this nondescript building by if you didn't know. "Jump," whose real name is John Griffin, is an author of thriller novels under the pen name John R. Maxim, and this place is a magnet for area writers and football fans during the season.

The Metropolitan Lounge (⊠*Park Plaza, Greenwood Dr., South End* ☎*843/785–8466*) is the most sophisticated of several fun places on Park Plaza. With a Euro-style that appeals to all ages, it is known for its martini menu. On weekends, there is dancing in an anteroom separated by a wrought-iron gate. Here you will see all ages, from golf guys to the island's sassy, young, beautiful people.

Monkey Business (⊠*Park Plaza, Greenwood Dr., South End* ☎*843/686–3545*) is a dance club popular with young professionals. On Friday there's live beach music.

One of the island's latest hot spots, **Santa Fe Cafe** (⊠*Plantation Center in Palmetto Dunes, 700 Plantation Center, North End* ☎*843/785–3838*) is where you can lounge about in front of the adobe fireplace or sip top-shelf margaritas on the rooftop. The restaurant's clientele is predominately local residents and tends to be older than those who frequent the Boathouse because of its Southwestern atmosphere, unique on the island, and its guitarist(s).

Turtle's (⊠*The Westin Hilton Head Resort & Spa, 2 Grass Lawn Ave., North End* ☎*843/681–4000*) appeals to anyone who still likes to hold their partner when they dance.

Island Gators

The most famous photo of Hilton Head's brilliant developer, Charles Fraser, ran in the *Saturday Evening Post* in the late 1950s. It shows him dressed as a dandy, outfitted with a cane and straw hat, with an alligator on a leash.

These prehistoric creatures are indeed indigenous to this subtropical island. What you will learn if you visit the Coastal Discovery Museum, where the old photograph is blown up for an interpretive board on the island's early history, is that someone else had the gator by the tail (not shown) so that he would not harm Fraser or the photographer.

Nowadays, in Sea Pines Center, there is a life-sized, metal sculpture of an alligator that all the tourists, and especially their kids, climb upon to have their pictures taken. And should you happen to see a live gator while exploring the island or playing a round of golf, please don't feed it. Although, if you have the courage, you might want to take a snapshot.

SHOPPING

Shopping is starting to become a key component of the Hilton Head experience. While husbands play golf, the stores fill up with their wives. There are no mega–malls on the island; rather, Hilton Head's shopping areas are tasteful enclaves. The mid-island Mall at Shelter Cove is the largest; further north, the village of Wexford has an interesting collection of stylish shops. Sea Pines Center is also memorable, not only for its shops but also its park benches, landscaping, and outdoor alligator sculpture. There are some 700 stores on the island, and they run the gamut, including fine jewelry boutiques, upscale men's shops, sporting goods stores, art galleries, designer consignment shops, and charity-based thrift shops. Nearly half a dozen consignment shops featuring gently-used clothing, furniture, sports equipment, and art; because Hilton Head Islanders are characteristically well-heeled and well turned-out, many shed their clothes each season like molting birds. There's also an outlet mall over the bridge in Bluffton, while Old Town Bluffton has its own eclectic and artsy mix of shops selling mainly crafts, gifts, and art.

ART GALLERIES

Linda Hartough Gallery (⊠*Harbour Town, 140 Lighthouse Rd., South End* ☎*843/671–6500*) is all about golf. There's everything from landscapes of courses to golden golf balls to pillows embroidered with sayings like "Queen of the Green."

The **Red Piano Art Gallery** (⊠*220 Cordillo Pkwy., Mid-Island* ☎*843/785–2318*) showcases 19th- and 20th-century works by regional and national artists.

GIFTS

The **Audubon Nature Store** (⊠*The Village at Wexford, U.S. 278, Mid-Island* ☎*843/785–4311*) has gifts with a wild-life theme.

Outside Hilton Head (⊠*The Plaza at Shelter Cove, U.S. 278, Mid-Island* ☎*843/686–6996 or 800/686–6996*) sells Paw-leys Island hammocks (first made in the late 1800s) and other items that let you enjoy the great outdoors.

JEWELRY

The **Bird's Nest** (⊠*Coligny Plaza, Coligny Circle and N. Forest Beach Dr., South End* ☎*843/785–3737*) sells locally made shell and sand-dollar jewelry, as well as island-theme charms.

The **Goldsmith Shop** (⊠*3 Lagoon Rd., Mid-Island* ☎*843/785–2538*) carries classic jewelry and island charms.

Forsythe Jewelers (⊠*71 Lighthouse Rd., South End* ☎*843/342–3663*) is the island's leading jewelry store.

BEAUFORT

38 mi north of Hilton Head via U.S. 278 and Rte. 170; 70 mi southwest of Charleston via U.S. 17 and U.S. 21.

Charming homes and churches grace this old town on Port Royal Island. Come here on a day-trip from Hilton Head, Savannah, or Charleston, or to spend a quiet weekend at a B&B while you shop and stroll through the historic district. Tourists are drawn equally to the town's artsy scene (art walks are regularly scheduled) as well as the area's water sports possibilities. Actually, more and more transplants have decided to spend the rest of their lives here, drawn to Beaufort's small-town charms, and the area is burgeoning. A truly Southern town, its picturesque backdrops have

Beaufort

Exploring

Beaufort Museum
& Arsenal, **2**

Henry C. Chambers
Waterfront Park, **4**

John Mark Verdier House
Museum, **3**

St. Helena's
Episcopal Church, **1**

Restaurants

Emily's Restaurant
& Tapas Bar, **4**

Plums, **6**

Saltus River Grill, **7**

Hotels

Beaufort Inn, **5**

Best Western
Sea Island Inn, **2**

Cuthbert House Inn, **1**

Rhett House Inn, **3**

KEY

1 *What to See*

① *Where to Stay & Eat*

lured filmmakers here to film *The Big Chill, The Prince of Tides,* and *The Great Santini,* the last two being Hollywood adaptations of best-selling books by author Pat Conroy. Conroy has waxed poetic about the Lowcountry and calls the Beaufort area home. The city closest to the Marine base on Parris Island, Beaufort also has a naval hospital.

GETTING HERE & AROUND

Beaufort is 25 mi east of Interstate 95, on U.S. 21. The only way here is by private car.

Visitor Information **Beaufort Visitors Center** (⊠*2001 Boundaray St., Beaufort* ☎*843/525–8523*).

Regional Beaufort Chamber of Commerce (⊠*1106 Carteret St., Box 910, Beaufort* ☎*843/986–5400* ⊕*www.beaufortsc.org*).

EXPLORING BEAUFORT

Built in 1795 and remodeled in 1852, the Gothic-style building that was the home of the Beaufort Volunteer Artillery now houses the **Beaufort Museum & Arsenal.** Prehistoric relics, Native American pottery, and Revolutionary War and Civil War exhibits are on display. At present it

Pat Conroy, Writer, on Beaufort

While ambling down Bay Street, you can't help but notice the life-size, paper cutout of author Pat Conroy in the window of Bay Street Traders. It is their way of saying that they stock his work. Conroy has had signings for all seven of his books at this landmark bookstore, and adds laughingly: "They say I am their cottage industry!"

Many Conroy fans consider Beaufort *his* town because of his autobiographical novel *The Great Santini*, which was set here. He, too, considers it home base: "We moved to Beaufort when I was 15. We had moved 23 times. (My father was in the Marines.) I told my mother, 'I need a home.' Her wise reply was: 'Well, maybe it will be Beaufort.' And so it has been. I have stuck to this poor town like an old barnacle. I moved away, but I came running back in 1993."

A number of Hollywood films have been shot here, not just Conroy's. "The beautiful white house on The Point was called the 'Big Santini House' until the next movie was shot and now it is known as 'The Big Chill House.' If a third movie was made there, it would have a new name."

"One of the great glories of Beaufort is found on St. Helena Island," he says. "You get on Martin Luther King Jr. Blvd. and take a right at the Red Piano 11 Gallery to the Penn Center. Before making the right turn, on the left, in what was the Bishop family's general store, is Gullah Grub, one of the few restaurants that serve legitimate Gullah food."

He continues: "At the end of St. Helena, toward the beach, take Seaside Road. You will be in the midst of the Gullah culture. You end up driving down a dirt road and then an extraordinary avenue of oaks that leads to the Coffin Point Plantation, which was the house where Sally Field raised Forrest Gump as a boy."

is undergoing a major renovation and is slated to open in Spring 2009 with exciting new exhibits. The admission price may go up. ✉ *713 Craven St.* ☎ *843/379–3331* ✉ *$3* ☽ *Mon.–Sat. 11–4.*

Henry C. Chambers Waterfront Park, off Bay Street, is a great place to survey the scene. Trendy restaurants and bars overlook these seven landscaped acres along the Beaufort River. There's a farmers' market here on Saturday, April through August, 8 to noon.

John Mark Verdier House Museum, built in the Federal style, has been restored and furnished as it would have been between its construction in 1805 and the visit of Lafayette in 1825. It was the headquarters for Union forces during the Civil War. A combination ticket that gets you into the Beaufort Museum & Arsenal (under renovation until Spring 2009) and the John Mark Verdier House Museum saves you $1. ✉*801 Bay St.* ☎*843/379–6335* ✑*$5* ⊙*Mon.– Sat. 10–3:30.*

The 1724 **St. Helena's Episcopal Church** was turned into a hospital during the Civil War, and gravestones were brought inside to serve as operating tables. ✉*505 Church St.* ☎*843/522–1712* ⊙*Tues.–Fri. 10–4, Sat. 10–1.*

St. Helena Island, 9 mi southeast of Beaufort via U.S. 21, is the site of the Penn Center Historic District. Established in the middle of the Civil War, Penn Center was the South's first school for freed slaves; now open to the public, the center provides community services, too. This island is both residential and commercial, with nice beaches, cooling ocean breezes, and a great deal of natural beauty.

The **York W. Bailey Museum** has displays on the Penn Center, and on the heritage of Sea Island African-Americans; it also has pleasant grounds shaded by live oaks. The Penn Center (1862) was one of the first schools for the newly emancipated slaves. These islands are where Gullah, a musical language that combines English and African languages, developed. This is a major stop for anyone interested in the Gullah history and culture of the Lowcountry. ✉*16 Martin Luther King Jr. Blvd., St. Helena Island* ☎*843/838–2432* ⊕*www.penncenter.com* ✑*$5* ⊙*Mon.–Sat. 11–4.*

★ Secluded **Hunting Island State Park** has nature trails and about 3 mi of public beaches—some dramatically and beautifully eroding. Founded in 1993 to preserve and promote its natural existence, it harbors 5,000 acres of rare maritime forests. Nonetheless, the light sands decorated with driftwood and the raw, subtropical vegetation is breathtaking. Stroll the 1,300-foot-long fishing pier, among the longest on the East Coast, or you can go fishing or crabbing. You will be at one with nature. The fit can climb the 181 steps of the **Hunting Island Lighthouse** (built in 1859 and abandoned in 1933) for sweeping views. The nature center has exhibits, an aquarium, and lots of turtles. The park is 18 mi southeast of Beaufort via U.S. 21; if you want to stay on the island, be sure to call for reservations. From April 1 to October

8

Pat Conroy, Writer, on Fripp Island

"What has Fripp Island meant to me?" Pat Conroy, one of the Lowcountry's famous writers, answered: "The year was 1964. I was living in Beaufort. And when the bridge to Fripp Island was built, I was a senior in high school. My English teacher *and* my chemistry teacher moonlighted as the island's first security guards. It was a pristine island; there were no houses on it yet, and it was as beautiful as any desert island.

"In 1978, my mother moved over there, and all our summers were spent on the island. It was to be her last home. That sealed the island in our family history. In 1989, I bought a house there, both because it is a private island and [because it] is good for a writer, but also so that our family—my brothers and sisters—could always have a home on Fripp to come to."

31, there is a one-week minimum stay; November 1 to March 31, the minimum is two nights. Cabins that sleep up to six or eight ($–$$) must be reserved far in advance for summer weekends (there are only 12). Expect to pay about $25 for campsites with electricity, $17 without. ✉*1775 Sea Island Pkwy., off St. Helena Island, Hunting Island* ☎*843/838–2011* ⊕*www.southcarolinaparks.com* 🖼*$4* ⊘*Park: Apr.–Oct., daily 6 AM–9 PM; Nov.–Mar., daily 6–6. Lighthouse daily 11–4.*

WHERE TO EAT

★ Fodor'sChoice✕**Bateaux.** *Eclectic.* This contemporary restau-
$$$$ rant, which was formerly on Lady's Island, has a new home in a historical brick building in Port Royal, 6 mi southwest of Beaufort. The location affords waterfront views, which are best from the second story, although some downstairs tables also offer a glimpse of the blue. The move has brought major changes: lunch is no longer served, and "Chip" Ulbrich is no longer a partner. For now, owner Richard Wilson is in the kitchen. He continues creating imaginative Southern cuisine, and the menu keeps evolving. The food is fresh, elegant, and artistically presented. Foodies love that they can get foie gras in crepes and other dishes. Seafood is the obvious specialty; try the shrimp and scallops over red-pepper risotto with fried prosciutto and spinach. The staff is well-trained and knowledgeable. ✉*610 Paris Ave., Port Royal* 🗂*Box 2179, Port Royal, 29935* ☎*843/379–0777* 🖃*AE, MC, V* ⊘*Closed Sun. No lunch.*

$$$ ✕**11th Street Dockside.** *Seafood.* The succulent fried oysters, shrimp, and fish are some of the best around. In addition to Lowcountry fried seafood, more healthful options are available, including a steamed seafood hot pot filled with crab legs, oysters, shrimp, and lobster; by request only you can get Frogmore stew (with shrimp, potatoes, sausage, and corn). Everything is served in a classic wharfside environment, where you can eat on a screened porch and have water views from nearly every table. The restaurant is open from 4:30 to 10 every day. ⊠*1699 11th St. W, 6 mi southwest of Beaufort, Port Royal* ☎*843/524–7433* ☐*AE, D, DC, MC, V* ⊗*No lunch.*

$$$ ✕**Emily's Restaurant & Tapas Bar.** *American.* Long, narrow, and wood-paneled, Emily's is a lively restaurant, definitely a haunt where the cool locals hang out. It has full dining service, mainly simple fare—heavy on steaks, which come with a generous salad. Crowds linger over the tapas, including spring rolls, garlic beef, and even baby lamb chops. This is a great place to come early or late, since the kitchen serves from 4 PM to 10 PM. (and on weekends, the bar may be open later). At this writing, the restaurant was considering whether to start opening at lunch and the piano bar had gone quiet but was still hoping for a comeback. ⊠*906 Port Republic St.* ☎*843/522–1866* ☐*AE, MC, V* ⊗*Closed Sun. No lunch.*

$–$$ ✕**Plums.** *American.* Down the alley behind Shipman's Gallery is this homey frame house with plum-colored awnings shading the front porch. Plums still uses old family recipes for its crab-cake sandwiches and curried chicken salad, but now it also offers a blue cheese and portobello mushroom sandwich. Dinner has creative and affordable pasta and seafood dishes. The crowd is a mix of locals and tourists, often with children. Its downtown riverfront location, fun atmosphere, and reasonable prices are the draw. There's live music on weekends, starting at around 10 PM and geared to the younger crowd. ⊠*904½ Bay St.* ☎*843/525–1946* ☐*AE, MC, V.*

★ Fodor'sChoice✕**Saltus River Grill.** *Eclectic.* Owner Lantz Price
$$$$ has given this 19th-century loft a classy sailing motif, with portals and oversized photos of sailboats. The hippest eatery in Beaufort wins over epicureans with its cool design (subdued lighting, mod booths, dark-wood bar), waterfront patio, and Modern Southern menu. Come early (the kitchen opens at 4 PM) and sit outdoors on the river with

8

your cocktails. There are separate menus for sushi and oysters. A flawless dinner might start off with the skillet crab cakes with corn relish and beurre blanc sauce, then segue to the skewered, grilled quail with Oriental glaze. The wine list is admirable, and the staff is adept at pairings. Desserts change nightly; if offered, the pineapple upside-down cake can be the perfect end to your meal. ⌧*802 Bay St.* ☎*843/379–3474* ▭*AE, D, MC, V.*

$-$$ ✕**Shrimp Shack.** *Seafood.* On the way to Fripp and Hunting islands, follow the cue of locals and stop at this endearing little place where Ms. Hilda, the owner, will take good care of you. All seating is outdoors, and once seated, you can't see the water. The menu includes all of the typical Lowcountry fried plates, as well as South Carolina crab cakes, boiled shrimp, and gumbo, but it is best known for it shrimp burgers, sweet-potato fries, and sweet tea. Dinner is served only until 8 PM. Doors open at 11 AM. ⌧*1929 Sea Island Pkwy., 18 mi southeast of Beaufort, St. Helena* ☎*843/838–2962* ▭*No credit cards* ⊘*Closed Sun.*

WHERE TO STAY

$$—$$$ ✕▦**Beaufort Inn.** This peach-painted 1890s Victorian inn charms you with its gables and wraparound porches. Pine-floor guest rooms have period reproductions, striped wallpaper, and comfy chairs. Several have fireplaces and four-poster beds. This is a homey place right in the heart of the historic district, and most rooms have views of the surrounding buildings. Room options in the main inn range from a standard queen-size room to suites, which are the most popular. Deluxe suites have living rooms and are in separate cottages. There's also one two-bedroom, two-bathroom apartment in a separate, historic building overlooking Bay Street. Garden Cottages are modern buildings and don't have the same traditional feel, but they do have garden or courtyard views; decor here is more contemporary with heavier, darker woods, and replica claw-foot tubs. Regrettably, the restaurant has closed, which is a loss to Beaufort's culinary scene. **Pros:** located in the heart of the historic district; Continental breakfast has a chef-attended omelet station; the evening social hour includes snacks, refreshments, and wine. **Cons:** atmosphere may feel too dated for those seeking a more contemporary hotel; no more restaurant; deluxe suites have the worst views of all—the parking lot. ⌧*809 Port Republic St.* ☎*843/521–9000* ⊕*www.beaufortinn.com* ⇺*28 rooms* ⌂*In-room: DVD. In-*

hotel: bicycles, no kids under 8, parking (free), no-smoking rooms ▭*AE, D, MC, V* ⦿|*BP.*

$ ⊞**Best Western Sea Island Inn.** At this well-maintained motel in the downtown historic district, you are within walking distance of shops and restaurants. Guests can see the bay from the front terrace. Ample rooms have two queen or king beds. Cookies and coffee are always available in the lobby. **Pros:** only accommodation in historic district that is not a B&B; directly across from marina and an easy walk to art galleries and restaurants; Continental breakfast (early) and hot breakfast included. **Cons:** complaints about dim lighting in rooms; not an upscale property. ✉*1015 Bay St.* ☎*843/522–2090 or 800/528–1234* ⦿*www.sea-island-inn. com* ⟿*43 rooms* ⚛*In-room: refrigerator, Internet. In-hotel: pool, gym, Internet terminal, no-smoking rooms* ▭*AE, D, DC, MC, V* ⦿|*BP.*

$$$– ⊞**Cuthbert House Inn.** Named after the original Scottish
$$$$ owners, who made their money in cotton and indigo, this
★ 1790 home is filled with 18th- and 19th-century heirlooms. It retains the original Federal fireplaces and crown and rope molding. When Beaufort was occupied by the Union army during the Civil War, this home was used as the generals' headquarters. Guest rooms and oversized suites have endearing architectural details, comfortable with hand-knotted rugs on the pine floors and commanding beds piled high with quilts. Choose one that looks out on the bay and the glorious sunset. The Mariner's Suite has a veranda, too. Beautifully lit at night, this antebellum house, with white pillars and dual verandas, typifies the Old South. Wedding parties can rent out the whole inn, and many couples spend their honeymoon nights here, but it appeals foremost to an older generation. A renovation of all rooms was in progress at this writing and was expected to be finished by mid-2009. **Pros:** owners are accommodating; other guests provide good company during the complimentary wine service. **Cons:** some furnishings are a bit busy; some artificial flower arrangements; stairs creak. ✉*1203 Bay St.* ☎*843/521–1315 or 800/327–9275* ⦿*www. cuthberthouseinn.com* ⟿*6 rooms, 2 suites* ⚛*In-room: refrigerator, DVD, Wi-Fi. In-hotel: bicycles, no kids under 12, no-smoking rooms* ▭*AE, D, MC, V* ⦿|*BP.*

$$$ ⊞**Fripp Island Resort.** This resort sits on the island made
☾ famous in *Prince of Tides*, with 3½ miles of broad, white
★ beach and unspoiled sea island scenery. It has long been

Sea Monkeys

There is a colony of monkeys living on a little isle near Fripp Island. If you are in a boat cruising or on a fishing charter and think you might be seeing monkeys running on the beach, it may not be your imagination. The state of South Carolina leases one of these tiny islands to raise monkeys, both those that are used for medical re-

search and also rare Golden Reese's monkeys that are put up for sale as exotic pets. This deserted island and the sub-tropical climate and vegetation have proved ideal for their breeding. But you can't land on the island or feed the monkeys, so bring binoculars.

known as one of the more affordable and casual of the island resorts. It is private and gated, a safe haven, where kids are allowed to be free, to go crabbing at low tide, bike the trails, and swim, swim, swim. Families love the narrated nature cruise and love Camp Fripp, the nature center, not to mention all the teen activities. Most residents are retired and happily tool around in golf carts. Golf carts, mopeds, and bikes can be rented. This is no swinging-singles destination, but it is a good getaway for sporty couples who like to kayak and canoe. Of course, you can play highly-rated golf or tennis and go fishing out of the marina as well. There are more than 200 individual villas here instead of a hotel, though there are a variety of small efficiencies. There's a pavilion with shops and a choice of restaurants, often with live entertainment, from the rollicking Bonito Boathouse to the sophisticated Beach Club. ⊠ *1 Tarpon Blvd., 19 mi south of Beaufort, Fripp Island* ☎ *843/838–3535 or 877/374–7748* ⊕ *www.frippislandresort.com* ⟿ *210 units* ⚹ *In-room: kitchen, DVD (some). In-hotel: 5 restaurants, golf courses, tennis courts, pools, bicycles, children's programs (ages 3–12), laundry facilities, parking (free), no-smoking rooms* ⊟ *AE, D, DC, MC, V* ⏅ *EP.*

★ Fodor'sChoice ☆**Rhett House Inn.** Art and antiques abound in a
$$$–
$$$$ circa-1820 home turned storybook inn. Look for the little luxuries—down pillows and duvets, a CD player in each room, and fresh flowers. The best rooms open out onto the veranda (No. 2) or the courtyard garden (No. 7). The interior decor is Beaufort traditional coupled with Manhattan panache. Breakfast, afternoon tea, evening hors d'oeuvres, and dessert are included in the rate. Visiting

celebrities have included Barbra Streisand, Jeff Bridges, and Dennis Quaid. The remodeled (not so historic) house across the street has eight more rooms, each of which has a gas fireplace, a whirlpool bath, a private entrance, and a porch. **Pros:** all guests come together for breakfast and other social hours; more private in annex. **Cons:** annex does not have the charisma of the main inn; in the main house you can hear footsteps on stairs and in hallways. ✉*1009 Craven St.* ☎*843/524–9030* ⊕*www.rhetthouseinn. com* ⤳*16 rooms, 1 suite* ⚭*In-hotel: restaurant, bicycles, no kids under 5, parking (free), no-smoking rooms* ▤*AE, D, MC, V* ⊙*BP.*

NO ROOM AT THE INN. The military has a commanding presence in Beaufort, and throughout the year there are various graduation ceremonies on Wednesday and Thursday. Lodgings can fill up fast, so make sure to call ahead.

PRIVATE VILLAS ON FRIPP ISLAND

$–$$ 🖩**Beach Club Villa 172.** Since its development in the 1960s, Fripp Island has been known as one of the more moderately-priced, private resort islands. Yes, like everything, prices have risen, but this condo/villa is an example of how to keep costs down. A couple of decades old, this building is well-maintained, the roof recently replaced, and the view is of marshland and a canal with an access to a private crabbing dock. Individually owned, like most of the units on Fripp, the unit has been renovated with an updated furniture package, flat-screen TVs, stainless-steel appliances, and a granite countertop. Condos like this one are well-suited to small families, golf buddies, and corporate groups. Daily maid service is an option. **Pros:** price is right; conveniently located to main facilities; on the first floor, so there are no stairs to climb. **Cons:** the better views are on the second and third floors; not as commodious as a house; not on the ocean; no barbecue grills are allowed. ✉*172 Beach Club, Fripp Island* ⊕*www.frippislandresort. com* ⤳*2 bedrooms, 2 baths* ⚭*Dishwasher, DVD, VCR, Wi-Fi, daily maid service, on-site security, laundry facilities* ▤*AE, D, M, V.*

$$$$ 🖩**424-Ocean Point Lane.** A view of the indigo ocean is a straight shot across the 18th hole of the Ocean Point Golf Course from this villa. Watch sons learn how to play golf from their fathers, and spy dolphins cruising in close. Light streams in through the front wall of glass that extends

from the open living/dining room to the cozy loft on the second floor. A sunny, happy home, it is contemporary and individualistic. The two master suites, one on each floor, make sharing democratic, with privacy a plus. It's just footsteps from the pool complex, and along the way you can talk to the docile marsh deer. Daily maid service is an option. **Pros:** spacious; captivating views and sea breezes on the second-floor deck; wonderfully quiet yet with a superior media system. **Cons:** interior decor somewhat dated; kitchen isn't large; not on the beach. ⊠*424 Ocean Point La., Fripp Island* ☎*843/838–1696* ⊕*www.fripp islandresort.com* ⬢*3 bedrooms, 3.5 baths* ⬡*Dishwasher, DVD, VCR, Wi-Fi, daily maid service, on-site security, laundry facilities, no-smoking* ⊟*AE, D, MC, V 2-night min. (1-week Jun.–Aug.).*

SPORTS & THE OUTDOORS

BIKING

Beaufort is great for biking. In town, traffic is moderate and you can cruise along the waterfront and through the historic district. However, if you ride on the sidewalks or after dark without a headlight, you run the risk of a city fine of nearly $150. If you stopped for happy hour, say at Emily's, and come out as the light is fading, walk your bike back "home." Some inns rent them to guests, but alas, they may not be in great shape and usually were not the best even when new.

If you want to have decent tires, call **Lowcountry Bicycles** (⊠*102 Sea Island Pkwy., 29907* ☎*843/524–9585*). For just $5 you can rent bike headlights on your rental wheels that will cost just $15 for a half day, $30 a full day, $80 a week. Adult bicycles only are available, either a 3-speed or 8-speed.

CANOE & BOAT TOURS

★ Beaufort is where the Ashepoo, Combahee, and Edisto rivers form the A.C.E. Basin, a vast wilderness of marshes and tidal estuaries loaded with history. For sea kayaking, tourists meet at the designated launching areas for fully-guided, two-hour tours.

Adults pay $40 at **Beaufort Kayak Tours** (⊠*600 Linton La.* ☎*843/525–0810* ⊕*www.beaufortkayaktours.com*).

A.C.E. Basin Tours (⊠*1 Coosaw River Dr., Coosaw Island* ☎*843/521–3099* ⊕*www.acebasintours.com*) might be the best bet for the very young, or anyone with limited mobility, as it operates a 38-foot pontoon boat tour. A tour costs $35.

GOLF

Most golf courses are about a 10- to 20-minute scenic drive from Beaufort.

In a gated community, **Dataw Island** (✉*Dataw Club Rd., off U.S. 21, 6 mi east of Beaufort, Dataw Island* ☎*843/838–8250* ⊕*www.dataw.org* ⅃ *Cotton Dike: 18 holes. 6799 yds. Par 72. Morgan River: 18 holes. 6646 yds. Par 72. Green Fee: $69–$120*) has Tom Fazio's Cotton Dike Course, with spectacular marsh views, and Arthur Hill's Morgan River Course, with ponds, marshes, and wide-open fairways. The lovely 14th hole of the Morgan River Course overlooks the river. You must be accompanied by a member or belong to another private club. To tap into the reciprocal system, one's home-club pro has to call Dataw's golf pro to make arrangements.

Fripp Island Golf & Beach Resort (✉*201 Tarpon Blvd., Fripp Island* ☎*843/838–2131 or 843/838–1576* ⊕*www.fripp islandresort.com* ⅃ *Ocean Creek: 18 holes. 6643 yds. Par 71. Ocean Point: 18 holes. 6556 yds. Par 72. Green Fee: $89–$99*) has a pair of championship courses. Ocean Creek Golf Course, designed by Davis Love, has sweeping views of saltwater marshes. Designed by George Cobb, Ocean Point Golf Links runs along the ocean the entire way. This is a wildlife refuge, so you'll see plenty of it, particularly marsh deer. In fact, the wildlife and ocean views may make it difficult for you to keep your eyes on the ball. Nonguests should call the golf pro to make arrangements to play.

Sanctuary Golf Club at Cat Island (✉*8 Waveland Ave., Cat Island, Beaufort* ☎*843/524–0300* ⅃ *18 holes. 6625 yds. Par 71. Green Fee $60–$90*) is a semiprivate club, so members get priority. Its scenic course is considered tight with plenty of water hazards. The course reopened after a major renovation in fall 2008 of greens, tees, bunkers, and even the driving range.

NIGHTLIFE & THE ARTS

The **Hallelujah Singers** (✉*806 Elizabeth St.* ☎*843/379–3594*), Gullah performers, perform at Lowcountry venues. They foot stomp and clap hands and sing spirituals.

The late-night hangout **Luther's** (⊠910 Bay St. ☎843/521–1888) rocks on weekends.

SHOPPING

ART GALLERIES

At **Bay Street Gallery** (⊠719 Bay St. ☎843/525–1024 or 843/522–9210), Laura Hefner's oils of coastal wetlands magically convey the mood of the Lowcountry.

At **Four Winds Gallery** (⊠709 Bay St.< ☎843/838–3295) Marianne Norton imports folk art, antiques, sculpture, photography, furniture, rugs, textiles, and weavings, connecting cultures and artists and artisans around the world. Southern art, both Gullah and New Orleans artwork, is new. (Ask about her four rooms to let at 1103 Craven Street, for about $100 a night.)

The colorful designs of Suzanne and Eric Longo decorate the **Longo Gallery** (⊠103 Charles St. ☎843/522–8933).

The **Rhett Gallery** (⊠901 Bay St. ☎843/524–3339) sells Lowcountry art by four generations of the Rhett family, as well as antique maps and Audubon prints.

DAUFUSKIE ISLAND

13 mi (approx. 45 minutes) from Hilton Head via ferry.

From Hilton Head you can take a 45-minute ferry ride to nearby Daufuskie Island, the setting for Pat Conroy's novel *The Water Is Wide,* which was made into the movie *Conrack.* The boat ride may very well be one of the highlights of your vacation. The Lowcountry beauty enfolds before you, as pristine and unspoiled as you can imagine. Since the island is in the Atlantic, nestled between Hilton Head and Savannah, you can also pick up a launch from Savannah, and that's another delightful ride. Many visitors do come just for the day, to play golf and have lunch or dinner; you might indulge your senses in the New Age Breathe Spa, or kids might enjoy biking or horseback riding.

Most of the island's development is at the Daufuskie Island Club & Resort and Melrose, which is now a private club, but the island also has acres of unspoiled beauty. On a bike, in a golf cart, on horseback, or in a horse-drawn carriage you can easily explore the island. You will find remnants of churches, homes, and schools—all reminders of antebellum times. Guided tours include sights such as an 18th-century cemetery, former slave quarters, a local winery, and the Haig Point Lighthouse. The scenic boat ride and the physically beautiful island itself will become etched in your memories.

GETTING HERE & AROUND

The only way to Daufuskie is a ferry from Hilton Head or Savannah. It's possible to come on a day-trip. On arrival you can rent a golf cart or bicycle or take a tour. If you are coming to Daufuskie Island for a multiday stay with luggage and/or groceries, and perhaps a dog, be absolutely certain that you allow a full hour to park and check in for the ferry, particularly on a busy summer weekend. Whether you are staying on island or just day-tripping, the ferry costs $40 round-trip from Hilton Head ($45 from Savannah).

WHERE TO STAY

$$$$ ⬚**Daufuskie Island Resort & Breathe Spa.** Overnight visitors can stay at the Inn at Melrose, in rooms that are twice as large as most of the hotels on the main island. Rooms are traditional but contemporary in style and have a separate sitting area. Families might be tempted to opt for the even larger space of the cottages, with the two-bedroom options the most popular. (It is a pet-friendly resort, too, though pets are allowed only in some cottages.) Corporate groups usually take both inn rooms and cottages. Note that those run high-occupancy in the summer, especially on the weekends and for holidays such as Thanksgiving. In June, especially, it is a destination resort for weddings. Sophisticated dining at Jack's Grill (named after J. Nicklaus) and its golf motif is the adult choice, whereas families enjoy the Beach Club Restaurant. ⊠*Embarkation Center, 421 Squire Pope Rd., North End* ☎*843/341–4820 or 800/648–6778* ⊕*www.daufuskieresort.com* ⊅*52 rooms* ⌖*In-room: kitchen (some), refrigerator, Internet. In-hotel: 4 restaurants, room service, bars, golf courses, tennis courts, pools, gym, spa, beachfront, water sports, bicycles, laundry facilities, parking (free), some pets allowed, no-smoking rooms* ⊟*AE, D, MC, V* ⑩ *EP.*

8

SPORTS & THE OUTDOORS

Calibogue Cruises (⊠*Broad Creek Marina, 164B Palmetto Bay Rd., Mid-Island* ☎*843/342–8687* ⊕*www.freeport-marina.com*) has several Daufuskie tour options, including guided tours with lunch and gospel-music performances starting at $40.

Vagabond Cruises (⊠*Harbour Town Marina, South End* ☎*843/785–2662* ⊕*www.vagabondcruise.com*) conducts daytime boat rides, from dolphin tours to runs to Savannah, sails on the *Stars & Stripes* of America's Cup fame, and dinner cruises.

EDISTO ISLAND

62 mi northeast of Beaufort via U.S. 17 and Rte 174; 44 mi southwest of Charleston via U.S. 17 and Rte. 174.

On rural Edisto (pronounced *ed*-is-toh) Island, find magnificent stands of age-old oaks festooned with Spanish-moss border, quiet streams, and side roads; wild turkeys may still be spotted on open grasslands and amid palmetto palms. Twisting tidal creeks, populated with egrets and herons, wind around golden marsh grass. A big day on the island may include shelling and shark-tooth hunting.

Edisto is one of the less-costly, more down-home of the Carolina sea islands. Adults sing their hearts out on karaoke nights while their kids sip rocking root beer floats. And now bingo is big, and not just for seniors.

The small "downtown" beachfront is a mix of public beach-access spots, restaurants, and old, shabby-chic beach homes that are a far cry from the palatial villas rented out on the resort islands. The outlying Edisto Beach State Park is a pristine wilderness and camper's delight. The one actual resort was bought by Wyndham and, although it houses time-share units, they also have a number of rental accommodations.

GETTING HERE & AROUND

Edisto is connected to the mainland by a causeway. The only way here is by private car.

Visitor Information Edisto Island Chamber of Commerce (⊠*430 Rte. 174, Box 206, Edisto Island* ☎*843/869–3867 or 888/333–2781* ⊕*www.edistochamber.com*).

★ **Fodor's Choice** **Edisto Beach State Park** covers 1,255 acres and
☺ includes marshland and tidal rivers, a 1½-mi-long beachfront, towering palmettos, and a lush maritime forest with
a 3½-mi trail running through it. The park has the best
shelling beach on public property in the Lowcountry. Overnight options include rustic furnished cabins (with basic,
no-frills decor) by the marsh and campsites by the ocean
(although severe erosion is limiting availability). Sites are
$23 with electricity, $17 for no electricity. This park stays
extremely busy, so with only seven cabins (the park system
struggles to maintain their livability), you have to reserve
far in advance. They are so sought after that reservations
sometimes go on the lottery system. The campsites are
another story: reservations are on a first-come, first-served
basis. Deluxe resort development has begun to encroach
around the edges of the park. ⊠*Route 174, off U.S. 17*
☎*843/869–2156* ⊕*www.southcarolinaparks.com* ⊠*$4*
⊙*Early Apr.–late Oct., daily 8 AM–10 PM; late Oct.–early
Apr., daily 8–6.*

The ruins of **Sheldon Church,** built in 1753, make an interesting stop if you're driving from Beaufort or Charleston
to Edisto Island. The church burned down in 1779 and
again in 1865. Only the brick walls and columns remain.
With its moss-draped live oaks, it has an eerie Lowcountry
beauty about it. At dusk it takes on a preternatural cast,
the kind of atmosphere that gives rise to the ghost stories
that Southern children are raised on. On the weekends in
and around June, you can almost always witness a wedding. No matter, it is a good spot to get off the highway
and stretch a spell. You can pick up a snack or some fixin's
at the filling station nearby at Gardens Corner. It was
modernized about 10 years back, but this highway landmark is still shades of decades past. ⊠*18 mi northwest of
Beaufort; Hwy. 17 S.*

8

WHERE TO EAT

¢–$ ✕**Po' Pigs Bo-B-Q.** *Southern.* Step inside the super-casual
★ restaurant for pork barbecue that has South Carolinians
raving. Sample the different sauces (sweet mustard, tomato,
or vinegar) and wash it all down with a tall glass of sweet
tea. Don't miss down-home sides like squash casserole, pork
skins, lima beans and ham, and red rice. The blink-and-
you-miss-it location is on the tail end of an undeveloped
road. ⊠*2410 Rte. 174* ☎*843/869–9003* ⊟*No credit cards*
⊙*Closed Sun.–Tues.*

WHERE TO STAY

¢ ⬚**Atwood Vacations.** For complete privacy, rent out a family-owned cottage on Edisto, which will be much more comfortable than the bare-bones options that the park maintains. The list of properties include everything from one-bedroom condos to six-bedroom homes. All kitchens are stocked with appliances and dishes, but you need to bring your own bed linens. Two-day minimum stays are required. ⊠*495 Rte. 174* ☎*843/869–2151* ⊕*www.atwood vacations.com* ⚷*In-room: kitchen* ⊟*AE, MC, V* ⦿*EP.*

$ ⬚**Wyndham Ocean Ridge Resort.** Looking for resort amenities in a get-away-from-it-all escape? You've found it here, at the only resort on the island. This is the former Fairfield Ocean Ridge, which was taken over by Wyndham in 2006. It is a time-share, so all of the attractive units are individually owned and decorated according to the owner's taste. Nonowners can still rent these units, but, alas, the number available is less than in the past, so reserve as far in advance as possible. There is a two-day minimum stay in-season (April 1–August 30), and you will pay a $25 reservation fee. Summers are solidly booked, especially the weekends; in the off-season, the major holidays find few available units. Although few of the accommodations (efficiencies to five-bedroom villas and houses) are on the beach, most are just a short walk away from it. Be sure to ask if this is important to you. There is no daily maid service, nor can you pay extra for it, although towels can be switched out. The family-oriented staff knows how to keep kids amused. A shuttle transports guests to the resort's beach cabana, which is delightful, with plenty of chaises. Wyndham has done an admirable renovation on The Plantation Golf Course. ⊠*1 King Cotton Rd. Box 27, 29438* ☎*843/869–2561; 843/869–4527 or 877/296–6335 for reservations* ☎*843/869–2384* ⊕*www. wyndhamoceanridge.com* ⟿*38 units* ⚷*In-hotel: restaurant, bar, golf course, tennis courts, pool, children's programs (ages 6–14), beachfront, bicycles, no-smoking rooms* ⊟*AE, D, MC, V* ⦿*EP.*

Travel Smart
Charleston

WORD OF MOUTH

"If you're just staying downtown, a car is not necessary. If you plan on heading out of the historic area, a car might be the most economical way, even for just a day."

—dsgmi

GETTING HERE & AROUND

We're proud of our Web site: Fodors.com is a great place to begin any journey. Scan Travel Wire for suggested itineraries, travel deals, restaurant and hotel openings, and other up-to-the-minute info. Check out Booking to research prices and book plane tickets, hotel rooms, rental cars, and vacation packages. Head to Talk for on-the-ground pointers from travelers who frequent our message boards. You can also link to loads of other travel-related resources.

You can fly into either Charleston or Hilton Head (which shares an airport with Savannah). Charleston (though not Hilton Head) is reachable by train or bus as well, but you'll certainly need a car if you want to explore beyond Charleston's historic downtown, where it's more convenient to get around on foot. Taxis or pedicabs can take you around the city and may be more convenient than driving, especially if your hotel or B&B offers free parking.

■TIP➔ **Ask the local tourist board about hotel and local transportation packages that include tickets to major museum exhibits or other special events.**

▮ BY AIR

Several airlines offer regularly scheduled service to Charleston.

Airlines & Airports **Airline and Airport Links.com** (⊕www.

airlineandairportlinks.com) has links to many of the world's airlines and airports.

Airline-Security Issues **Transportation Security Administration** (⊕www.tsa.gov) has answers for almost every question that might come up.

AIRPORTS

Charleston International Airport, about 12 mi west of downtown. Charleston Executive Airport on John's Island does have some scheduled service, but it's mostly used by private aircraft.

Airport Information **Charleston Executive Airport** (⊠2700 Fort Trenholm Rd., John's Island ☎877/754–7285). **Charleston International Airport** (⊠5500 International Blvd., North Charleston ☎843/767–1100). **Mt. Pleasant Regional Airport** (⊠700 Airport Rd., Mount Pleasant ☎843/884–8837).

GROUND TRANSPORTATION

Several cab companies serve the airport, including the Charleston Black Cab Company, which has London-style taxis with uniformed drivers that cost $50 for two-five passengers to downtown. Airport Ground Transportation arranges shuttles, which cost $14 per person to downtown. Do not expect to be picked up by the same service when returning to the airport. If you want to add a little excitement to your life, call Star Limousine Service. They have the largest and most varied fleet in town. Choose from many vehicles including a stretch limo or a vintage Rolls-Royce.

Airport Transfers **Airport Ground Transportation** (☎843/767–1100). **A Star Limousine** (☎843/745–6279). **Charleston Black Cab Company** (☎843/216–2627 or 843/216–1206).

FLIGHTS

Charleston International Airport is served by American Eagle, Continental, Delta, United Express, Northwest, US Airways, and Air Tran, which has service only to Atlanta.

Wings Air, a commuter airline that flies to and from Atlanta, flies into the Charleston Executive Airport.

Airline Contacts **AirTran** (☎800/247–8726) or 678/254–7999 ⊕www.airtran.com). **American Airlines** (☎800/433–7300 ⊕www.aa.com). **Continental Airlines** (☎800/523–3273 for U.S. and Mexico reservations, 800/231–0856 for international reservations ⊕www.continental.com). **Delta Airlines** (☎800/221–1212 for U.S. reservations, 800/241–4141 for international reservations ⊕www.delta.com). **Northwest Airlines** (☎800/225–2525 ⊕www.nwa.com). **United Airlines** (☎800/864–8331 for U.S. reservations, 800/538–2929 for international reservations ⊕www.united.com). **USAirways** (☎800/428–4322 for U.S. and Canada reservations, 800/622–1015 for international reservations ⊕www.usairways.com).

▌ BY BUS

Greyhound connects Charleston with other destinations.

Contacts **Charleston Bus Station** (✉3610 Dorcester Rd., North Charleston ☎843/744–4247). **Greyhound** (☎843/744–4247 or 800/231–2222 ⊕www.greyhound.com).

▌ BY CAR

You'll need a car in Charleston if you plan on visiting destinations outside of the city's historic district, or if you plan to take trips to Beaufort or Hilton Head.

Although you'll make the best time traveling along the South's extensive network of interstate highways, keep in mind that U.S. and state highways offer some delightful scenery and the opportunity to stumble on funky roadside diners, leafy state parks, and historic town squares. Although the area is rural, it's still densely populated, so you'll rarely drive for more than 20 or 30 mi without passing roadside services, such as gas stations, restaurants, and ATMs.

GASOLINE

Gas stations are not hard to find, either in the city limits or in the outlying areas.

PARKING

Parking within Charleston's Historic District can be difficult. Street parking is irksome, as meter readers are among the city's most efficient public servants. Some parking garages and lots, both privately and publicly owned, still charge around $1.50 an hour, although a number of them in key locations now charge $1 per half-hour; the less expensive ones charge a maximum of between $10 and $12 a day if you park overnight. Some private lots now charge as much as $10 (some $8) per day as a flat rate, whether you are there one hour or six hours. Most of the hotels charge a fee to park your car. Nevertheless, if you have a car, it's usually best to park it and simply take taxis or shuttles around the Historic District. Save the car for trips outside of town.

RENTAL CARS

All of the major car-rental companies are represented in Charleston, either at the airport or in town.

Contacts Alamo (☎843/767–4417 ⊕www.alamo.com). **Avis** (☎843/767–7030 ⊕www.avis.com). **Budget** (☎843/577–5195 ⊕www.budget.com). **Hertz** (☎843/767–4552 ⊕www.hertz.com). **National** (☎843/767–3078 ⊕www.nationalcar.com).

RENTAL CAR INSURANCE

Everyone who rents a car wonders whether the insurance that the rental companies offer is worth the expense. No one—including us—has a simple answer. If you own a car, your personal auto insurance may cover a rental to some degree, though not all policies protect you abroad; always read your policy's fine print. If you don't have auto insurance, then seriously consider buying the collision- or loss-damage waiver (CDW or LDW) from the car-rental company, which eliminates your liability for damage to the car. Some credit cards offer CDW coverage, but it's usually supplemental to your own insurance and rarely covers SUVs, minivans, luxury models, and the like. If your coverage is secondary, you may still be liable for loss-of-use costs from the car-rental company. But no credit-card insurance is valid unless you use that card for *all* transactions, from reserving to paying the final bill. All companies exclude car rental in some countries, so be sure to find out about the destination to which you are traveling. It's sometimes cheaper to buy insurance as part of your general travel insurance policy.

ROADSIDE EMERGENCIES

Discuss with the rental car agency what to do in the case of an emergency, as this sometimes differs between companies. Make sure you understand what your insurance covers and what it doesn't, and it's a good rule of thumb to let someone at your accommodation know where you are heading and when you plan to return. Keep emergency numbers (car rental agency and your accommodation) with you, just in case.

ROADS

Interstate 26 traverses the state from northwest to southeast and terminates at Charleston. U.S. 17, the coastal road, also passes through Charleston. Interstate 526, also called the Mark Clark Expressway, runs primarily east–west, connecting the West Ashley area, North Charleston, Daniel Island, and Mount Pleasant.

BY BOAT & FERRY

Boaters—many traveling the intra-coastal waterway—dock at Ashley Marina and City Marina, in Charleston Harbor, or at Wild Dunes Yacht Harbor, on the Isle of Palms. The Charleston Water Taxi is a delightful way to travel between Charleston and Mount Pleasant. Some people take the $10 round-trip journey for fun. It departs from the Charleston Maritime Center. Do not confuse their address at 10 Wharfside being near the area of Adger's Wharf, which is on the lower peninsula. The water taxi departs every hour from 2:30 PM to 5:30 PM.

Boat & Ferry Contacts **Ashley Marina** (⊠Lockwood Blvd., Medical University of South Carolina ☎843/722–1996). **Charleston Water Taxi** (⊠Charleston Maritime Center, 10 Wharfside St., Upper King ☎843/330–2989). **City Marina** (⊠Lockwood Blvd., Medical University of South Carolina ☎843/723–5098).

BY PUBLIC TRANSPORTATION

The Charleston Area Regional Transportation Authority, the city's public bus system, takes passengers around the city and to the suburbs. Bus 11, which goes to the airport, is convenient for travelers. CARTA operates DASH, which runs buses that look like vintage trolleys along three downtown routes. A single ride is $1.25, and a day-long pass is $5. You should have exact change.

Contacts **CARTA** (⊠3664 Leeds Ave., North Charleston ☎843/747–0922 ⊕www.ridecarta. com).

BY TAXI

Fares within the city average about $5 per trip with the regular cab companies. An upscale cab like the Charleston Black Cab Company can cost up to $10 to get around the city. Other taxis include Safety Cab and Yellow Cab, which are available 24 hours a day.

The bike-peddling companies will take you anywhere in the historic district for $4.50 per person per 10 minutes. It is a fun way to get around in the evening especially if you are barhopping. Three can squeeze into the one seat.

Contacts **Charleston Bike Taxi** (☎843/532–8663). **Charleston Black Cab Company** (☎843/216–2627 or 843/216–1206). **Charleston Ped-Cab** (☎843/577–7088). **Charleston Rickshaw Company** (☎843/723–5685). **Safety Cab** (☎843/722–4066). **Yellow Cab** (☎843/577–6565).

BY TRAIN

Amtrak has service from such major cities as New York, Philadelphia, Washington, Richmond, Savannah, and Miami. Taxis meet every train; a ride to downtown averages $25.

Contacts **Amtrak** (⊠4565 Gaynor Ave., North Charleston ☎843/744–8264).

ESSENTIALS

▋ COMMUNICATIONS

INTERNET

Most area lodgings have in-room data ports or in-room broadband, and some have wireless connections in the rooms or public areas. Internet cafés are rare, but many coffee shops, including Starbucks, will let you use their wireless connection for a fee. The FedEx Kinko's branch on Orleans Road has computers you can use for 25¢ a minute.

Contacts **Cybercafes** (⊕www. cybercafes.com). **FedEx Kinkos** (⊠73 St. Philip St., Upper King ☎843/723–5130 ⊠873 Orleans Rd., West Ashley ☎843/571–4746).

PHONES

The area code in Charleston is 843.

▋ EMERGENCIES

Medical University of South Carolina Hospital and Roper Hospital have 24-hour emergency rooms. Roper Hospital recently completed a multimillion-dollar renovation of its emergency room.

Emergency Services **Emergency Services** (☎911).

Hospitals **Medical University of South Carolina Hospital** (⊠169 Ashley Ave., Medical University of South Carolina ☎843/792–2300). **Roper Hospital** (⊠316 Calhoun St., Upper King ☎843/724–2000).

Late-Night Pharmacy **Eckerds** (⊠261 Calhoun St., Upper King ☎843/805–6022).

▋ HOURS OF OPERATION

Like most American cities, Charleston businesses generally operate on a 9 to 5 schedule. Shops downtown will often open at 10 AM and close at 6 PM, with some conveniently staying open until 7; around the market area, clothing stores stay open as late as 9, while the fresh-made candy shops and souvenir stores may stay open even later.

▋ MAIL

The main post office is downtown on Broad Street, while a major branch is at West Ashley. To ship packages, FedEx Kinkos has a downtown branch and another at West Ashley. The UPS Store has locations in Mount Pleasant and West Ashley.

Post Offices **Downtown Station** (⊠83 Broad St., South of Broad ☎843/577–0690). **West Ashley Station** (⊠78 Sycamore St., West Ashley ☎843/766–4031).

Parcel Shipping **UPS Store** (⊠1000 Johnnie Dodds Blvd., Mount Pleasant ☎843/856–9099 ⊠1836 Ashley River Rd., West Ashley ☎843/763–6894).

MONEY

As in most cities, banks are open weekdays 9 to 5. There are countless branches in the downtown area, all with ATMs.

CREDIT CARDS

Throughout this guide, the following abbreviations are used: **AE,** American Express; **D,** Discover; **DC,** Diners Club; **MC,** MasterCard; and **V,** Visa.

Reporting Lost Cards **American Express** (☎800/528–4800 ⊕www.americanexpress.com). **MasterCard** (☎800/627–8372 ⊕www.mastercard.com). **Visa** (☎800/847–2911 ⊕www.visa.com).

SAFETY

Charleston is considered a very safe, midsize city. You can feel quite secure in the downtown Historic District (from Broad Street up King Street or even Mary Street) even up until midnight during the week and later on weekends. In neighborhoods where there are housing projects (especially off upper King Street in the direction of Spring Street), you would not want to walk around carefree, either by day or night. A lot of late-night street crime is directed at those who drink too much, making themselves easy marks for robbery. Do lock your car doors, and do not leave valuables in sight. Full shopping bags, luggage, and laptops will be particularly tempting in hard economic times.

■TIP→ **Distribute your cash, credit cards, IDs, and other valuables between a deep front pocket, an inside jacket or vest pocket, and a hidden money pouch. Don't reach for the money pouch once you're in public.**

Contact **Transportation Security Administration** (TSA; ⊕www.tsa.gov).

TAXES

In Charleston, sales tax on most purchases is 7.5%. Hotels are taxed at 12.5% (11.5% in Mount Pleasant). In restaurants, the tax is 9.5% for food, beer, and wine (14.5% for liquor); however, in Mount Pleasant, food, beer, and wine are taxed at 8.5%, liquor at 13.5%.

TIPPING

In fine dining restaurants, it is customary to tip 15% to 20%. In less expensive, family restaurants, 15% is the norm. For taxis, a tip of 10% to 15% is typical. Passengers are often more generous to pedicab drivers as they are pedaling those bicycles.

TOURS

Tours in Charleston run the gamut, from aerial tours to city and ecotours, and also numerous boat and harbor trips; in a city that is known as a walker-friendly destination, walking tours are numerous and popular. A large percentage of tourists opt for a horse and carriage tour, mostly on large wagons with a dozen or so other visitors, but private horse-and-buggy trips by day or night are definitely a romantic option. Whatever you chose, it is a good way to orient yourself in the city and best taken at the beginning of your stay.

AIR TOURS

Flying High Over Charleston provides aerial tours of the city and surrounding areas. Trips begin at $60 per person.

Contacts **Flying High Over Charleston** (✉Mercury Air Center, W. Aviation Ave., North Charleston ☎843/569–6148 ⊕www. flyinghighovercharleston.com).

BOAT TOURS

Charleston Harbor Tours offers tours that give the history of the harbor; it's the oldest harbor tour boat company (since 1908) and gives a good narrated tour of the harbor; however, these tours do not stop at Fort Sumter. Spiritline Cruises, which runs the ferry to Fort Sumter, also offers harbor tours and dinner cruises ($47 to $52). The latter leave from Patriots Point Marina in Mount Pleasant and include a three-course dinner and dancing to a live band. Sandlapper Tours has tours focused on regional history, coastal wildlife, and ghostly lore; you must make reservations by phone in advance since there is no ticket office where the harbor tours depart. All harbor cruises range between $15 and $25. On the authentic, 84-foot-tall *Schooner Pride* (capacity 49 persons), you can enjoy a diesel-free sail and the natural sounds of Charleston harbor on a two-hour harbor cruise, a sunset cruise, or the new romantic full-moon sails; tours range from $27 to $39.

Contacts **Charleston Harbor Tours** (✉Charleston Maritime Center, 10 Wharfside St., Upper King ☎843/722–1112, 800/979–3370; 212/209–3370 ⊕www.charleston harbortours.com). **Sandlapper Tours** (✉Charleston Maritime Center, 10 Wharfside St., Upper King ☎843/849–8687 ⊕www.sand lappertours.com). **Schooner Pride** (✉Aquarium Wharf, Upper King ☎843/559–9686 or 843/722–1112 ⊕www.schoonerpride.com). **Spiritline Cruises** (✉360 Concord St. [Aquarium Wharf], Upper King area ☎843/881–7337 or 800/789–3678 ⊕www.spiritlinecruises.com).

BUS TOURS

Adventure Sightseeing leads bus tours of the historic district. Associated Guides of Historic Charleston pairs local guides with visiting tour groups. Doin' the Charleston, a van tour, makes a stop at the Battery. Sites and Insights is a van tour that covers downtown and nearby islands. Gullah Tours focuses on sights significant to African-American culture. Chai Y'All shares stories and sights of Jewish interest.

Contacts **Adventure Sightseeing** (☎843/762–0088 or 800/722–5394 ⊕www.touringcharleston.com). **Associated Guides of Historic Charleston** (☎843/724–6419 ⊕www.historiccharleston.org). **Chai Y'All** (☎843/556–0664). **Doin' the Charleston** (☎843/763–1233 or 800/647–4487 ⊕www.dointhe charlestontours.com). **Gullah Tours** (☎843/763–7551 ⊕www.gullah tours.com). **Sites and Insights** (☎843/762–0051 ⊕www. sitesandinsightstours.com).

CARRIAGE TOURS

Carriage tours are a great way to see Charleston. Carolina Polo & Carriage Company, Old South Carriage Company, and Palmetto Carriage Tours run horse- and mule-drawn carriage tours of the historic district. Each tour, which follows one of four routes, lasts about one hour. Most carriages queue up at North Market and Anson streets. Charleston Carriage and Polo, which picks up passengers at the Doubletree Guest Suites Historic Charleston on Church Street, has a historically authentic carriage that is sought after for private tours and wedding parties.

Contacts **Charleston Carriage & Polo Company** (☎843/577–6767 ⊕www.cpcc.com). **Old South Carriage Company** (☎843/723–9712 ⊕www.oldsouthcarriagetours. com). **Palmetto Carriage Tours** (☎843/723–8145).

ECOTOURS

Barrier Island Ecotours, at the Isle of Palms Marina, runs three-hour pontoon-boat tours to a barrier island. Coastal Expeditions has half-day and full-day naturalist-led kayak tours on local rivers. Charleston Explorers leads educational boat tours that are great for kids.

Contacts **Barrier Island Ecotours** (✉Isle of Palms Marina, off U.S. 17, Isle of Palms ☎843/886–5000 ⊕www.nature-tours.com). **Charleston Explorers** (✉40 Patriots Point Rd., Mount Pleasant ☎843/723–5656 ⊕www.charleston explorers.org). **Coastal Expeditions** (✉514-B Mill St., Mount Pleasant ☎843/884–7684 ⊕www.coastal expeditions.com).

PRIVATE GUIDES

To hire a private guide to lead you around the city and outlying plantations, contact Charleston's Finest Historic Tours. Janice Kahn has been leading customized tours for more than 30 years. Christine Waggoner, of Promenade with Christine, offers tours in French and English.

Contacts **Charleston's Finest Historic Tours** (☎843/577–3311). **Janice Kahn** (☎843/556–0664). **Promenade with Christine** (☎843/971–9364 or 843/200–1766).

WALKING TOURS

Walking tours on various topics—horticulture, slavery, or women's history—are given by Charleston Strolls and the Original Charleston Walks. Bulldog Tours has walks that explore the city's supernatural side. Listen to the infamous tales of lost souls with Ghosts of Charleston, which travel to historic graveyards.

Military history buffs should consider Jack Thompson's Civil War Walking Tour. The food-oriented tours by Carolina Food Pros explore culinary strongholds—gourmet grocers, butcher shops, and restaurants, sampling all along the way.

Contacts **Bulldog Tours** (✉40 N. Market St., Market area ☎843/568–3315 ⊕www.cobble stonewalkingtours.com). **Carolina Food Pros** (✉701 E. Bay St., Market area ☎843/723–3366

⊕www.carolinafoodpros.com).
Charleston Strolls (✉Charleston Pl., 130 Market St., Market area ☎843/766–2080 ⊕www.charlestonstrolls.com). **Ghosts of Charleston** (✉184 E. Bay St., French Quarter ☎843/723–1670 or 800/723–1670). **Jack Thompson's Civil War Walking Tour** (✉Mills House Hotel, 115 Meeting St., Market area ☎843/722–7033). **Original Charleston Walks** (✉58½ Broad St., South of Broad ☎843/577–3800 or 800/729–3420).

▌ TRIP INSURANCE

Comprehensive travel policies typically cover trip cancellation and interruption, letting you cancel or cut your trip short because of a personal emergency or illness. Such policies also cover evacuation and medical care in case you are injured or become ill on your trip. Some also cover you for trip delays because of bad weather or mechanical problems as well as for lost or delayed baggage. Another type of coverage to look for is financial default—that is, when your trip is disrupted because a tour operator, airline, or cruise line goes out of business. Generally you must buy this when you book your trip or shortly thereafter, and it's only available to you if your operator isn't on a list of excluded companies.

Expect comprehensive travel insurance policies to cost about 4% to 7% or 8% of the total price of your trip (it's more like 8%–12% if you're over age 70). Always read the fine print of your policy to make sure that you are covered for the risks that are of most concern to you. Compare several policies to make sure you're getting the best price and range of coverage available.

▌TIP→ **OK. You know you can save a bundle on trips to warm-weather destinations by traveling in the rainy season. But there's also a chance that a severe storm will disrupt your plans. The solution? Look for hotels and resorts that offer storm/hurricane guarantees. Although they rarely allow refunds, most guarantees do let you rebook later if a storm strikes.**

Insurance Comparison Sites
Insure My Trip.com (☎800/487–4722 ⊕www.insuremytrip.com). **Square Mouth.com** (☎800/240–0369 or 727/490–5803 ⊕www.squaremouth.com).

Comprehensive Travel Insurers
Access America (☎866/729–6021 ⊕www.accessamerica.com). **CSA Travel Protection** (☎800/873–9855 ⊕www.csatravelprotection.com). **HTH Worldwide** (☎610/254–8700 ⊕www.hthworldwide.com). **Travelex Insurance** (☎888/228–9792 ⊕www.travelex-insurance.com). **Travel Guard** (☎800/826–4919 ⊕www.travelguard.com). **Travel Insured International** (☎800/243–3174 ⊕www.travelinsured.com).

▌ VISITOR INFORMATION

The Charleston Area Convention & Visitors Bureau runs the Charleston Visitor Center, which has information about the city as well as Kiawah Island, Seabrook Island, Mount Pleasant, North Charleston, Edisto Island, Summerville, and the Isle of Palms. The Historic Charleston Foundation and the Preservation Society of Charleston have information on house tours.

Contacts **Charleston Visitor Center** (✉375 Meeting St., Upper King ☎423 King St., 29403 ☎843/853–8000 or 800/868–8118 ⊕www.charlestoncvb.com). **Historic Charleston Foundation** (☎Box 1120, 29402 ☎843/723–1623 ⊕www.historiccharleston.org). **Preservation Society of Charleston** (☎Box 521, 29402 ☎843/722–4630 ⊕www.preservationsociety.org).

INDEX

NOTES

NOTES

NOTES

NOTES

ABOUT OUR WRITER

Eileen Robinson Smith, a veteran Fodor's writer for more than 15 years, spend part of her childhood in South Carolina and chose to return and live there as an adult. Though Yankee born, she has always had strong Southern leanings, and her love for the Lowcountry of the coastal South has grown with time. After living in the Caribbean for years, a hurricane blew her back to her lakeside home in Charleston in the early 1990s, where she remains. Although she still spends several months a year in the islands writing for our Caribbean and Dominican Republic guides, her home base is Charleston. Specializing in food and travel, she has contributed to such magazines as *Conde Nast Traveler, Caribbean Travel & Life, American Eagle's Latitudes,* Delta's *Sky,* and many more magazines. She is a former editor of *Charleston* magazine.